Third Edition. Version 1.5.1, March 2016

Credits

I want to thank the developers of the Meta Programming System, who have developed MPS since the early 2000. This book would not have been possible without them.
MPS Project leaders, in chronological order: Sergey Dmitriev, Igor Alshannikov, Konstantin Solomatov and Alexander Shatalin. **Current team members:** Alexander Shatalin, Fedor Isakov, Mihail Muhin, Michael Vlassiev, Václav Pech, Simon Alperovich, Daniil Elovkov, Victor Matchenko, Artem Tikhomirov, Mihail Buryakov, Alexey Pyshkin, Maria Lebedeva and Sergej Koscejev. **Earlier members of the MPS team:** Evgeny Gryaznov, Timur Abishev, Julia Beliaeva, Cyril Konopko, Ilya Lintsbah, Gleb Leonov, Evgeny Kurbatsky, Sergey Sinchuk, Timur Zambalayev, Maxim Mazin, Vadim Gurov, Evgeny Geraschenko, Darja Chembrovskaya, Vyacheslav Lukianov, and Alexander Anisimov. **And these external contributors:** Sascha Lisson, Thiago Tonelli Bartolomei and Alexander Eliseyev.

I am particularly grateful to the executives at JetBrains s.r.o who open-sourced an internal research project and made it possible for a growing community of programmers to become more familiar with a truly different and very promising approach to software development. Special Thanks go to Václav Pech and Alexander Shatalin for providing feedback about earlier drafts of this book and offering clarifications when I had trouble figuring out certain less-traveled aspects of MPS.

I need to thank Philippe for his patience during the winter 2013, when I used all these week-ends to write the first volume of this book series. I apologize to my relatives, colleagues and friends if they felt that I have been less available to them during the time it took to complete this book.

Finally, I want to thank Stanislav Povelikin (http://spdesign.org) for turning some of my illustration ideas into beautiful cover designs for this book series.

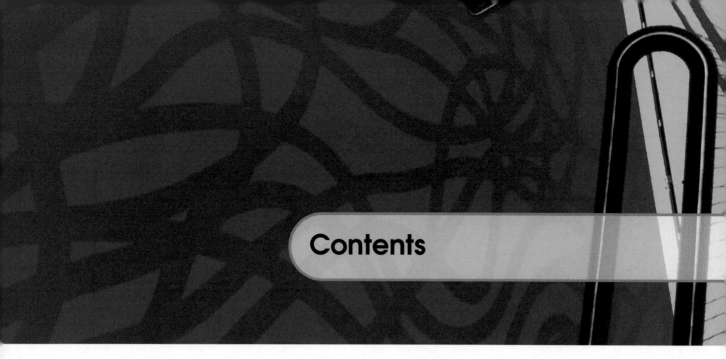

Contents

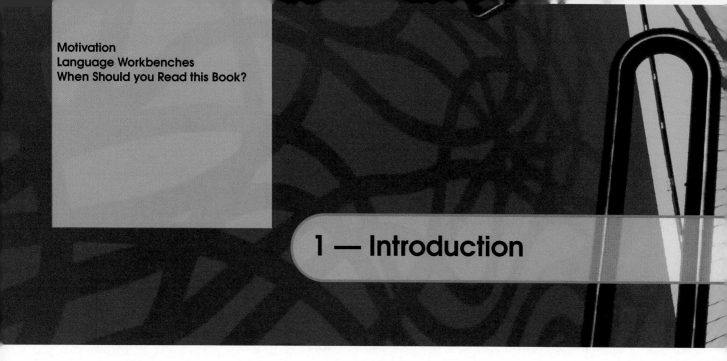

Motivation
Language Workbenches
When Should you Read this Book?

1 — Introduction

1.1 Motivation

After contributing three text-book chapters and knowing the effort involved in drafting and finishing each of them, I thought long and hard before deciding to embark on a book project. My key motivation for writing this book was that I needed a reference text that would make it easier to teach others how to use the Meta Programming System (MPS).

MPS represents a new paradigm to programming and software design. Intentional programming [Sim95] and meta programming [Dmi04], were conceived to overcome some of the challenges of traditional language design and development approaches.

I first came across MPS in the fall of 2006 when I downloaded one of the first Early Access Program (EAP) releases[1]. The description of the project suggested that the tool could help solve a number of problems I was encountering in the field of bioinformatics and this potential sparked my interest[2]. I quickly realized that the version of MPS I experimented with was not for the faint of heart. There was very limited documentation at the time and the only tutorial available with the EAP appeared incomplete. While I spent some time trying to understand this version of MPS, I had to give up when difficulties arose that I could not resolve[3] and when other priorities surfaced. I would have liked then, to find a resource such as I hope this book will be for newcomers to MPS. Of course, the MPS documentation has greatly improved since the version I tested in 2006. I am writing these lines in the winter of 2013. Despite these improvements, I think that there is still a need for a resource that will help beginners become familiar with MPS in a short amount of time. I hope this book will fill this gap and provide both a reference and a gentle introduction to a very unique and promising tool.

---

[1] See http://icb.med.cornell.edu/wiki/index.php/Language_Oriented_Programming

[2] More information about my research in bioinformatics can be found on the laboratory web site: http://campagnelab.org

[3] See http://icb.med.cornell.edu/wiki/index.php/MPS/Examples/TextLanguage

1.2 Language Workbenches

Language Workbenches are software engineering tools developed in the last ten years that help their users create new languages and the tools to write programs in these languages.

> **Definition 1.2.1 — Language Workbench (LW).** A Language Workbench is a software tool designed to help its users develop new computer languages.

Some LWs focus on non-technical users and provide languages to help organize knowledge. Intentional Software (`http://www.intentsoft.com/`) is a commercial Language Workbench that falls in this category [Sim95; SCC06]. Another prominent language workbench aimed at software programmers is the Jetbrains Meta Programming System (MPS) [Dmi04; Voe13; VS10]. MPS is developed as an open-source project (source code is available at `https://github.com/JetBrains/MPS`). This workbench was developed to provide the tools necessary to design new programming languages.

1.3 When Should you Read this Book?

If you are reading this book, you are either taking one of my courses or more likely are trying to use MPS to help with software engineering or programming problems that you encounter in your hobbies or professional life. MPS offers a different paradigm from the traditional programming tools that you may be used to and this section aims to explain what type of problems MPS can help you with.

You will find that MPS is a useful tool if your project requires that you do one or more of the following:

1. Develop a Domain Specific Language (DSL),

   > **Definition 1.3.1 — Domain Specific Language (DSL).** A Domain Specific Language is a language designed to meet the needs of a specific application domain [For+04]. Examples of widely used DSLs include HTML and SQL.

2. Develop an Application Specific Language (ASL),

   > **Definition 1.3.2 — Application Specific Language (ASL).** An Application Specific Language is a language designed to meet the needs of a specific application program. An example is the PlantUML language used to describe UML diagrams so that the PlantUML program can render them. Some well-designed ASL which are reused by several programs have evolved towards DSLs. An example is the DOT language, initially used for input to GraphViz, which has evolved towards a DSL for representing graphs and is supported by several programs.

3. Need to automate the generation of source code,
4. Need to automate the generation of configuration files,
5. Need to develop a software framework for a specific application domain. Instead of developing a framework, consider modeling the domain as a set of languages in MPS that generate to the code that you want the framework for.

> **Definition 1.3.3 — Software Framework.** A Software framework is an abstraction in which software providing generic functionality can be selectively changed by additional user-written code, thus providing application-specific software. [Gac+04]

6. Need to write long boiler-plate code sections as part of usual development that are very repetitive. If you find that the interesting part of your programs are buried among a lot of implementation code, you should consider modeling the interesting part of the program with MPS and generate the implementation part automatically from the short language description.

7. For data analysis. Since the publication of the first edition of this book, my laboratory has shown that the MPS LWcan be applied to facilitate data analysis by non-specialists. If data analysis is an area of interest, you can learn more about this application in these publications and pre-prints: [BC15; CDS15; KSC16]

You can find detailed discussions of the activities and the motivation for using a Language Workbench in the book "DSL Engineering" by Markus Voelter and colleagues[Voe+13]. The book that you are reading now is concerned with teaching you how to perform these activities and helping you quickly become productive with the MPS Language Workbench.

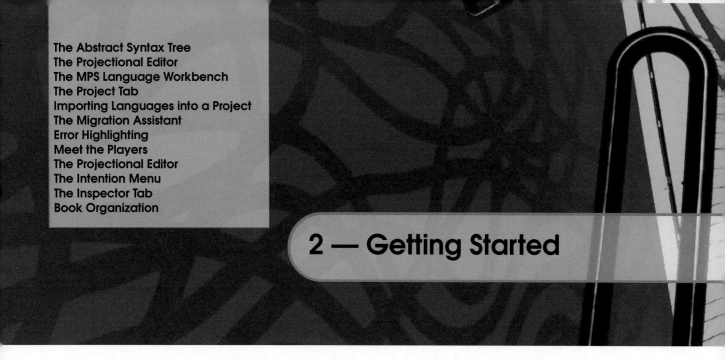

2 — Getting Started

Traditional compiler technology relies on lexers and parsers to read programs expressed as text files [Lam+06] and transform them into data structures called Abstract Syntax Trees (AST). This process is illustrated on Figure 2.1, top panel.

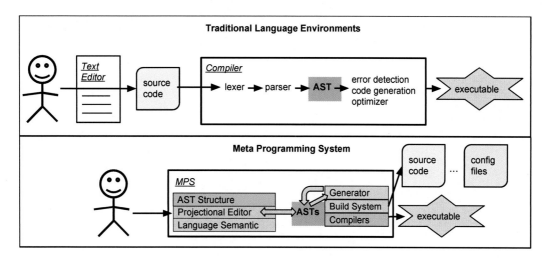

Figure 2.1: **Two Paradigms.** This figure compares the MPS programming paradigm to a more traditional programming approach. The top panel shows how programmers develop programs with a traditional language environment consisting of a text editor and compiler. The bottom panel shows how a programmer interacts directly with the MPS system.

ASTs are the data structures that a compiler processes to generate executable code. In contrast, in the paradigm used by the Meta Programming System, the user interacts directly with one or several ASTs using a projectional editor. Figure 2.2 presents the relationships between the text representation of an arithmetic expression and a corresponding AST. The MPS approach works directly with the AST, without the need to express programs as text. This brings several advantages:

1. Language extensions are simple to develop. Extending a lexer and parser for a complicated language requires specialized skills, while extending a language in MPS consists in defining new AST concepts, with their associated editor(s) and semantic. Extending a language consists in describing its structure and creating an editor for the new language concepts. This process is much simpler than that needed to extend a compiler for an existing language because, the larger the language, the more difficult it becomes to develop a text syntax that avoids ambiguities.

2. Different languages can be composed effectively without the risk of introducing ambiguities in the concrete syntax.

2.1 The Abstract Syntax Tree

Definition 2.1.1 — Abstract Syntax Tree (AST). An abstract syntax tree (AST) is a data structure traditionally used by compilers to represent and manipulate programs. An AST starts with a root node. The root node can contain child nodes. Nodes in the tree can be of different types, often arranged in one or more concept hierarchies. Figure 2.2 presents an example of an AST.

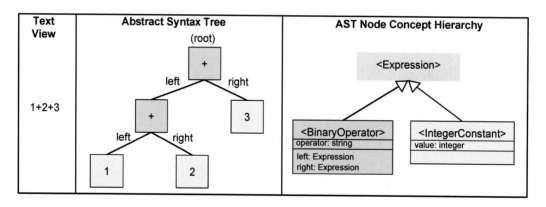

Figure 2.2: **Understanding the AST.** This figure presents the relationship between a program text view for an arithmetic expression (left), the corresponding Abstract Syntax Tree (middle) and the associated fragment of the node concept hierarchy (right). The expression shown adds three integer constants $(1 + 2 + 3)$. The root of the AST is a BinaryOperator node (operator: +). Lines connecting nodes of the AST indicate aggregation relationships. For instance, the root note has a left child of type BinaryOperator, and a right child of type IntegerConstant, with value 3.

Definition 2.1.2 — AST Concept Hierarchy. The AST Concept Hierarchy describes types of the nodes that make up possible ASTs, and their relationships to other AST nodes concepts. The AST concept hierarchy is analogous to a data schema since its structure defines which ASTs can be constructed.

In the MPS tool, the AST Concept Hierarchy can be defined in the Structure Aspect, which will be presented in Chapter 3. In contrast to the traditional approach shown at the top of Figure 2.1, MPS implements a projectional editor.

2.2 The Projectional Editor

> **Definition 2.2.1 — Projectional Editor (PE).** A projectional editor is a user interface that makes it possible to create, edit and interact with one or more ASTs.

Good user interfaces are usually difficult to develop, but MPS makes it easy to create a robust projectional editor for new languages. This book describes how to develop a projectional editor in Chapter 5.

2.3 The MPS Language Workbench

Figure 2.3 presents a snapshot of the MPS workbench. This snapshot should help you orient yourself around the MPS user interface. In the next section, we will look at the Project Tab in detail.

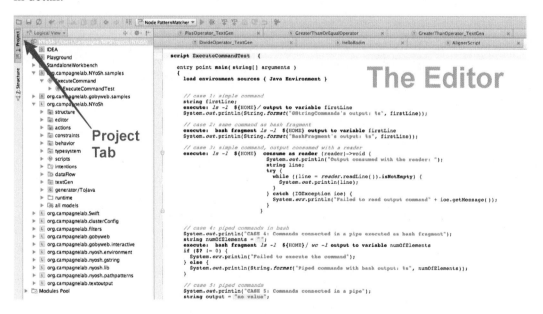

Figure 2.3: **The MPS Language Workbench.** The snapshot presents the user interface of the MPS Workbench. When starting to work with MPS, it is useful to focus on the Editor and Project Tabs. The Editor is shown to the right and the Project Tab to the left. Note that you need to open an existing project, or create a new one to see this view.

2.4 The Project Tab

A key user interface element of MPS is the Project Tab. This tab gives you access to a logical organization of the languages included or imported in a project. When working with MPS,

Figure 2.4: **The Project Tab Explained.**
Solutions and Models. Orange icons with a S inside them denote Solutions. The name of the Solution follows the orange square. Solutions contain models, which themselves contains ASTs.

Language and Language Aspects. The yellow square icons with an L in them represent languages. The name of the language is shown to the right of the icon. Solution and language icons are prefixed with a little triangle. Click on the triangle to open the solution or language. Click again to collapse the solution or language. Opening a solution presents the models in the solution (ExecuteCommand is a model in the *org.campagnelab.NYoSh.sample* solution). In contrast to solutions, opening a language exposes a list of language aspects. Several aspects will be described in detail in the following chapters. See Table 2.1 for a brief description of the function of these aspects.

Modules Pool. Shown in green at the bottom is the Modules Pool. Note the other Languages and Solutions shown under Modules Pool are not part of the project, but provided by the platform or by some active MPS plugin. It is a great place to look for languages that you might wish to use in your own languages or solutions.

you will often use the Project Tab to modify properties of languages or solutions that make up an MPS project. Let's take a moment to become familiar with this MPS user interface element. A blown-up Project Tab is shown in Figure 2.4 to show details and explain the meaning of the icons included in the tab.

Developing a new language in MPS consists in adding and configuring nodes in these various language aspects. Note that some aspects are not created by default when creating a new language. You can add new aspects to a language by right clicking on a language name and selecting New ⟩ * Aspect (see Figure 2.5).

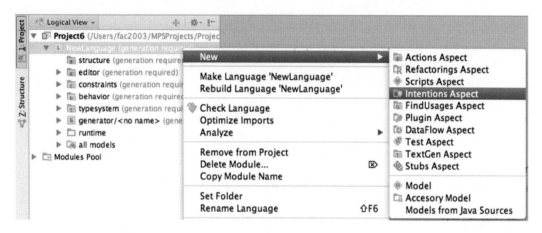

Figure 2.5: **Create New Aspect.** Some language aspects are not created by default for new languages and can be created as shown in this snapshot.

The function of the various MPS languages aspects shown in the Project Tab are explained in Table 2.1.

It is useful to realize that MPS aspects are implemented as MPS models, which contain ASTs and are created and edited with the same mechanisms that are available for languages developed with MPS. For instance, the structure aspect for the language *org.campagnelab.Swift* is implemented as a model stored under languages/org.campagnelab.Swift/languageModels/structure.mps and contains ASTs expressed in the *jetbrains.mps.lang.structure* language.

2.5 Importing Languages into a Project

When you create an empty MPS project, you might find it useful to import other languages into the project alongside the languages that you are developing. For instance, you could open the sample projects shipped with MPS as standalone projects, but it is often more convenient to import some languages from these projects into your own project. You then become able to switch back and forth between languages in the same workench window and are able to copy and paste across languages.

Let's assume you created an empty MPS project (or a project with one solution and/or language). You can import languages into this project by right clicking on the name of the project, at the very top of the Project pane and selecting 'Project Paths'. This opens the

Language Aspect	Function
Structure	Defines the AST Node Concept Hierarchies.
Editor	Define mini-editors for each concept of the structure aspect.
Actions	Provide means to customize the editing behavior of the editor.
Constraints	Provides means to restrict which AST nodes can be child or parents or other nodes and help define scopes.
Behavior	Provides method declarations and definitions for concepts of the structure aspect.
Typesystem	Makes it possible to implement a typesystem for the language.
Migration	Holds Migration classes to evolve the language during its life-time (MPS 3.2+, see Volume II [Cam15]).
Scripts	Holds Language Migration Scripts to evolve the language during its life-time (older mechanism: MPS 3.1 and earlier, see Volume II).
Intentions	Defines language intentions: context-dependent AST transformations that the user can activate on demand.
DataFlow	Defines the language data flow rules which govern which statements are reachable, which variables are read from or written to.
Test	Provides the means to test languages by developing unit tests to check type calculations and error detection.
Refactorings	Provides the means to offer refactoring tools for the language to end-users[Ele+01].
TextGen	Provides means to transform AST nodes to text.
Generator	Provides means to transform AST nodes to other languages.
Plugin	Holds code that when compiled integrates with MPS to extend its user interface and functionality (see Volume II).

Table 2.1: Function of the most common MPS Language Aspects.

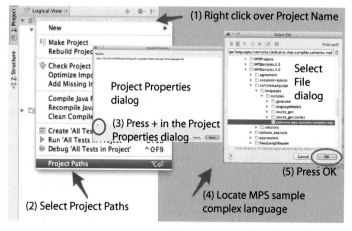

Figure 2.6: **Adjusting Project Paths.** You can import new languages and solutions into a project by following these instructions. Notice the names of the user interface dialogs as we will refer to them by name in the future.

dialog shown in Figure 2.6. Try it now by creating a new project, and adding the Complex language to your new project[1].

 This chapter is organized in such a way that the tutorial triggers a number of situations that you may encounter with MPS, and give you the tools to resolve the problems that arise in these situations. For instance, I will show you how to create an empty project and add languages to this project. It would be much simpler to tell you to open the sample project directly in MPS, but I think you can figure this out on your own. The tutorial instead shows how to import languages into an empty project to help you understand different concepts that you will need to work productively with MPS. Equipped with this understanding, you will be free to use the easier path, and will know what to do when you run into problems.

2.6 The Migration Assistant

When opening a project with MPS, you may be prompted to run the Migration Assistant and see a dialog like the following:

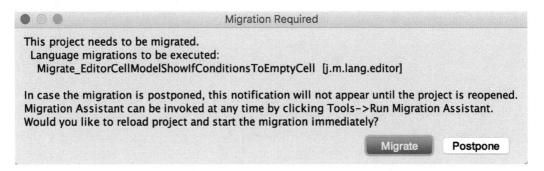

This will happen for instance if the version of MPS that you are using is more recent that the version used to save the project.

The migration assistant will fail to run if the project has any missing dependencies, so it is best to postpone running the assistant until you are sure the project includes all dependencies. If the migration assistant is triggered at this stage of the tutorial, click the Postpone button.

When you have added all dependencies to the project, you can restart the migration assistant manually with the menu Migration 〉 Run Migration Assistant. The migration assistant will run as needed any time you open a project.

2.7 Error Highlighting

After adding the language following the instructions of Figure 2.6, you should notice that the *jetbrains.mps.samples.complex* language is highlighted in red. MPS uses this cue to indicate an error in the language. See Figure 2.7 to learn how to find the cause of this error.

---

[1]The complex language should be located under ~/MPSSamples.3.0/complexLanguage/languages/complex/ jetbrains.mps.samples.complex.mpl, where ~/ indicates your home directory.

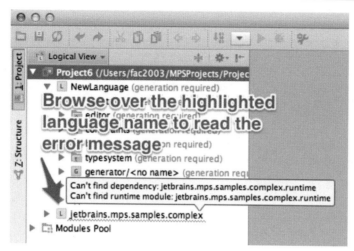

Figure 2.7: **An Example of Error Message.** Browsing over the name of the language highlighted in red reveals the error message. In this case, MPS indicates that the run-time solution associated with the complex sample language cannot be found in the project. To fix this error, you can add the complex runtime solution to the project following the approach you used to add the complex language.

(R) The complex solution should be located under ~/MPSSamples.3.3/complexLanguage /solutions/jetbrains.mps.complex.runtime/jetbrains.mps.samples.complex.runtime.msd, where ~/ indicates your home directory. Note that the directory includes the version number for MPS, which may be different in your installation.

Once you have followed similar steps to those shown in Figure 2.6 and added the runtime solution, you should notice that the error has been resolved. Dependencies encoded in languages and solutions must be resolved explicitly within a project for solutions and languages that are not available under Modules Pool.

Modules pool contain languages shipped with the MPS platform or bundled with plugins that are active in the MPS workbench. You can inspect the plugins active in your session by opening MPS ⟩ Preferences and locating the Plugins section. MPS can download plugins through a remote repository, or you can install plugins manually by installing plugin distributions under the plugins directory of the MPS distribution. Follow the installation instructions given with each plugin.

2.8   Meet the Players

An MPS project can contain a number of parts, organized in a hierarchical fashion. Typical parts are shown below, organized starting with Languages and Solutions:

- Languages
    - Structure Aspect
        * Concepts
        * Interface Concepts
        * Enumeration Types
        * Constrained Data Types
        * Primitive Data Types
    - Other Aspects [See Aspect Chapters for description of parts]

- Solutions
  - Models
    * AST Roots
      · AST Nodes

In this hierarchical structure, parts are organized from parent to descendants, where descendants are contained in a parent. For instance, Solutions contain Models that contain AST Roots, which contain AST Nodes and their descendants.

MPS Project parts can also be connected across this hierarchy. For instance, Solutions contain models described in specific Languages.

> **Definition 2.8.1 — Language.** An MPS Language describes what types of ASTs can be created with the language. A language includes a set of AST Node Concepts, semantic and behavior, represented in one or more MPS Aspects. A language is a kind of MPS Module.

> **Definition 2.8.2 — Solution.** An MPS Solution holds a set of models. Solutions are convenient packaging units that make it possible to reference a set of models as a unit from other Solutions or Languages. A solution is a kind of MPS Module.

> **Definition 2.8.3 — Model.** In MPS, a Model is a container for a set of AST Roots. Models are serialized to disk in XML (.mps extension) or binary format (extension .mpb)

> **Definition 2.8.4 — AST Root.** An AST root is an AST node that can be used as an immediate descendant of a Model. AST Roots are analogous to source files in a traditional programming paradigm, but different because AST Roots are serialized to disk when saved and deserialized when loaded.

The specific set of languages associated with a given Solution is recorded in a dimension orthogonal to the part hierarchy. Each solution includes references to the set of languages needed to write ASTs in the Solution.

> (R) Remember that MPS Projects are organized as a large AST (whose root node is the project node). Links between Solutions and Languages are an example of reference across an AST. AST References will be described in Chapter 3.

Create a New Project

Follow the instructions on Figure 2.8 to create a new project with one solution.

Now, import the MPS Sample *math* language into the new project. We described how to import languages in a project in Section 2.5. You will need to import the complete set of dependencies shown below to resolve errors:

1. jetbrains.mps.baseLanguage.math
2. jetbrains.mps.baseLanguage.math.pluginSolution
3. jetbrains.mps.baseLanguage.math.runtime

After configuration, the project properties on my machine look like this:

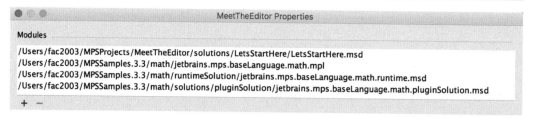

In MPS, all code exists inside a model. You can create a model inside the solution by selecting the solution name in the Project Tab. Right-click on the solution name and select [New] [Model] in the popup menu. The New Model Dialog appears. Type LetsStartHere.Math in the Model Name field and press OK. You are then presented with a Model Properties Dialog for the LetsStartHere.Math model. The next section describes how to edit model properties with this dialog.

2.8.1 The Model Properties

The Model Properties dialog has three tabs: Dependencies, Used Languages and Advanced. Enter math and *baseLanguage* in the Used Languages tab in a similar manner to that used for the Solution. See Figure 2.9 for directions.

The Dependencies Tab makes it possible to define dependencies on other languages that must be present before this language can be built and used. The Used Languages Tab defines what languages are used directly inside the model. Changing the set of languages inside this tab will directly control which root nodes you can create inside a model. Finally, the

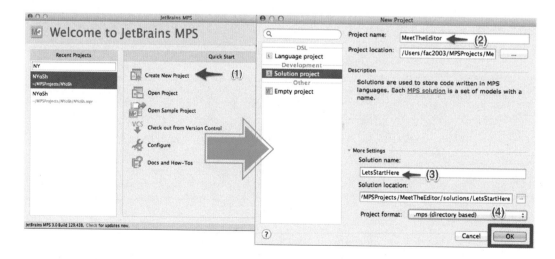

Figure 2.8: **Create A New Project with a Solution.** This snapshot provides directions to create a new project, starting at the window displayed when you first start MPS. If you already have one or more projects opened, close these projects to see this dialog. Alternatively, you can select [File] [New Project] from the menu in any project to bring up the New Project Dialog (steps (2-4)). Create the project as instructed to continue learning how to use the editor.

Advanced Tab offers the option to not generate the model (useful if the model stores code that you know will yield errors, and you need to skip it in an automated build), and other options to customize what languages participate to generation. It also shows the path where the model is serialized on disk inside the project.

Figure 2.9: **Model Properties.** Follow these directions to specify model properties for the MeetTheEditor.Math model. The set of used languages should look as shown when you are done. The language names are greyed out because they are currently not used anywhere in the model. When a language is used in a model, the language name will appear solid black in this dialog.

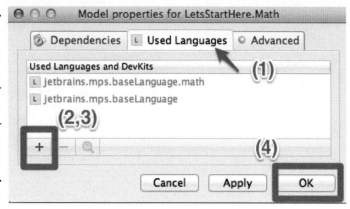

> **Definition 2.8.5 — Used Languages.** Each MPS module has a set of Used Languages. Only languages that are declared under Used Languages can be used to write ASTs in this module.

2.9 The Projectional Editor

Let's try the *math* and *baseLanguage* languages by creating a root node under the `MeetTheEditor.Math` model. See Figure 2.10 for step by step instructions.

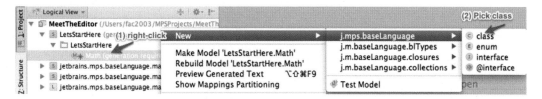

Figure 2.10: **Create an AST Root.** This snapshot provides directions to create an AST Root node. Select a `class` root node from *j.mps.baseLanguage*. If you open the Model Properties dialog again, you may notice that *baseLanguage* is no longer greyed out (the language is now used in an AST node of the model). If you also open the Module properties dialog, you will see Used Languages for the module includes *baseLanguage*. Module Used Languages are calculated dynamically since MPS 3.3 (the set is the union of all used languages in the models of the solution/language).

2.9.1 The Editor Window

After you have created the class AST Root node, you will see in the editor tab the content shown in the top left corner of Figure 2.11. Follow the directions in this figure to enter two complex variable declarations.

Figure 2.11: **Walkthrough the *math* language Editor Example.** Immediately after creating a class AST Root node, follow these directions to learn how to edit the AST in the editor. In step 11, notice how the editor presents two possible completion choices after you have typed the '*' character.

If you are familiar with the Java programming language, you will recognize the class language construct, but may be puzzled by the complex variable type. This type appears in the editor as if it was a primitive type of the language, but the Java language does not offer such a type [Gos+05]. The explaination is that we are not editing Java code in a text editor, but are editing an AST in MPS by composing two languages. The *base-Language* (language) provides most of the Java language syntax and behavior, while the *jetbrains.mps.baseLanguage.math* (*math*) extends *baseLanguage* with features to make it easier to work with mathematical abstractions. The complex primitive type is offered by the *math* language. Similarly, typing the I letter in the editor enters the imaginary number *i* and makes it possible to use this complex number in expressions.

> (R) Well-designed MPS languages present a smooth editor experience and include notations that feel natural to the intended end-users of the languages. In the previous walk-through the complex data type is well-integrated with *baseLanguage*: (i) it is possible to declare new variable declarations of type complex, as if the complex type was a primitive type of the language, (ii) the complex instance *i* can be used inside expressions of the language. This book aims to describe how to develop languages with MPS that feel natural to use for end users of the language.

2.9.2 Everything you See is a Projection

The content of the editor window is a projection. It is a data structure that is projected for display according to some choices made by the designer(s) of the language editors.

In contrast with textual editors, a projectional editor like MPS lets you change how data structures are projected onto the editor display. To demonstrate this, we will use a feature introduced in MPS 3.3, which offers a reflective editor for any part of an AST. When it is active, the reflective editor displays every attribute of the AST node.[2] To change projection, try selecting different parts shown in the editor, and activate the Reflective Editor. You can do this by right-clicking on the node and selecting `right-click` ⟩ `Show Reflective Editor`. The display will change and show all the attributes of the node you have selected. You can revert to the previous editor by selecting `right-click` ⟩ `Show Regular Editor`. The reflective editor is useful when you need to inspect or edit part of a node that are not shown by the editor provided by the language.

> **Exercise 2.1** Try selecting the reflective editor when the cursor is positioned over `main` (as in the root node shown in Figure 2.11). This will display the reflective editor and show all properties, children and references of the main method.   ∎

2.9.3 Executing the AST Root

Some MPS languages are designed to generate code that can be executed. This is the case of the *math* language because it generates to *baseLanguage* and *baseLanguage* generates to Java source code. MPS make it possible to generate and run Java code directly within the workbench (the second volume of this book explains how to implement this functionality for other languages [Cam15]). Figure 2.12 shows how to execute the program that we created in Figure 2.11.

Figure 2.12: **Running the Complex Math Example.** Follow these steps to generate, compile and execute the complex example. (1) Right click on the main method. Select Run 'Class HelloWorld' in the popup menu. Execution occurs in the Run tab (3), at the bottom of the MPS workbench. Comparing the output to the program shows a seamless integration of the complex type in *baseLanguage*.

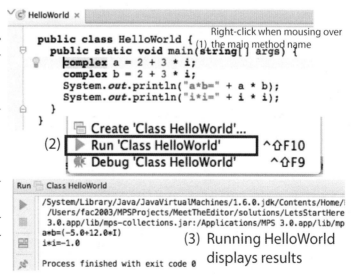

---

[2]This editor is called reflective because it uses a reflection mechanism to be able to access and render node content irrespective of node type.

2.9.4   **Code Generation**

What kind of code does MPS execute when you select Run 'Class HelloWorld'? The answer is code generation. The *math* language includes a Generator Aspect that transforms the concepts of the *math* language into concepts of *baseLanguage* (model to model transformation is described in Chapter 15). Because MPS ships with a Build System capable of compiling Java code seamlessly, and because *baseLanguage* classes with a `public static void main` method can be executed by the workbench you can seamlessly run the generated code in the workbench. Let's have a look at the generated code. You can do this with $\boxed{\text{solution name}}$ $\boxed{\text{AST Root}}$ $\boxed{\text{right-click}}$ $\boxed{\text{Preview Text Output}}$. See Figure 2.13 for detailed steps.

```
package LetsStartHere.Math;

/*Generated by MPS */

import jetbrains.mps.baseLanguage.math.runtime.Complex;

public class HelloWorld {
  public static void main(String[] args) {

    Complex a = new Complex(2, 3);
    Complex b = new Complex(2, 3);

    System.out.println("a*b=" + a.mul(b));
    System.out.println("i*i=" + Complex.I.mul(Complex.I));
  }
}
```

Figure 2.13: **The Complex Math Example Generated to Java Source Code.** To generate this output from the editor window, locate the HelloWorld AST Root, right click and select 'Preview Generated Text'. An alternative way to preview the generated code is to right click on the Model or AST Root node in the Project Tab. Select 'Preview Generated Text'. Note that models may generate multiple output text files if they contain several AST roots. Compare the generated output to the content of Figure 2.12.

The Generator Aspect is explained in Chapter 15 and describes how to generate text output or to transform an AST expressed in one language into another one. While many approaches have been developed over the years to generate code, including StringTemplate[Par] and Velocity Template[Con], MPS provides a principled and very effective platform to generate code from concise language notations. MPS Generators scale easily as projects grow and benefit from full editor support in the templates. This is a strong advantage that has no equivalent in existing code generation tools based on templates.

2.10 The Intention Menu

Intentions are a convenient way to interact with the AST when there is no simple way to map an action to a word[3] or set of keys[4]. An intention menu is available on nodes that provide intentions. In MPS, the intention menu is shown as a yellow light bulb (💡) in the left margin of the editor when the cursor is immobile on a node for a few seconds. You can also trigger the display of the intention menu with the keyboard. Use `option` + `↵` on mac, or `ctrl` + `↵` on Windows or Linux. When the intention menu appears, select the intention that you want to run, or navigate to the code that runs the intention by using the intention submenu.

2.11 The Inspector Tab

The Inspector Tab is located at the bottom right of the main MPS window.[5] It can be opened by clicking on the `🔲 2: Inspector` icon. The Inspector Tab shows the Inspected Cell Layout for a node. The Inspected Cell Layout can be defined when developing a custom AST node editor (see Chapter 5 Section 5.2.4). For existing MPS Concepts, the Inspector Tab will often provide a means to edit properties associated with a node which are not shown in the main editor window. This can be done to avoid clutter or to provide a complementary editing dimension when working with some kinds of AST nodes. This is particularly useful when working with the Editor and Generator languages.

2.12 Book Organization

This book is organized in a succession of reference chapters interleaved with chapters that present applications of the concepts covered in the reference chapters. Reference chapters focus on clear definitions and exhaustive explanations of MPS capabilities. Application chapters highlight some of the most important points through a worked example.

   If you have read an earlier version of this book and only need to lookup new material introduced in a new edition, I suggest to use the index and look for the entry "New in MPS X.Y". For instance, the third edition of this book contains an entry called "New in MPS 3.3" which points to the pages introduced to discuss features new in MPS 3.3.

Conventions

This book uses the following typographical conventions:

1. *italic* identifiers refer to MPS languages (e.g., *baseLanguage* or *jetbrains.mps.base Language*). Note that I also use italic to refer to interface concept names, but there should be no ambiguity with language names.

---

[3] Section 5.3.1 describes how to run actions when some text is typed.

[4] Section 5.3.2 describes how to run code when a key combination is pressed.

[5] In MPS 3.1+, you may need to enable the inspector tab before you can open it. You can enable/disable tabs by clicking or browsing over the 🔲 icon in the lower left corner of MPS 3.1 window. While you are adjusting the 3.1 user interface, you should also enable the Toolbar (`View ⟩ Toolbar`) because you will need it often (for some reason, it is disabled by default in MPS 3.1). The Toolbar is enabled if you see a checkbox next to it in the `View` menu.

2. `typewriter text` is used either to show a concept name, or to make it easier to see fragments of code when they are embedded in the text.

3. Keystrokes are shown as follows: option + SPACE . This means that you should press the option key together with the SPACE key on the keyboard. Note that the return key is shown as ↵ .

4. Menus that you should select to perform some action are shown as Solution ⟩ right-click ⟩ Model Properties . Note that MPS has a menu bar, but attaches menus over several types of user interface elements.

5. The 💡 symbol represents the icon that appears in the left margin of the editor and makes it possible to execute an intention or navigate to the code of the intention.

6. The 2: Inspector icon is used to suggest that your should look at the content of the Inspector Tab.

3 — The Structure Aspect

3.1 Overview

The Structure Aspect is a component of a Language that makes it possible to define the structure of possible ASTs that can be expressed with that language. The Structure Aspect is expressed with the *jetbrains.mps.lang.structure* language. This language can be used to define AST Concept Node hierarchies. Figure 3.1 presents the different AST Root nodes that can be defined in a Structure Aspect. The following sections describe these types of Root Nodes in detail.

Structure aspects can be queried and modified with the *jetbrains.mps.smodel* language.

Figure 3.1: **AST Roots of the Structure Aspect.** This figure presents the type of AST Roots that can be created under a Structure Aspect. To test this, create a new MPS Language, right-click on the Structure Aspect, browse over New. Selecting a type of AST Root node will create this root in the structure of the language.

3.2 Concepts

You can create a new Concept in a structure aspect by selecting New ⟩ Concept, as shown in Figure 3.1. Creating a new Concept presents the content shown in Figure 3.2 in the editor. Immediately after creating the concept you should type the concept name. The name will be used under the structure aspect in the Project Tab and can be used in large projects to locate the concept with Navigate 〉 Go To Root Node [ctrl + N or ⌘ + N]. Naming the concept will resolve the error shown in Figure 3.2.

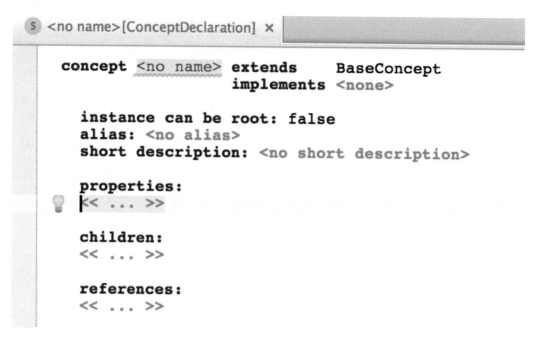

Figure 3.2: **New Concept AST Root.**

3.2.1 The extends Clause

The extends clause provides a reference to the super-concept. By default, Concepts are created with BaseConcept as their super concept, but this can be changed to a more specific super-concept. The extends clause encodes the equivalent to the is-a relationship of the Unified Modeling Language. When concept B extends concept A, it indicates that concept B has all the attributes of concept A, plus some.

3.2.2 The implements Clause

The implements clause provides references to Interface Concepts that the concept implements. Interface Concepts are described in Section 3.3. Interface Concepts can be used as type markers or to indicate that the concept must implement some behavior methods. See Chapter 7 for more details about endowing Concepts and Interface Concepts with behavior methods.

3.2.3 Instance can be root

This boolean attribute indicates whether the concept can be used as an AST Root node. Only concepts for which the attribute 'Instance can be root' is true will be shown in the New 〉 〉Concept menu of a solution that uses the language.

Changing the 'Instance can be root' attribute does not require a rebuild of the language to take effect. Notice how the New 〉 Concept menu of solution models is immediately updated when you modify this attribute.

3.2.4 The Concept's alias

The alias attribute is used to construct the auto-completion menu. This attribute should contain a string that it would be natural to type when trying to create an instance of this concept. In the math example of Section 2.8, the alias of the Complex concept was simply 'complex'. Note that the string can contain any UTF-8 character and symbol names are handy to encode operators (for instance + is an adequate alias for concepts that represent additions for some concept types).

3.2.5 The Concept's short description

Use this attribute to document the function of this concept. The short description is presented to the right of the auto-completion menu and helps end-users of your languages distinguish among concepts that could share the same alias. Keep this description short as only a few words fit comfortably on screen in the auto-completion menu. The auto-completion menu defaults to showing the concept language name for concepts that have no short description.

3.2.6 Properties

Properties hold values that are owned by the concept. You can create a new property in a Concept by positioning the cursor within « ... » immediately below properties: and pressing ⏎. When some properties are defined, the symbol « ... » is not shown, but you can position the cursor to the right of any property and press ⏎ to insert a new property. Properties have a name and a type. Properties are analogous to UML class properties. By default, property types can be

- **Primitive types**: (i) integer (ii) string or (iii) boolean . Custom primitive types can be created if necessary. See Section 3.6 to learn how to define new primitive types.
- **Enumeration types**: defined with the 'Enumeration Types' AST Root node. See Section 3.4 to learn how to define new enumeration types.
- **Constrainted data types**: defined with the 'Constrained Data Types' AST Root node. These types are a restriction of an existing type, which limit the range of values that are acceptable. See Section 3.5 to learn how to define new constrained data types.

3.2.7 Children

Children define aggregation relationships between the concept and its possible parts. You can add new children to a Concept by positioning the cursor within « ... » immediately below children: and pressing ⏎. When some children relationships are already defined, the symbol « ... » is not shown, but you can position the cursor to the right of any child relation and press ⏎ to insert a new child association. Concept children associations have a role, a type, and a cardinality. They optionally can specialize a child association from a super-concept. These elements are analogous to the UML aggregation associations:

- **Role**: Describes the function for the child in the parent concept. The role is used to access the children as in concept.role when concept is a reference to a node of the Concept.
- **Type**: A reference to another Concept that is acceptable as a child in this role.
- **Cardinality**: One of (a) 0..1 (b) 1 (c) 0..n or (d) 1..n . A cardinality of 0..1 means that the child is optional in this role and can occur at most once. A cardinality of 1 means that the child is required in this role and can occur exactly once. A cardinality of 0..n means that the child is optional in this role and can occur several times. A cardinality of 1..n means that the child is required in this role and can occur several times.
- **Specializes**: You can indicate that the child association specializes one defined in a super-concept. To this end, the *specializes* attribute can be added to a children role of a concept by locating the cursor to the right of cardinality, typing a space and pressing ctrl + SPACE . Select "specializes" and indicate which super-concept association this link specializes.
- **Unordered**: For associations with multiple cardinality (i.e., 1..n or 0..n), you can specify that the order of the children does not matter. This is achieved by adding the *unordered* attribute to the association. To this end, locate the cursor to the right of cardinality, typing a space and press ctrl + SPACE . Select "unordered". The unordered keyword will be displayed next to the child association. You can delete the keyword to revert back to ordered children in this role.

(R) Specialization makes it possible to restrict the type of the target of a child association in a sub-concept. Assume concept *A* has sub-concepts *B* and *C*. You define a child in concept *A* called *myParts*, with type *Part*. The concept *Part* has sub-concepts *PartB* and *PartC*. Without specialization, any instance of *PartB* could be added to the *myParts* children of a *PartC* node. If you introduce specialization on *PartC*, you can restrict the myParts children link to nodes of the PartC concept. You can similarly restrict the *myParts* children role of the *B* concept to accept only *PartB* nodes.

3.2.8 References

References define relationships from this concept to other nodes of the AST. Contrary to children, references can point to nodes that are not connected to the Concept node by aggregation. It is only possible to create a reference to a node if this node already exists in some AST Root node. You can add new references to a Concept by positioning the cursor within « ... » immediately below references: and pressing ⏎ . When some references are already defined, the symbol « ... » is not shown, but you can position the cursor to the right of any reference declaration and press ⏎ to insert a new reference.

References have a role, a target concept, a cardinality and can optionally indicate that they specialize a reference link from a super-concept.

- **Role**: Describes the function for the reference in the parent concept. The role is used to access the reference as in concept.role.
- **Type**: A reference to another Concept that is acceptable as a reference in this role.
- **Cardinality**: One of (a) 0..1 or (b) 1. A cardinality of 0..1 means that the reference is optional in this role and can occur at most once. A cardinality of 1 means that the

reference is required in this role and can occur exactly once. Unbounded cardinalities are not possible for references. If you need them, simply create a Concept to hold a reference and this reference concept as child with the required cardinality.

- **Specializes**: A references can specialize a reference link from a super-concept. At least one reference link must exist for this option to be enabled. To indicate specialization, the *specializes* attribute can be added to a reference role of a concept by locating the cursor to the right of cardinality, typing a space and pressing ctrl + SPACE . Select "specializes" and indicate which super-concept reference this link specializes.

 In MPS, children and references are implemented as LinkDeclaration concepts. It is possible to refer to a reference or children link in the behavior aspect (see Chapter 7) with the expression `link/ConceptName/role/`.

3.2.9 Inspector Tab: Help and Icon

Note that you can configure some additional attributes of a concept by opening the inspector tab when the concept is selected. Click on the concept keyword and open the inspector Tab 2: Inspector to see these attributes.

URL

The URL attribute makes it possible to provide a URL that will be opened when the user requests help about a node of the concept. When a URL is provided, the user will be able to right click on a node of the concept in the editor and select "Show help for Node" or "Show help for Root Node" (when the node was created as a Root node). When this action is invoked, MPS will open the web browser to the page indicated in the URL attribute.

Icon

The icon attribute offers a file selection dialog that can be used to locate a png image file. When an icon path is selected, the file is copied to the language under the `icons/` directory and used to render a small icon in the Project Tab and on each editor tab where the concept is viewed. Small images of size 16 pixels by 16 pixels or up to 24 by 24 work well as icons.

3.2.10 Abstract Concepts

Concepts can be marked as abstract. This is useful when a concept is needed as an internal node of a concept hierarchy, but should not be instantiated directly. To mark a concept as abstract, position the cursor before the concept word and start typing the word 'abstract'. On the last typed letter of the word, the abstract modifier appears before the concept. An alternative way to make a concept abstract is to position the cursor over the concept name, show the intention menu, and select Intentions ⟩ Make abstract . You can remove the abstract modifier either by deleting the modifier word in the editor or with Intentions ⟩ Make Not Abstract .

3.2.11 Smart Reference

A concept that contains only one reference of cardinality [1] and that has no properties, alias or children is called a Smart Reference concept. Smart reference concepts are wrappers which make it possible to hold multiple references as children of a concept. The editor provides special support for smart references to help end-users locate instances that can satisfy the reference.

3.3 Interface Concepts

Interface Concepts offer a convenient mechanism to declare concept characteristics that can be used across several Concept types. For instance, this mechanism can be used for grouping properties that are commonly used together in an interface concept, and declaring any concept that need these properties to implement the Interface Concept.

You can create a new Interface Concept in a structure aspect by selecting New ⟩ Interface Concept , as shown in Figure 3.1. Creating a new Interface Concept presents the content shown in Figure 3.3 in the editor. Immediately after creating the interface concept you should enter a suitable name. The name will be used under the structure aspect in the Project Tab and can be used in large projects to locate the interface concept with Navigate ⟩ ⟩ Go To Root Node [ctrl + N or ⌘ + N]. Naming the interface concept will resolve the error shown in Figure 3.3.

Figure 3.3: **New Interface Concept AST Root.** Interface concepts can extend other interface concepts. They possess properties, children and references and can be used when groups of these attributes need to be reused across different Concept types. Interface Concepts with a name, but no properties, children or references are called Marker Interface.

3.3.1 The extends clause

Interface Concepts can extend other Interface concepts and these is-a relations are represented in the extends clause. The extends clause has [0..n] cardinality. To indicate that the interface concept extends more than one interface concept, simply press return over the content of the extend clause and use the editor completion to locate the appropriate InterfaceConcept.

3.3.2 Other attributes

Interface Concepts have properties, children and references with identical semantic to Concepts. Refer to sections 3.2.6-3.2.8 for details about these attributes.

3.3.3 Marker Interface

Definition 3.3.1 An interface concept with a name, but no properties, children or references is called a Marker Interface.

Marker interfaces are useful to tag Concepts that have a certain characteristic. Tagging concepts with a marker interface makes it possible to find all concepts that have the marker interface, and allow to hold a reference to the concept without knowing its concrete type.

3.4 Enumeration Types

Enumeration Types, or Enumerations for short represent fixed sets of named constant values. Enumerations are similar to enum types in languages like Java or C++.

Figure 3.4 presents the editor just after creating a new Enumeration Type (solution name ⟩ ⟩ New ⟩⟩ Enum Data Type). You should name the enumeration type immediately after creating it. A complete example of enumeration is shown in Figure 3.5

After naming the type you can add values to the enumeration. Start by positioning the cursor over <no type> shown after 'enumeration datatype:' in Figure 3.4. Press ctrl + Space to activate the auto-completion menu and pick integer as the member type over which to base the enumeration.

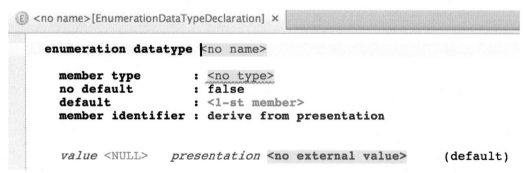

Figure 3.4: **New Enumeration Type.**

3.4.1 Member Type

This is the type of the values. You can choose one of (i) integer or (ii) string or (iii) boolean.

3.4.2 No Default/Default

These attributes control whether the enumeration type has a default value. When no default is set to true, the enumeration type has no default value. When no default is set to false, the enumeration type has the default value specified in the default attribute. In this case, placing the cursor over the 'default' attribute makes it possible to pick one of the defined values as default value (Press `ctrl` + `Space` to activate the auto-completion menu or start typing the name of the default value to use as default).

3.4.3 Member Identifier

This attribute govern how identifiers are generated for each enumeration element in the generated code. One of two choices is available: (i) derive from presentation or (ii) derive from internal value (iii) boolean. Switch the value of this attribute and do `Editor` `right-click` `Preview Generated Text` to see the impact on the generated code.

3.4.4 Enumeration Elements

The line that starts with value <NULL> in Figure 3.4 can be used to fill-in value and presentation for the first enumeration element. Press `↵` to create additional elements for this enumeration type. The element assigned as default value is marked with the (default) string to the right of the element name.

Value

Place the cursor over <NULL> to define the value of the element. The value must be compatible with the type selected under member type. As of MPS 3.02, mismatches between member type and element values are not detected in the editor and generation errors will result.

```
enumeration datatype FunLevel

    member type       : integer
    no default        : false
    default           : SO_SO
    member identifier : derive from presentation

    value 1     presentation BORING
    value 10    presentation SO_SO      (default)
    value 11    presentation NICE
    value 20    presentation GREAT
```

Figure 3.5: **Completed Enumeration Type.** This figure presents a completed enumeration type with three elements. The element called SO_SO is the default value of the type.

Presentation

Place the cursor over <no external value> and start typing the name of the enumeration element.

3.5 Constrained Data Types

Constrained Types are string types with restrictions on the value that the type can hold. Figure 3.6 presents the editor just after creating a new Constrained Type (`solution` `New` `Constrained Data Type`). You should name the constrained type immediately after creating it. A complete example of constrained type that restricts values to some kind of identified made up of letters, underscore and digits is shown in Figure 3.7.

Note that the constrained type generates a setter that checks the value set to the type matches the regular expression in the generated code, but it does not wire this check with the editor. Consequently, syntax errors will not be highlighted when values set on a property of the constrained type do not match the regular expression of the type.

Figure 3.6: **New Con-strained Data Type.**

⊙ <no name>[ConstrainedDataTypeDeclaration] ×

constrained string datatype: <no name>

matching regexp: <no value>

Figure 3.7: **New Con-strained Data Type Exam-ple.**

constrained string datatype: SomeKindOfIdentifier

matching regexp: [a-fA-F0-9_]+

3.5.1 Matching Regexp

Enter a regular expression in this expression to constrain the type of value that can be set on a property of the constrained type. The regular expression is directly inserted into Java code as a String literal and needs to be escaped appropriately. For instance \. must be written as \\. to correctly match dots in the value of the type (writing \. will cause a syntax error in the generated code).

3.6 Primitive Data Types

The default MPS primitive data types (see Section 3.2.6 on page 37) can be extended by creating a new Primitive Data Type in a language.

Figure 3.8 presents the editor just after creating a new Primitive Data Type (solution name ⟩ New ⟩ Primitive DataTypeDeclaration).

⊙ <no name>[PrimitiveDataTypeDeclaration] ×

primitive datatype: <no name>

Figure 3.8: **New Primitive Data Type.**

Primitive DataType

This attributes names the primitive data type. Enter a type name. We recommend to follow naming conventions consistently across types and concept names.

3.7 Annotation Link

Annotation links were available in earlier versions of MPS, but are marked as deprecated in MPS 3+. To create annotations in recent versions of MPS, see Section 17.1.

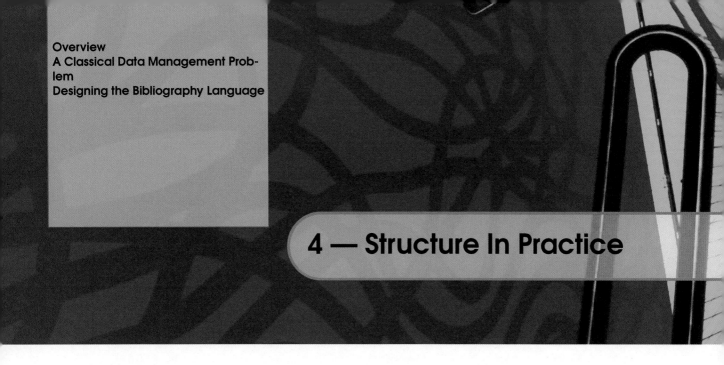

4 — Structure In Practice

4.1 Overview

This chapter illustrates the use of the MPS structure aspect. As an example, we look at the problem of storing bibliographical references.

4.2 A Classical Data Management Problem

Tracking bibliography is a classical data management problem since computers have been used for typesetting scholarly publications. In a nut-shell we aim to store the bibliographical details about books, articles and web sites that we wish to refer to in a the context of a new publication (such as this book).

Many tools have been developed over the years to keep track of bibliography. To cite just a few, BIBTEX is a text format that was integrated to the TEX and LATEX systems. For instance, BIBTEX is used to store the bibliography of this book. The BIBTEX format looks like a succession of bibliographical records like this:

```
@article{Simi2014,
    title = {Composable languages for bioinformatics:
            the NYoSh experiment},
    author = {Simi, Manuele and Campagne, Fabien},
    journal = {PeerJ},
    volume = "2",
    page = "e241",
    year = {2014}
    url = "http://dx.doi.org/10.7717/peerj.241"
}
```

You can see the above reference formatted in the bibliography of this book [SC14]. Storing data as text is particularly inconvenient because text editors are unable to validate that the format of the text matches some specification. Even TEX editors like TEXPad are unable to highlight syntax problems in a BIBTEX formatted file. When writting this book, I would often forget commas that the BIBTEX format requires between two fields of the bibliographical record. Finding such errors is surprisingly difficult when the parsers report a problem several lines later.

To illustrate the Structure Aspect we will model a collection of bibliographical records with MPS. In the following chapters, we will add functionality to this toy example to create an editor and generate a collection to the BIBTEX text format. In the generator in practice chapter (Chapter 16), we will show how to convert this model to an XML format with model to model transformation.

4.3   Designing the Bibliography Language

A first step in the design is to think about the concepts that we will need to implement and their relationships. Figure 4.1 provides a UML diagram of the *Bibliography* language that we will create.

This UML diagram can be easily mapped into the MPS Structure language because the concepts are well aligned. The is-a relationships will be modeled either with the extends or implements clause of Concepts (see Section 3.2.1 and 3.2.2). Aggregations will be represented with children elements. Figure 4.1 presents a snapshot of the structure aspect for some of the concepts of the *Bibliography* language.

These declarations are sufficient to start using the language in a solution. Let's create such a solution. Using the Project Tab, create a solution called *Biblio*, then do Project > > right-click > New Solution . Import the *Bibliography* language for use in the solution. Create a new model into this solution and also import the language. Finally, add a Bibliography Root to the Model Project Tab > Solution > Biblio > right-click > New > bibliography . Remember that this menu is visible only for these concepts that have the attribute 'instance can be root' set to true.

You should now be able to edit the Bibliography. Try to enter the details of Simi2014 as shown in Figure 4.3. Play with the editor and notice how the completion menu works and offers only concepts when they are compatible with the structure declared in the concepts. Remember that ↵ is used to create new nodes. When a new node is an instance of an abstract concept (i.e., BiblioElement), the editor shows a pink box that activates the auto-completion menu and lets you pick an appropriate concrete implementation of the abstract concept. You can pick by either typing the name of the alias for the concrete concept, or by activating the auto-completion menu option + SPACE and selecting an option.

> (R)   Note that in MPS 3.02, when a concept does not implement INamedConcept and a
>   default editor is used, a property field of type string is picked to render right after the
>   concept type name. In Figure 4.3, the author's middleName property is shown right
>   after the author keyword, which is sub-optimal. There are two work-arounds: define
>   an editor for the author concept, or make Author implement INamedConcept.

While working with the editor, you may notice a problem with the way we have defined the *Bibliography* language. If you wanted to create another BiblioRecord about an article

Figure 4.1: **UML Diagram of the Bibliography Language.** Boxes denote concepts and the letter in the box specified the type of concept. C letters denote Concepts, I letters denote Interface Concepts and A letters denote Abstract Concepts. The light cyan color denotes classes or interfaces that are part of the MPS platform. In this design, the Bibliography concept has a 1..n record children of type `BiblioRecord`. Each record has elements of type `BiblioElement`. BiblioElement is an abstract concept and has several concrete sub-concepts. Shown are `TitleElement` to hold the title of a publication as a string value, PublicationYearElement and `AuthorElement` to hold a list of authors.

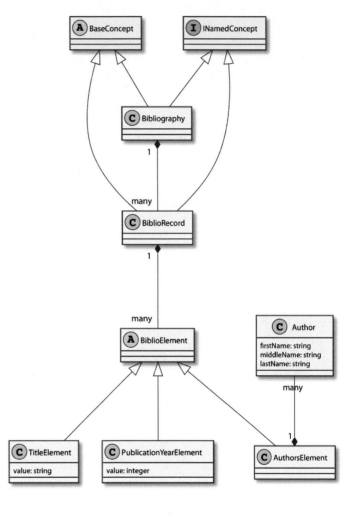

Figure 4.2: **Structure aspect definitions of the Bibliography language.** This figure presents the key concepts of the *Bibliography* language. Note the very close relationship between the structure language declarations and the UML diagram shown in Figure 4.1.

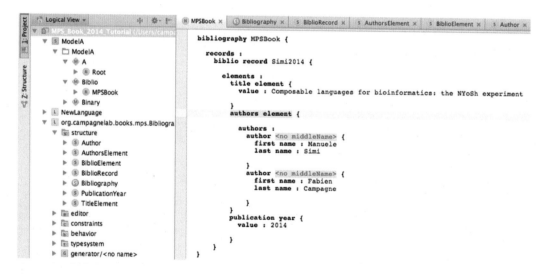

Figure 4.3: **Bibliography Root node shown with the default editor.** The details of the bibliographical record Simi2014 are shown as entered with the default MPS editor. The default editor can render any MPS concept whose structure has been defined. You can use it to test-run your language concepts and their connectivity before creating a custom editor. Notice that you can cut and paste part of the AST and have full undo/redo support. See Chapter 20 for the MPS editing Key Map.

authored by Manuele Simi, you would need to duplicate the author block. You can easily do this with copy and paste, but doing so will duplicate the data and make it hard to find all papers authored by the same author. A solution to this problem is to introduce an `AuthorRef` concept, which is a sub-concept of Author and references an author already defined in the AST. Figure 4.4 presents a revised UML diagram for the AuthorElement sub-concepts. The equivalent MPS Concepts are shown in Figure 4.5. Figure 4.6 presents a view of the editor where the authorRef concept references authors across the Biblography AST.

Figure 4.4: **UML Diagram of the AuthorElement Sub-Concepts after Refactoring.** This diagram presents the `AuthorElement` concept and sub-concepts after refactoring `Author` as the `Person` concept. The new design introduces an abstract concept `Author`, which is extended by `Person`, `AuthorRef` and an `EtAl` concept used to represent other authors (et al usage). `AuthorRef` is a smart reference to an `Author` node and enables to reference previously-defined `Author` nodes.

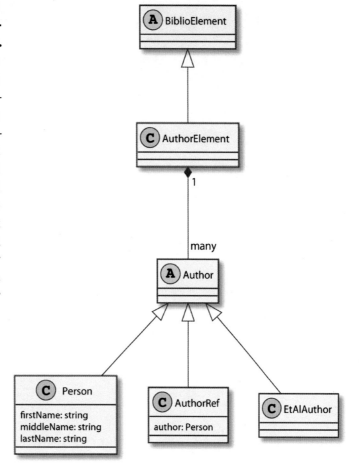

In the next chapter, you will learn about the Editor Aspect that makes it possible to develop custom editors for concepts of your languages. In Chapter 6 we will develop custom editors for the *Bibliography* language.

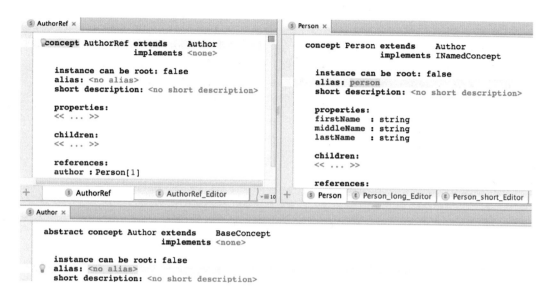

Figure 4.5: **Author concept refactored to support references across the AST.** We renamed the `Author`concept as Person, created an abstract concept `Author` and added a `AuthorRef` concept that extends `Author` and references a `Person` node.

```
bibliography MPSBook {

  records :
    biblio record Simi2014 {

      elements :
        authors element {

          authors :
            person Simi,Manuele {
              first name : Manuele
              middle name : <no middleName>
              last name : Simi

            }
            person Campagne,Fabien {
              first name : Fabien
              middle name : <no middleName>
              last name : Campagne
            }
        }
        title element {
          value : Composable languages for bioinformatics: the NYoSh experiment

        }
    }
    biblio record AnotherPublication {

      elements :
        title element {
          value : Understanding References to other parts of the AST
        }
        authors element {

          authors :
            author ref author : Campagne,Fabien
            author ref author : Simi,Manuele
        }
    }
}
```

Figure 4.6: **Default editor after the author reference refactoring.** The default editor is shown after we have added another publication to the bibliography, and the *Bibliography* language has been refactored to support author references. The nodes rendered as author ref is a smart reference to an author defined in the other `BiblioRecord`. The editor renders smart-references with the name of the concept (author) followed by the name of the referenced node. The blue arrow illustrates that references point to nodes across the AST.

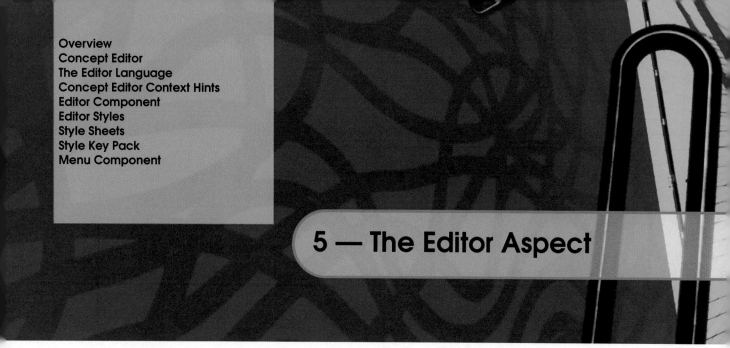

5 — The Editor Aspect

5.1 Overview

The Editor Aspect is a component of a Language that makes it possible to customize the rendering and editing of AST nodes in the editor. The Editor Aspect is expressed with the MPS *jetbrains.mps.lang.editor* language. This language can be used to create custom views for AST nodes. Figure 5.1 presents the different AST Root nodes that can be defined in an Editor Aspect.

When working with the editor aspect it is essential to know about the inspector tab, which is used extensively to edit style and configure connections between cells and the concept parts that they render. You can read more about the inspector tab in Section 2.11. Make sure you open the tab by clicking on the ⊕ 2: Inspector icon. The following sections describe the types of Root Nodes offered in the Editor Aspect.

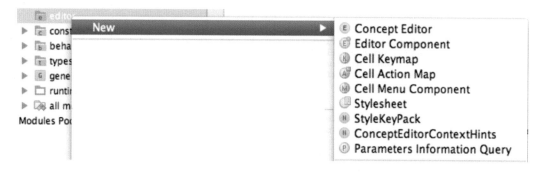

Figure 5.1: **AST Roots of the Editor Aspect.** This figure presents the type of AST Roots that can be created under an Editor Aspect. To test this, create a new MPS Language, right-click on the Editor Aspect, browse over New (Editor Aspect ⟩ right-click ⟩ New). Selecting a type of AST Root node will create this root in the editor aspect of the language.

5.2 Concept Editor

A concept editor is responsible for rendering and editing one node for one AST Concept.
MPS 3.0 introduced the ability to define multiple editors per concept. This feature gives the
ability to offer different views of the same concept for different needs. There are two ways
to create a new Concept Editor.

1. You can use Editor Aspect ⟩ right-click ⟩ New to create an orphan editor. Figure 5.2
   presents a snapshot of a new orphan editor.
2. You can click on a concept in the structure aspect to bring it into focus in the editor,
   click on the Editor tab (at the bottom of the editor window), and click in the window
   and pick Concept Editor Concept ⟩ Editor tab ⟩ Click ⟩ Concept Editor .

The second method is handy if you are already looking at the Concept. It will bind
the editor to the Concept automatically. If you use the first method, you need to enter the
Concept name after 'editor for concept'. You should do this immediately after creating the
Concept Editor because doing so will activate auto-completion in the editor language for
properties, children and references of the bound Concept.

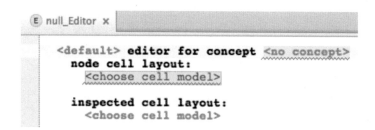

Figure 5.2: **Orphan Concept Editor.** An orphan Concept Editor was created with
Editor Aspect ⟩ right-click ⟩ New . It is recommended to immediately bind the editor to
a concept. To do so, provide a Concept reference after 'editor for concept'. The attribute
showing as <default>, at the top-left of the editor makes it possible to associate a context
hint to the editor. To add a concept hint, locate the cursor over the area marked <default>
and invoke auto-completion. A hint can be selected when it has been previously defined.
See Section 5.2.1 to learn how to do this.

5.2.1 Context Hint

This attribute associates the editor to a context hint. If a concept has several editors, context
hints are used to help MPS choose which editor to use when rendering a node of the concept
in a given editor window. Note that if several editors are bound to the same concept, the
editors must have different context hints. To add a context hint to an editor, you first need to
create a 'Concept Editor Concept Hints' node in the Editor Aspect (see Section 5.4). You
can then bind the editor to one of the hints defined in this node.

5.2.2 Editor For Concept

This is a reference to the Concept that this editor will present/edit. Auto-completion will show concepts from your language.

5.2.3 Node Cell Layout

This attribute provides a way to configure the view shown in the main editor window. Use the Editor Language to define the layout of nodes of the Concepts bound to this editor. The Editor Language is described in Section 5.3. A Node Cell Layout attribute consists of exactly one Cell from the Editor Language. Since cells can be collections, arbitrary editors can be presented.

5.2.4 Inspected Cell Layout

This attribute provides a way to configure the view that will be shown in the Inspector Tab ⊕ 2: Inspector when the cursor is positioned over a node of the concept. The same language is used here as that used to define Node Cell Layouts and a single Cell is similarly allowed. Use the Editor Language described in Section 5.3 to define the Inspected Cell Layout.

5.3 The Editor Language

The editor language consists of ways to define Editor Cells. An editor cell renders a node into the MPS editor window, typically, over a rectangular region. Several kinds of cells can be used to various effects. All cell types have common attributes, which include:

- **cell id** a string that is used to identify a specific editor cell. The string must be unique within a language.
- **action map** a reference to a Cell Action Map. Binding a cell action map to a cell enables the actions defined in the map in the context of the editor cell (when the user puts the cursor over the region that the cell rendered). See Section 5.3.1 for details.
- **keymap** a reference to an editor Cell Key Map. Binding a cell key map to a cell enables the key strokes defined in the map in the context of the editor cell (when the user puts the cursor over the region that the cell rendered). See Section 5.3.2 for details.
- **menu** is an attribute that makes it possible to extend the completion menu in the context of the cell. See Section 5.3.3 for details.
- **attracts focus** is an option to control whether the cell attracts the user focus when a node is created. Three options are possible: (a) noAttraction (b) attractsFocus (c) attractsRecursively and (d) firstEditableCell . The option attractsRecursively makes it possible to set focus recursivly on child cells. This is useful to set focus for instance on the last element of a chain of identifiers separated by dots, such as *a.b.c.d*, where each identifier is a child of another (i.e., b is a child of a, and d is a child of c). Attract focus recursively will correctly position the focus on the cell that renders d, making it possible to apply side transformation to insert another dot identifier on d, for instance.
- **show if** is a concept function that let you specify the condition when a cell is shown. Press ⏎ to insert the empty function body. The function has three parameters:

editorContext, scope, and node and returns a boolean. When the function returns `true` the cell is shown. When it returns `false` the cell is hidden. You can use this functionality to implement keywords that appear only when pressing a certain key.

5.3.1   Cell Action Map

Cell Action Maps provide a way to associate actions to specific events. You create a new Action Map with Editor Aspect ⟩ New ⟩ Cell Action Map . Figure 5.3 presents a freshly created Cell Action Map. You should immediately name the map after you created it. Remember that cell action maps must be bound to at least one cell of the editor before they become enabled. You can use the *action map* editor attribute (found under the 2: Inspector) to bind a cell action map to a given cell.

Applicable Concept

You can restrict a Cell Action Map to a concept by entering a concept reference here. MPS defines about thirty types of events that can happen to nodes, from INSERT (insertion of a new node) to DELETE (deletion of a node). Table 5.1 provides a partial list of the most common action types. The complete list of Cell Actions is available in the language *jetbrains .mps.ide.editor*.

```
action map <no name>

applicable concept: <any>

actions:

<< ... >>
```

Figure 5.3: **The Cell Action Map.** Cell Action Maps associate actions to specific event types. You can map actions to events by placing the cursor inside < ... >, below 'actions:', and invoking the completion menu to choose the appropriate event type.

```
keymap <no name>

everyModel false

applicable concept: <any>

keymap items:

<< ... >>
```

Figure 5.4: **The Cell Key Map.** Cell Key Maps associate keystrokes to specific event types. You can map key strokes to events by placing the cursor inside < ... > below 'keymap items:' and pressing ⏎.

Action Type	Event Descriotion
INSERT	A new node was inserted.
INSERT_BEFORE	A new node was inserted immediately before this node.
DELETE	The node is about to be deleted.
COPY	The node was copied to the clipboard.
PASTE	The node was pasted from the clipboard.
PASTE_BEFORE	A node was pasted from the clipboard immediately before this node.
PASTE_AFTER	A node was pasted from the clipboard immediately after this node.
BACKSPACE	The backspace key was pressed over the node.

Table 5.1: List of Common Cell Action Types.

5.3.2 Cell Key Map

Cell Key Maps, or key maps for short, associate key strokes to custom actions. You create a new Cell Key Map with [Editor Aspect ⟩ New ⟩ Cell Key Map]. Figure 5.4 presents a freshly created Cell Key Map. You should immediately name the map after you created it. Remember that key maps must be bound to at least one cell of the editor before they become enabled. You can use the *keymap* editor attribute (you can find it under the [2: Inspector]).

Applicable Concept

You can restrict a keymap to a concept by entering a concept reference here.

5.3.3 Element Menu

You can add parts to the auto-completion menu of this cell by adding elements to the *menu* attribute. Press enter to add a part and use the auto-completion menu to see which part types are available for the element. Section 5.9.2 presents a description of Cell Menu Components and menu parts.

The following subsections present categories of cells and their usage.

5.3.4 Collection Cells

Collection cells can have other cells as children. The type of collection determines how the editor will render the children of the cell. The following types of collection cells are available:

- [> ... <] **Horizontal Cells** Will show children cells horizontally arranged from left to right.
- [/ ... /] **Vertical Cells** Will show children cells vertically stacked from top to bottom.
- [- ... -] **Indent Cells** Will show children cells arranged according to the indentation layout. The indentation layout organizes children horizontally until the end of

line is reached. At that point the remaining children will be rendered on the next line, but prefixed with an indentation.

To add a Collection Cell, start typing an opening bracket '[' to use auto-completion and pick the correct collection type.

Inspector

Collections have a number of attributes that you can edit by opening the ⬛2: Inspector. These attributes let you change whether the collection will use braces or folding. When braces is active, selecting the collection will surround it with blue braces in the editor. If you choose to activate folding, the editor will show a small − or + symbol in the left margin that enables end users to fold/unfold the entire collection. Since MPS 3.3, the default folding state can be configured using the `collapse by default` attribute.

5.3.5 Constant Cells

A constant cell can be used to render keywords or other constant text in the editor. Press ["] to create a constant cell, or type 'constant'. Typing the character of the constant also will create a constant cell if no cell alias could match the text that you typed. For instance, if you wanted to create a constant with text [- you would need to use the ["] shortcut to create a constant cell, then type [-, since pressing [- directly would create a horizontal collection cell. The rendering of constant cells is affected by the style attached to the cell. See Section 5.7 for a description of styles.

5.3.6 Property Cells

Property Cells render the content of a specific property of the node attached to the editor. You can create a propery cell by typing [{], then using auto-completion to select the property. Assume the editor is bound to a concept with the *a* property (type string). In order to create an editor that renders the value of *a*, you type [{] under Node Cell Layout, then select the *a* property in the selection menu. This creates a property cell linked the a property of the concept, which is rendered as {a}. Property cells have several attributes that can be edited in the ⬛2: Inspector:

- **property** is the name of the property bound to the cell.
- **text*** is the default text shown when the property is not set on the node.
- **empty text*** is a boolean. When true, empty property values are shown as a narrow pink placeholder, where the user can type the property value. When false, the user is shown a strong message that the property is missing.
- **read only** is a boolean. When true, the editor prevents the user from editing the value of the property. When false (the default), the editor provides read/write access to the property.
- **allow empty** is a boolean. When true, no error message is shown when a property is empty. Even when empty text is true, no narrow pink placeholder is shown. Empty properties become invisible, but can still be edited if the user knows where they are and positions the cursor over them.

5.3.7 **Child Cell**

Child Cells delegate the rendering of a child to the appropriate concept editor. You can create a child cell by typing `%`, then using auto-completion to select the child by role. Assume the editor is bound to a concept with children of type Part in role 'part'. In order to create an editor that renders the value of *parts*, you type `%` under Node Cell Layout, then select the *parts* child role in the selection menu. This creates a child cell linked the a *parts* child of the concept, which is rendered as `%parts%`. Child cells have several attributes that can be edited in the `2: Inspector`:

- **link** is the role for the child bound to the cell.
- **filter** is a concept function that is called for every child in the bound role. The function has two arguments (scope, childNode) and returns a boolean. When the function returns `true`, the child is included in the list of children shown for the role. When the function returns `false` it is not.
- **cell layout** determines how the child in the bound role will be laid out. Choices include: flow, horizontal, indent, indent_old, superscript, table, vertical, vertical_grid. Experiment with changing this settings to see the effect in the editor.
- **uses braces** is a boolean which determines if braces ({ }) will be shown around each child.
- **uses folding** is a boolean which determines if folding is allowed for the entire set of children in the role. When folding is true, a plus or minus character is shown in a box in the left marging of the editor and makes it possible to fold child cells.

When the child has the multiplicity other than 0..1 or 1..1 that is compatible with multiple elements, the following attributes are also shown in the `2: Inspector`:

- **separator** is a string that defines the separator used when more than one element needs to be shown.
- **separator constraint** is one of none, flow, punctuation. Experiment changing this attribute to see the effect in the editor. Note that this option may only be useful with some layouts.
- **separator style** lets you select a style to apply to the separator. Styles are defined in Section 5.6.
- **reverse order** is a boolean that controls if children should be shown in reverse order (when true).
- **element factory** is a concept function that implements node creation. When a user inserts a new node in a collection, the editor will call this factory concept function to obtain the new node. You can implement this function to create a node of a specific type. This function can be used to return concepts for empty lines. See the MPS editor cookbook online for details (`http://tinyurl.com/le4qgu5`).
- **element action map** is a reference to an editor action map. Action maps are described in Section 5.3.1. Binding the action map to the cell will enable the actions of the Action Map in the editor context where the cell is displayed.
- **element menu** is an attribute that makes it possible to extend the auto-completion menu. See Section 5.3.3 for details.

- **add context hints** concept function to add a concept hint. See Section 5.4 for details.
- **remove context hints** concept function to remove a concept hint. See Section 5.4 for details.

5.3.8   Referent Cell

Referent Cells are used to show the values of some attributes of a concept's reference. You can create a referent cell by typing `%`, then using auto-completion to select the reference by role. The auto-completion menu will show a choice like `%reference%—>`. Select this choice to use the referent cell. After accepting this choice, you need to select the attribute of the reference node that you wish to display when the referent cell is rendered in the editor. Assume the editor is bound to a concept with reference of type Person in role 'user'. In order to create an editor that renders the name property of reference *user*, you type `%` under Node Cell Layout, then select the *user* reference in the selection menu. This creates a referent cell linked the user reference of the concept, which is rendered as `%user%—>`. You finally select the name property of the `Person` concept to display at the location of the referent cell in the editor. The completed referent cell will be displayed as `%user%—>name`.

Referent cells have several attributes that can be edited in the `2: Inspector`:

- **link** is the role for the reference bound to the cell.
- **text*** this attribute appears to have no effect for reference cells in MPS 3.
- **empty text*** is a boolean, but is attribute that appears to have no effect reference cells in MPS 3.

5.3.9   Swing Component Cell

Swing Components Cells are used to render an arbitrary Swing JComponent in the editor. You can create a Swing component cell by typing 'swing' in a new editor cell and accepting the *swing component* suggestion. An swing component cell is rendered as `$swing component$` when editing the editor of a concept, but renders the component in the live editor window (i.e., after you have rebuilt the editor and start using it to edit nodes of the concept in a solution).

Swing component cells have a single attribute that can be edited in the `2: Inspector`:

- **component provider** is a concept function that makes it possible to return a JComponent instance. The function has two arguments: node and editorContext, and returns a javax.swing.JComponent instance. You can use the function to render an arbitrary JComponent subclass. For instance, returning `return new JLabel("Icon");` will render a JLabel component showing the text Icon.

Reading node state from Swing code

If you implement a swing component to render a cell, you may find that you need to read or write information from the node of the concept associated with the Swing component. This is possible, but particular caution must be taken to guarantee that read/writes are synchronized with the rest of the data accesses that MPS performs.

If you need to read the state of the node, you need to enclose the code that accesses the node with a runReadAction block. The following code snippet is reproduced from the

Samples example (available in the MPS 3.1 distribution):

```
node.model/.getRepository().getModelAccess().runReadAction({
  =>
    foundColor = node.color.findColor();
    radius = node.radius;
});
```

The code fragment obtains the model from the node in the concept function that initializes the swing component. The model is downcast to its specific implementation (operator /). The downcast model can be used to retrieve the repository and start a model access transaction for read access. Inside the closure, the color and radius variables are obtained from the node and stored in the swing component variables. This transaction is run each time the swing component needs to refresh.

A similar method is available if you need to write information to the node. In this case, use the runWriteAction method of the *ModelAccess* implementation.

Note that MPS provides a simpler way to express read and write access to nodes. See the *jetbrains.mps.lang.access* language described in Section 17.8.

5.3.10   Image Cell

Image Cells are used to render an image in the editor. You can create an image cell by typing 'image' in a new editor cell. An image cell is rendered as `$image$` when editing the editor of a concept, but displays the image when the user is using the editor to edit a node. Image cells have several attributes that can be edited in the ⚉ 2: Inspector :

- **image provider** is a concept function that makes it possible to return a calculated image path. The function has two arguments: node and editorContext, and returns a string wich must be the path to the image to be displayed.
- **image file** This provides a way to enter a constant path to the image to be displayed. In case both image provider and image file are provided, image provider is used.
- **descent** is an integer that controls by how much the image is moved down from the position calculated by the current layout. Experiment with changing this value to position the image appropriately in the rendered editor.

5.3.11   Editor Component Cell

An Editor Component Cell delegates its rendering to an editor component. See Section 5.5 to learn how to create an editor component. Referencing editor components makes it easier to construct modular editors.

5.3.12   Model Access Cell

Model Access Cells are used to modify the state of a node following a get/set/validate pattern. You can create a model access cell by typing 'mod' in a new editor cell, invoking the auto-completion menu with ctrl + SPACE and accepting the *model access* suggestion. A model access cell is rendered as `$model access$` when editing the editor of a concept, but renders the string retrieved when calling the get concept function.

Model Access cells have several attributes that can be edited in the [2: Inspector]:

- **model accessor: get** is a concept function that makes it possible to calculate the text string that will be shown in the editor using information about the state of the node. The get function has two parameters: *editorContext* and *node* and returns a string.
- **model accessor: set** is a concept function that makes it possible to set the state of the node, using the text entered in the editor. The set function has three parameters: *text*, *editorContext* and *node* and returns no value. The parameter *text* contains the string the end user entered in the editor in this cell. If a validate function is defined, the set function will only be called when validate returns `true`.
- **model accessor: validate** is a concept function that makes it possible to validate whether the text entered by the end-user in the cell is valid. The set function has five parameters: *text*, *node*, *oldText*, *editorContext* and *node* and returns a boolean. The parameter *text* contains the string the end user entered in the editor in this cell. The parameter *oldText* contains the last text value when validate returned true, or the first invocation of get. The return value must be `true` if the text is a valid entry for this node, or false otherwise. The set function will only be called with text values that validate as true. Furthermore, when the validate value function returns `false`, the text is highlighted in red in the editor to provide immediate feedback to the end user. It is important to note that validate must be robust and catch any exception that parsing arbitrary text might trigger (e.g., NotANumberException should be handled in the function).

5.3.13   Indent Cell

Indent Cells are used to add indentation space in the editor. The amount of space added for each indentation cell is configurable in the MPS Preferences. For this reason, creating an indentation cell is preferable to adding a constant cell with spaces in it. You can create an indentation cell by typing [-]+[-]+[-]+[>]. This will yield a cell that looks like − − −>. Indent cells have no properties exposed in the inspector tab.

5.3.14   Custom Cell

A custom cell makes it possible to create new implementations of the editor cells. You can create a custom cell by typing 'custom' in a new editor cell, invoking the auto-completion menu with [ctrl]+[SPACE] and accepting the *custom cell* suggestion. A custom cell is rendered as `$custom cell$` when editing the editor of a concept, but renders the cell implementation returned by the get function.

Custom cells have one attribute that can be edited in the [2: Inspector]:

cell provider

is a concept function that makes it possible to return an implementation of AbstractCell-Provider. The function has two arguments: editorContext and node, and returns a Cell-Provider. You can use the function to render an arbitrary CellProvider subclass. You can find examples of cell provider implementations by navigating to the concept (⌘ + N) QueryFunction_CellProvider and looking for usage globally (include concept instances).

5.3.15   Next Applicable Cell

You can create a `next applicable cell` by typing 'next' in a new editor cell, invoking the auto-completion menu with ctrl + SPACE and accepting the *next applicable cell* suggestion.

This cell is useful when you need to delegate rendering to another editor attached to the same concept. In the next section, Editor Context Hints are described, which can be used to associate multiple editors to a single concept and decide when one editor should be used rather than another.

While this gives some flexibility, it can also be useful to define an editor as a wrapper around another editor of the same concept. For instance, consider the case where you already have an editor for concept A, and the editor is rather complicated. You need another editor, whose rendering will add some cells around the previous A editor. You could copy the previous A editor, call it something else and customize it. However, maintenance will be easier if you can simply reuse the previous editor inside a new editor. The `new applicable cell` allows to do just this. When inserted into an editor for concept A, the cell will identify the next editor suitable to render a node of A, given the Editor Context Hints active at this location of the display, then render it.

 The New Applicable Cell can be used when you have defined several alternative editors for the same concept. If no other editor is available for the concept, the reflective editor will be shown at the location of `new applicable cell`.

5.4   Concept Editor Context Hints

Concept Editor Context Hints, or context hints for short, help MPS decide which editor to show when a concept has multiple editors defined for it. You can create a new Context Hints in an editor aspect by selecting New ⟩ ConceptEditorContext Hints , as shown in Figure 5.5

Context hints can be set in different ways. First, Users can interactively choose to push hints to the editor. To do this, in the editor window, right-click ⟩ Push Editor Hints . Second, Language designers can change which editor hints are considered programmatically.

Changing hints programmatically is done by implementing one of two concept functions in the Inspector Tab of a collection cell. These concept functions are called 'add context hint' and 'remove context hint'. They both return a sequence of strings. Using these functions together you can force a collection to use a specific hint. You would do this by defining functions that add the hint you want to use and remove all others. To force the use of a specific hint in a collection, return the hint in the add method and set the remove function to the other hint (if you have exactly two defined), or set the remove function to *query* to edit the concept function directly. When removing with *query*, construct a sequence of strings with all the hints that you need to remove (for instance `new arraylist<string>{concept editor`

`hint/long/, concept editor hint/short/}` would remove two hints called long
and short).

> (R) Note that removing hints programmatically does not prevent the user from adding
> these hints back manually with `right-click` 〉 `Push Editor Hints`.

```
concept editor context hints |<no name>
   hints:
      <no hints specified>
```

Figure 5.5: **Concept Editor
Context Hints.** The figure
shows a freshly created AST
Root of type Concept Editor
Context Hints. Use this AST
Root to define context hints
for your language.

```
concept editor context hints |MyPersonHints
   hints:
      ID: long Presentation: Long Description for Persons
      ID: short Presentation: Short Description for Persons
```

Figure 5.6: **Complete Context Hints Example.** This example shows two hints defined for
alternate views of the `Person` concept. The editor associated with the 'long' hint presents
the full name of an author, while the editor associated with the 'short' hint displays only
the last name of the author. Hints do not define each editor, they simply name the type of
presentation implemented by each editor associated with the context hint.

5.5 Editor Component

An Editor Component is responsible for rendering and editing one part of a node. In contrast
to Concept Editors, which are responsible for rendering entire nodes, Editor Components
focus on rendering specific parts of a node. As such, Editor Components can be reused
across concept editors that need to render parts similarly. Editor components can also be
Overriden in new languages, which makes it possible for language designers to customize
the presentations of parts of nodes, when these parts are rendered with a component.

You can create a new Editor Component with `Editor Aspect` 〉 `right-click` 〉 `New` 〉 `Editor
Component`. Figure 5.7 presents a snapshot of a new editor component.

5.5.1 Overrides

Editor Components can override other components. Overriding an editor component makes
it possible to customize the presentation or editing of the concept that the original editor was
responsible for rendering. You can specify that the new component overrides a previously
defined component by using the *overrides:* attribute. Note that when a component A
overrides a component B, the concept rendered by A must be a sub-concept of the concept

rendered by component B. When *overrides:* is specified, you can specify an editor context hint with the 'Applicable Context Hint' attribute.

5.5.2 Applicable Concept

This attribute is a reference to the concept that the component will render. Bind the editor to a concept to enable auto-completion with the concept properties, children and references.

5.5.3 Component Cell Layout

This attribute provides a way to configure the view shown in the main editor window when this component is rendered. Use the Editor Language to define the layout of this component. The Editor Language is described in Section 5.3. A Component Cell Layout attribute consists of exactly one Cell from the Editor Language. Since cells can be collections, arbitrary editors can be presented.

Figure 5.7: **New Editor Component.** This figure presents a freshly created Editor Component. Note that editor components can override other components, which provides a way to customize the rendering of parts of a node.

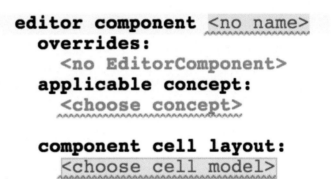

5.6 Editor Styles

Editor Styles can be applied to editor cells to affect how the cell is rendered. To apply a style to an editor, you select the editor (Concept Editor or Editor Component), click on a cell of the editor, open the inspector tab, and change the **Style:** attribute. See Figure 5.8 for a snapshot of the Style attribute in the inspector.

 MPS Stylesheets and Styles are reminiscent of Cascading Style Sheets (CSS). Both technology help separate presentation concerns from visual layouts. Use Style Sheets when developing MPS editors to avoid cluttering the editor with repetitive style items.

5.6.1 Base Style

The Base Style is the style that a cell is assigned to. It is a reference to a node of type Style. Styles are defined in StyleSheets, and described in Section 5.7. Base styles provide a set of rendering attributes that are applied to a cell, unless they are overriden. Style attributes can be overriden by specifying them inside the BaseStyle bracket.

5.6.2 Overriding Style Attributes

Style attributes can be Overriden by providing the style attribute inside the < ... > shown in Figure 5.8. In case no base style was assigned, this section can be used to set style attributes to a cell directly. While it is possible to define style attributes directly, it is good practice to design a style sheet for a language, or reuse an existing style sheet from another language (e.g., *baseLanguage* offers a stylesheet suitable for many programming languages).

```
Style:
<no base style> {
   << ... >>
}
```

Figure 5.8: **The Style Attribute.** This figure presents a snapshot of the Style attribute seen in the inspector tab. The attribute is shown when it is not assigned to any style.

5.7 Style Sheets

Style Sheets offer a way to define new editor styles. You can create a new Style Sheet with `Editor Aspect` > `New` > `Style Sheet`. Figure 5.9 presents an empty style sheet. You should name the style sheet immediately after creating it. Pressing `↵` over the 'No Styles' area will create a new Style. See Figure 5.10 for an example of a complete, but minimalist, style sheet.

5.7.1 Style

Style affect the presentation of editor cells. A style has a name, which is used to attach styles to specific editor cells. Until MPS 3.0, a style could extend another style (use the intention menu when the cursor is positioned over the style name to introduce the extends clause). A change introduced in MPS 3.1 replaces the extend keyword with the `dominates over` keywords. This change clarifies that a stylesheet overrides any style elements defined in a style that it extends/dominates over.

Finally, a style can define a list of style attributes (MPS calls these *style items*).

You can learn more about available style items by using the auto-completion menu. The list of style items available in MPS will be displayed. When you have identified a style item that you would like to learn more about, navigate to the concept that implements it (`right-click` > `Go To + Concept Declaration`). When you see the concept in the editor, use `Concept Name` > `right-click` > `Find Usage`. Make sure your find usage settings look for Concept Instances in the global scope. Find usage will then return examples of usage of the style item.

Changes Introduced in MPS 3.1

MPS 3.1 introduces some changes to styles. A key change is the introduction of the `apply-if` style construction. This construction makes it possible to apply a style only when a condition evaluates to true.

apply-if   This style statement accepts a style reference and a concept function that must return a boolean value. The style referenced is applied only when the condition concept function returns `true`. The signature provides access to the editor context and to the node that the editor is displayed for.

apply   This style statement accepts a style reference and applies the style items. Note that if several apply statements are used and the same style items are defined in these styles, the apply statement that comes last will take effect.

Colors

Some style items require the specification of a color. In this case, a number of pre-defined colors are offered in the auto-completion menu. If you need a color that is not pre-defined, pick any predefined color, then use the intention on the color name to introduce a query concept function. The function must return a java.awt.Color instance initialized with the required color.

Predifined Styles

It is possible to define and reference a predefined style. Predefined styles are referenced by key. Each key must be defined in a Style Key Pack. See Section 5.8 to learn how to create a Style Key Pack.

Figure 5.9: **New Style Sheet.** This figure presents a freshly created new style sheet. See Figure 5.10 for a completed style sheet.

```
stylesheet <no name> {
    No styles
}
```

Figure 5.10: **Complete Style Sheet.** This figure presents a complete style sheet. The style sheet contains three styles. The first one is called SomeBlandPresentation and defines no style attributes. The second style is called Fancy and includes style attributes that set the background to yellow and text foreground to black. The third style extends and overrides ("dominates over") the Fancy style to bold text.

```
stylesheet FancyStyles {
    style SomeBlandPresentation {
        Add style items
    }

    style Fancy {
        background-color : yellow
        text-foreground-color : black
    }

    style BoldFancy dominates over Fancy {
        font-style : bold
    }
}
```

5.8 Style Key Pack

Style Key Pack define a set of keys that are typically used to reference predefined styles. You can create a new Style Key Pack with `editor aspect ⟩ New ⟩ StyleKeyPack`. This creates an empty pack that you should name immediately. You can define new keys by pressing `↵` when the cursor is over the « ... ». Type a string to use as key. Press `↵` to add more keys. By convention, all MPS keys should be written in uppercase with words separated by underscore.

5.9 Menu Component

Cell Menu Components represent menu actions that can be added to the auto-completion menu of an editor cell. You can create a new Cell Menu Component with `editor aspect ⟩ New ⟩ Cell Menu Component`. This creates an empty menu component that you should name immediately. Figure 5.11 presents a freshly created Cell Menu Component. In addition to creating a menu component as an editor AST Root, you can also add the component directly under the menu attribute of a Cell (see Common attributes in `2: Inspector`). The difference between these two options is that the AST Root makes it easier to reuse a menu when it needs to be attached to several editor cells.

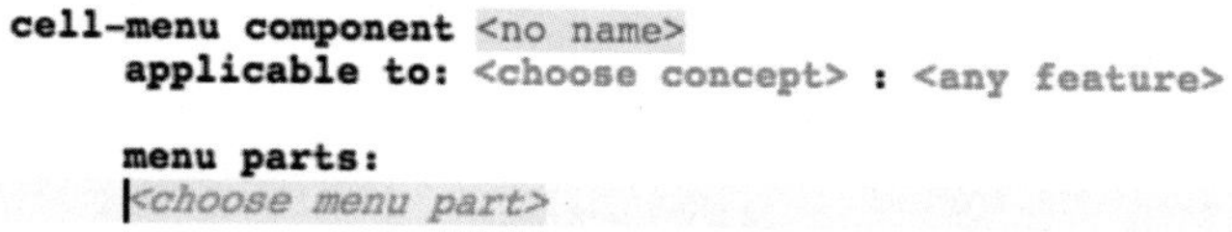

```
cell-menu component <no name>
    applicable to: <choose concept> : <any feature>

menu parts:
|<choose menu part>
```

Figure 5.11: **New Menu Component.** This figure presents a freshly created Cell Menu Component.

5.9.1 Applicable To

These attributes let you define the concept for which the menu will be available. You can restrict the menu to a specific property, child or reference of the concept by specifying the role in the `<any feature>` attribute.

5.9.2 Menu Parts

Positioning the cursor over `<choose menu part>` and activating the auto-completion menu displays a selection of menu parts. Figure 5.12 presents the parts available in MPS 3.

Generic Item

The simplest type of menu part is a generic item. This item adds a text item to the menu and invokes a concept function when the user activates the menu item. The concept function is called *handler*. The menu part should be added to a text property that is editable, or the user will not be able to type the property and activate the menu. When the menu is associated to an abstract concept, it is convenient to attach the menu to the alias property and make the alias editable. Figure 5.13 shows how to create a Generic Item that adds a Node author when the first name of the author is typed in the alias property of the abstract `Author` concept.

Figure 5.12: **Menu Parts Auto-completion Menu.** The auto-completion menu presents several types of menu parts.

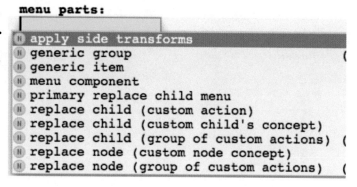

Figure 5.13: **Generic Menu Item.** The figure shows how to connect a generic menu item to the alias property of the abstract Author concept (editor shown in panel (A)). There are three components: Panel (A), the editor of the abstract `Author` concept displays the alias property. (B) The inspector tab is used to make the `#alias#` cell editable and to connect the menu part to this cell. (C) The Cell Menu Component defines a Generic Menu Item that associates a concept function to the text 'fabien'. The matching text is displayed in the auto-completion menu. When the text is selected in the auto-completion menu, the function will replace the abstract `Author` node with a `Person` node initialized with data.

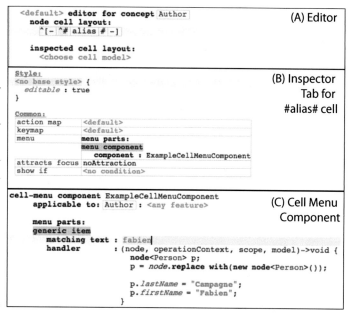

Generic Group

The Generic Group menu is useful when you need to create a set of menu items that only differ by one item. For instance, if we wanted to provide one auto-completion menu item for each of *n* authors, we would construct a Generic Menu Item similar to the one shown in Figure 5.14.

```
menu parts:
generic group
   parameter object type : string
   parameter objects     : (operationContext, scope, node)->list<string> {
                              return new arraylist<string>{"Proust", "Camus", "Hemingway"};

                           }
   presentation          : custom
   matching text         : <default>
   description text      : (parameterObject)->string {
                              "Add an author: " + parameterObject;
                           }
   handler               : (parameterObject, node, model, scope, editorContext, operationContext)->void {
                              node<Person> p;
                              p = node.replace with(new node<Person>());

                              p.lastName = parameterObject;
                              switch (parameterObject) {
                                 case "Proust" :
                                    p.firstName = "Marcel";
                                    break;
                                 case "Camus" :
                                    p.firstName = "Albert";
                                    break;

                                 case "Hemingway" :
                                    p.firstName = "Ernest";
                                    break;

                                 default :
                                    break;
                              }
                           }
```

Figure 5.14: **Generic Group Menu.** The figure shows how to construct Generic Group menu items. We start by defining the parameter type and set this attribute to string. The 'parameter objects' concept function is then updated to list<string> to reflect the chosen parameter type. We write the function implementation to return a list of three author names. In the handler, we recognize each author name and setup the corresponding Person instance. Note that we use *baseLanguage.jdk7* which provides a switch statement with string expression. We changed the presentation from default to custom and return a presentation string that includes the author name.

Menu Component

The Menu Component attributes allows to provide a reference to another menu component. The component must be already defined to set a reference to it. The menu items of the referenced menu will be added to the auto-completion menu of the cell in focus.

The Replace Node menu items will add an option to the auto-completion menu to replace the node with another of a specific concept. Figure 5.15 presents an example that extends the menu to replace the Author node with a Person node. The Replace Node menu comes in several variants called:

1. Replace Node (custom node concept). This variant is described in Figure 5.15.
2. Replace Node (group of custom actions). This variant can be used when the replace-

ment nodes vary by one parameter. It is similar to the Generic Group Menu, but less general as the handler simply returns a node to use as replacement. The example shown in Figure 5.14 is easier to implement with Replace Node (group of custom actions) because you don't need to write code to replace the node in the AST.

Figure 5.15: **Replace Node Menu Item.** The Replace Node menu item indicates that the auto-completion menu should contain an item to replace the node with a node of the specified concept.

```
cell-menu component ExampleCellMenuComponent
          applicable to: Author : <any feature>

          menu parts:
          replace node (custom node concept)
              replace with : Person
```

Apply Side Transform

The Apply Side Transform menu part indicates which direction side transforms should be applied on the editor cell attached to the menu. Three choices are available: *right* transform (default) and *left* transform and *both sides*. Note that side transformations will only be enabled if the apply side transform menu item is present to bind the cell to the side transformation. Side transform actions are described in Chapter 10.

Replace Child

These menu items are provided to extend the completion menu for chidren of the node, using information from the node. For instance, assume that concept A has a child of type B in role *b*. You may want to extend the auto-completion menu that will let end-users locate assign a new child in role b, with information from concept A.

6 — The Editor in Practice

In this chapter, we go back to the Bibliography example introduced in Chapter 4 and learn how to create custom editors for editing bibliographies. Refer to the previous Chapters for reference material about the editor. Remember that at the end of Chapter 4, we visualized the Bibliography node with the MPS default editors (see Figure 4.3). In this chapter, you will learn how to customize editors for the concepts of the *Bibliography* language.

6.1 Editor for the Person Concept

Let's create an editor for the Person concept. This concept defines three properties that store the author first, middle and last names. Furthermore, the Person concept implements INamedConcept, and therefore also has a name property. The editor shown in Figure 6.1 uses an indent collection as root cell. The collection contains property cells that display the first, middle and last name of the Person in order, followed by an opening parenthesis, the name property and a closing parenthesis.

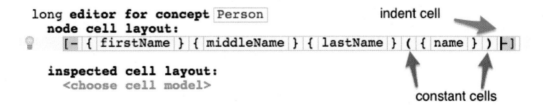

Figure 6.1: **Editor for the Person Concept.** The editor displays the four properties of the Person concept. Notice that the editor is bound to the Person concept, and associated with the *long* editor hint. The inspected cell layout is left empty since we don't need to edit a person node in the inspector tab.

If you look back at Figure 4.3, you will see that the default editor renders each Person as a block of six lines starting with the "person" keyword and ending with the "}" bracket. After entering the editor shown in Figure 6.1, if you rebuild the editor, and view the MPSBook AST Root node we created in Chapter 4, you will see the editor display in Figure 6.2.

> **authors :**
> Manuele <no middleName> Simi (Simi,Manuele)
> Fabien <no middleName> Campagne (Campagne,Fabien)

Figure 6.2: **Rendering of the Bibliography with the Person Editor.** A Person node is now displayed on a single line. Notice that the middleName name property is missing for these two authors and highlighted in red in this editor. Also notice that the authors collection is shown with one element per line.

The editor highlights the middleName property with an error message. This is the default behavior for concept properties. However, the author Manuele Simi does not have a middle name and we would prefer the editor to handle this relatively common case more gracefully. Let's prevent the editor from showing an error message in this case. We can adjust the middleName property cell by opening the ⊞ 2: Inspector and changing some attributes in the *Property cell:* section. Follow the instructions in Figure 6.3.

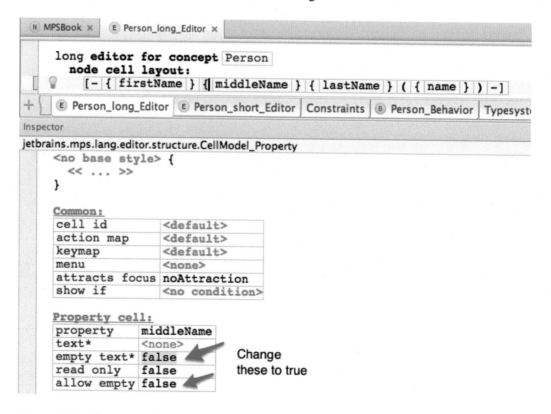

Figure 6.3: **Changing the middleName Cell Properties.** Put the cursor over the middle-Name property cell and open the inspector tab. Edit the properties "allow empty" and "empty text*" to set their values to true. Rebuild the language when you are done.

You should then see the rendering of `Person` nodes change to that displayed in Figure 6.4. An empty space remains between the author's first and last names. Typing in the middle of this space will correctly enter a middleName if needed.

Figure 6.4: **Person Editor Display After Adjusting Middle Name.** This displays the editor rendering for the bibliography after we have adjusted the middleName property presentation.

```
authors :
   Manuele  Simi ( Simi,Manuele )
   Fabien   Campagne ( Campagne,Fabien )
```

(R) MPS lets you define a subset of editors, and combines these custom editors with the default editors to render an AST Root. This makes it possible to develop editors one concept at a time, while rebuilding the project often to see how this impacts the user experience when editing ASTs.

Figure 6.4 is still a bit untidy. If you look carefully, there is a space between the parentheses and the name of the concept. We can remove this space by assigning style items to the constant cells used to render the parenthesis. Start by selecting the constant cell with the left parenthesis, open the ⊞ 2: Inspector , and enter the style shown in Figure 6.5. Use similar steps for the constant cell that renders the right parenthesis. Rebuild the editor. The editor rendering should now look like Figure 6.6.

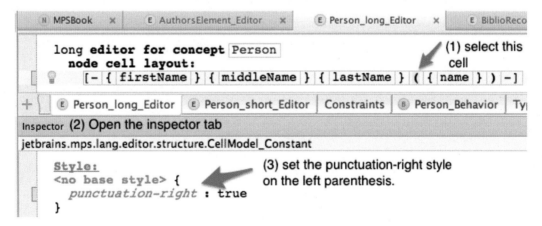

Figure 6.5: **Punctuation Style Items.** Follow these instructions (1-3) to add the punctuation style to the parenthesis constant cells.

6.2 Authors Collection

You may have noticed that authors are currently shown one Author per line. In bibliographies, it is customary to separate author names by comma and list names one after another. Let's

```
authors :
    Manuele   Simi (Simi,Manuele)
    Fabien   Campagne (Campagne,Fabien)
```

Figure 6.6: **Final Person Editor Rendering.** Notice how the spaces between the parentheses and the name have been removed. This is the effect of the punctuation-left/right style items.

change the AuthorsElement to achieve this presentation. AuthorsElement contains children of type Authors in role 'authors'. Go ahead and create an editor bound to the AuthorsElement concept (if needed, see Section 5.2 to learn how to do this). Figure 6.7 provides instructions for configuring the editor. We use an indent layout because it will nicely fit as many authors as possible per line, and wrap lines as needed.

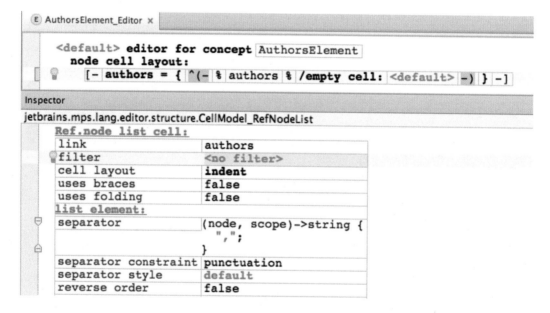

Figure 6.7: **Custom Editor for AuthorsElement.** The figure shows the editor for the concept AuthorsElement. We use an indent collection [- as root cell. We add a constant cell to show `authors = {`. After this, we add a child cell to display the authors role. In the ⚙ 2: Inspector , the child cell is configured to use an indent cell layout and provide a comma separator. Set the separator constraint to punctuation. Finally, we add a constant cell to close the bracket with the } character. Note that the ^ character in front of the %authors% cell is a visual indicator that the cell has an action map attached to it (the link to the action map is not shown in this figure).

After these changes, the editor will render as shown in Figure 6.8. Compare this display to the fully default editor rendering shown in Figure 4.3.

```
bibliography MPSBook {

  records :
    biblio record Simi2014 {

      elements :
        authors = { Manuele  Simi (Simi,Manuele), Fabien  Campagne (Campagne,Fabien) }
        title element {
          value : Composable languages for bioinformatics: the NYoSh experiment

        }
    }
}
```

Figure 6.8: **Rendering with Person and AuthorsElement Custom Editors.**

6.3 Editor for the TitleElement Concept

Let's change the editor for the `TitleElement` Concept. We aim to render the title in the BIBTEX format, that is with `title = "Title of the work here"` . Figure 6.9 shows this very simple MPS editor.

Figure 6.9: **TitleElement Editor.** We use a constant cell to render `title = "`. Then show the title property, then close the double quotes with another constant tag.

```
<default> editor for concept TitleElement
  node cell layout:
    [- title = " { value } " -]
```

6.4 Editor for the AuthorRef Concept

The editor to show references to other authors is also very simple. It displays the name of the author. Figure 6.10 shows this editor.

 In this case, we could have started the editor with the Reference Cell to the author name directly, because the editor really needs only one cell. However, it is advantageous to put an indent collection as root cell, because this makes it easier to insert other cells in the future in any position. If you started directly with the author reference, and needed later to add another cell next to it, you would have to delete the author reference, or cut/paste to preserve any configuration in the inspector. Starting with an indent collection cell avoids such problems.

Figure 6.10: **AuthorsRef Editor.** This simple editor shows the name of the person node referenced through the *author* role.

```
<default> editor for concept AuthorRef
  node cell layout:
    [- ( % author % -> { name } ) -]
```

6.5   Editor for the BiblioRecord Concept

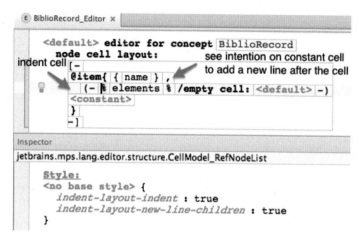

Figure 6.11: **BiblioRecord Editor.** The indent cell is added with an intention after you have entered the child cell for *elements*. New lines are added with constant cell. Create a constant cell by typing ⇧ + " , then add the new line with the "Add New Line" intention (cursor needs to be on the constant cell).

Let's focus now on the editor for the BiblioRecord concept. We aim to render the record in the BiBTEX style. Figure 6.11 shows such an editor. Note the use of the style item indent-layout-new-line-children. This style instructs the indent cell to show each element of the collection on a new line. New lines respect the indentation because we have added an indent cell immediately before the elements collection cell.

6.6   Editor for the Bibliography Concept

Finally, we provide an editor for the Bibliography concept (shown in Figure 6.12). The result of developing the editors presented in this chapter is shown in Figure 6.13. The rendering is now very close to the BiBTEX format, but completely editable. The editor has undo/redo capability and supports "Find Usage".

Figure 6.12: **Bibliography Editor.**

```
Bibliography MPSBook {
  @item{ Simi2014 ,
    authors = { Manuele  Simi (Simi,Manuele), Fabien  Campagne (Campagne,Fabien) }
    title = "Composable languages for bioinformatics: the NYoSh experiment"
  }
}
```

Figure 6.13: **Bibliography Editor Rendering.** Final view of the bibliography.

6.7 **Exercises**

Exercise 6.1 Use the Bibliography editors to add another item. Instead of entering a `Person` as author, use the `AuthorRef` concept to refer to an author previously defined. Try 'Find Usage' on the author referenced to verify that you see the reference in the list. ■

Exercise 6.2 Create an editor to render the PublicationDate concept in the BIBTEX format (e.g., `year = <value>`). ■

Exercise 6.3 Extend the auto-completion menu to offer auto-completion for the following authors: Donald Knuth, Andrew S. Tanenbaum, Brian W. Kernigan and Dennis M. Ritchie. Use the first name of these as the matching text so that when an end-user enters their first name, a complete Person instance is inserted in the author list of a `BiblioRecord`. See the auto-completion menu, Section 5.9 in the previous chapter for hints about how to proceed. ■

Overview
Concept Behavior
Internal Concept Declaration Holder
A baseLanguage Primer
The SModel language
Learning more
The Quotation language
AntiQuotations

7 — The Behavior Aspect

7.1 Overview

The Behavior Aspect is a component of a Language that makes it possible to endow the concepts of a language with behavior, that is, with code expressed in the *baseLanguage* and *SModel* languages and attached to some concepts. The Behavior Aspect is expressed with the MPS *jetbrains.mps.lang.behavior*. Figure 7.1 presents the different AST Root nodes that can be defined in a Behavior Aspect. These types of Behavior AST Root nodes are described in the following sections.

Figure 7.1: **AST Roots of the Behavior Aspect.** This figure presents the type of AST Roots that can be created under a Behavior Aspect. To test this, create a new MPS Language, right-click on the Behavior Aspect, browse over New. Selecting a type of AST Root node will create this root in the behavior of the language.

7.2 Concept Behavior

Concept Behavior nodes provide a way to define or declare methods for a concept. You can create a new Concept Behavior in a behavior aspect by selecting New ⟩ Concept Behavior, as shown in Figure 7.1. Creating a new Concept Behavior presents the content shown in Figure 7.2 in the editor. Immediately after creating the concept behavior you should bind the behavior to a concept. You can bind the behavior to a concept by entering a concept reference in the attribute marked <no concept>.

7.2.1 Constructor

Concept Behaviors define a constructor for the bound MPS concept. The code in the constructor block will be executed when a 'new initialized node' is created. In contrast to

```
concept behavior <no concept> {

    constructor {
        <no statements>
    }

    <<concept methods>>
}
```

Figure 7.2: **New Concept Behavior AST Root.** You can type *baseLanguage* statements in the constructor block. Press ⏎ when the cursor is over <<concept methods>> to insert a new method.

Java, it is worth noting that constructors are executed only in certain circumstances.

7.2.2 Methods

Behavior methods make it possible to associate methods to specific concepts or their descendants. The body of each method is often written with *baseLanguage*. Other languages can also be useful when writing method bodies. For instance, the *jetbrains.mps.smodel* language is useful to manipulate an AST (we call this language *SModel* in the rest of this book). See Section 7.5 to learn more about the *SModel* language. Many other languages can be used when writing behavior methods, including languages that you define specifically for your projects. Remember that before you can use a language to implement behavior methods or constructors, you need to add this language to the list of used languages for the Behavior aspect (see Section 2.8.1).

Methods Visibility

Behavior methods have a visibility that is analogous to the Java method visibility. Method visibility include: *public*, *protected* and *private*. You can change the visibility by putting the cursor over the visibility keyword (visibility is public by default) and typing a new visibility keyword. Method visibility allow you to control which languages can invoke the method of the behavior concept. When the method is public, any language who declares using a language that contains the behavior can use the method. When the method is protected, the method can only be called from behavior for concepts in the same language as the one the behavior is attached to. When the method is private, the method can only be called from within other methods of the same behavior concept.

Methods Modifiers

Behavior methods can be marked as *virtual*, *abstract*, *final*, or *static*. Marking a method with one of these modifiers is done by moving the cursor over the name of the method and invoking an intention. For instance, invoking the intention called "Make abstract" will add the *abstract* modifier to the behavior method.

- **virtual** This modifier has the same meaning as in the virtual modifier in the C++ language [Str00]. Methods marked with the *virtual* modifier can be extended in sub-concepts. This means that if concept *B* extends concept *A*, and both concept *B* and *A* offer a definition for the method called run(), the method run() must be marked as *virtual* in concept *A*. When implementing a virtual method for a sub-concept, you can mark the method of the subconcept as overriding the *virtual* method. You can do this by opening the ⬛ 2: Inspector and filling in the overrides attribute.

- **abstract** Methods marked with the *abstract* modifier do not have a body in the concept where they are marked abstract. Sub-concepts are expected to provide a body for the method.
- **final** This modifier has the same meaning as in the Java language [Gos+05]. Methods marked with the *final* modifier cannot be overriden in sub-concepts.
- **static** This modifier has the same meaning as in the Java language [Gos+05]. Static behavior methods are not attached to an instance of the concept, as such they cannot access the *this* instance. Methods marked with the *static* modifier can be called from a concept reference with the expression `concept/MyConcept/.staticMethodName`.

7.3 Internal Concept Declaration Holder

This AST Root node is internal to MPS and does not appear useful from the point of view of the end user.

7.4 A baseLanguage Primer

The MPS platform offers several languages that can be used immediately and are useful when implementing aspects for new languages. The language called *jetbrains.mps.baseLanguage* (baseLanguage for short) is a one to one mapping of the Java language 1.6 [Gos+05] to the MPS platform. While Java 1.6 may seem limiting when Java 1.7 and 1.8 have been released, it is not so because (*i*) it is easy to extend *baseLanguage* with new language constructs, and (*ii*) many useful extensions found in Java 1.8 are already offered in the MPS platform. For instance, the following languages are available in MPS 3+:

- **closures** Adds closure support in *baseLanguage*.
- **tuples** Adds support for tuples to *baseLanguage*. Used in the build language, for instance to represent input and output of compilation steps.
- **collections** Used by *SModel*, a powerful collections language with functional paradigm such as fold and reduce operations. Uses closures.
- **dates** Offer a way to represent dates and periods of time and to calculate with them.
- **regexp** Offer regular expressions tightly integrated with *baseLanguage*.

These languages are described in the MPS online reference manual. See `http://tinyurl.com/qc5xksy`, section **Platform Languages** for these languages. We will use some of these languages to write examples in this book and will then refer to the appropriate sections of the online reference manual.

7.5 The SModel language

The *SModel* language is designed to enable the traversal and modification of an MPS AST. *SModel* is often used in the Behavior aspect, but can also be used to implement intentions, actions, generators, or any concept function that needs to traverse or manipulate the AST.

7.5.1 Traversing the AST with SModel

SModel has a few general characteristics worth mentioning. In contrast to Java expressions, *SModel* expressions do not fail when trying to dereference *null*. Consider an expression like *a.b.c.d*, where *b* has value *null*. In Java, trying to access *d* through this chain will throw a `NullPointerException`. In *SModel*, the same chain will return *null*.

The behavior is extended to include collection access, so that any *null* occurence in a chain that ends with a collection will return an empty collection. For instance, in the chain *a.b.c.list( )*, the empty list is returned when either *a*, *b* or *c* evaluate to *null*.

This behavior makes it easier to traverse ASTs where some references are *null* without having to clutter traversal code with checks for *null*. You can check wether a chain element evaluated to *null* by using the methods *isNull( )* and *isNotNull( )* as in:

```
if (node.elements.first.isNull()) {
    // do something
}
```

7.5.2 Node Children, Descendants and Parents

When you have a reference to a node, you can traverse the AST up or down using *SModel*. You can access the parent of the node with the expression:

```
node.parent
```

You can access the children of the node with the expression:

```
node.children
```

This will return a list of immediate children of the node. In contrast, if you are interested in collecting the children of the node recursively, you can use `node.descendants <concept=Type>`, where type will indicate which concepts you wish to collect. For instance, to collect all the Person descendants of a BiblioRecord, you would do:

```
nlist<Person> persons = biblioRecord
                .descendants<concept = Person>;
```

See section 7.5.4 for a description of the `nlist<>` type.

7.5.3 Traversing References

In a way similar to accessing children of a node, you can obtain all the references that a node holds to other nodes with the following expression:

```
sequence<reference>=node.references
```

This expression returns a sequence, which is an immutable list defined in the *jetbrains.mps .collections* language.

7.5.4 SModel Types

The *SModel* language defines a number of types, which are described in the following sub-sections.

node<Concept>

Represents a node of the AST of type Concept. For instance, since the *Bibliography* language defines the concept `BiblioRecord`, we can hold a node of type `BiblioRecord` with the variable declaration:

```
node<BiblioRecord> record=node;
```

node<>

This type will represent a node of the AST of any concept type. This type can be used when you do not know the type of the concept a priori. For instance, to define a behavior method that accepts any node:

```
void process(node<> node) {
  ...
}
```

nlist<Concept>

Represents a list of AST nodes. You can use this type when you need to hold a list of nodes. For instance, in the *Bibliography* language, if you need to hold a list of bibliographical elements, you can use type `nlist<BiblioElement> elements= ....`

```
nlist<BiblioElement> list=record.elements;
```

concept<Concept>

A type suitable to hold a named concept. For instance:

```
concept<Bibliography> c= concept/Bibliography/
void process(concept<> c) {
  ...
}
```

New in MPS 3.2: A substantial change was introduced in MPS 3.2. Up to MPS 3.1, as far as the `concept<>` type was concerned, a language implementation and its sources were considered equivalent. For instance, you could use `concept<A>` to refer to a concept in language implementation (generated from sources by invoking build/rebuild), or to refer to the concept A inside the language sources (visible in the structure aspect of the language). MPS 3.2 introduces a distinction between these two types. If you need to refer to a concept in a language implementation (that is, a concept generated during the build process) you should use `concept<>`. Instead, if you need to refer to a concept under the structure aspect, visible even before the language is built, you must use `node<AbstractConceptDeclaration>` to hold a reference to that concept. You should be aware of this difference if you are upgrading a language from a previous version of MPS because MPS 3.1 `concept<>` has been renamed `conceptNode<>` and marked deprecated. It will be removed in a future version of MPS, so you are encouraged to replace `conceptNode<>` with the appropriate way to refer to the concept. There is no automatic migration for this change because MPS cannot determine which semantic your code requires. It is up to you to determine if when you wrote `concept<>` in MPS 3.1, you meant the concept in the language implementation (the most likely case if you are not working in the MPS team or do not need to modify concepts under the structure aspect directly), or if you mean the concept under the structure aspect. Use the following rule of thumb to determine what to replace `conceptNode<>` with in your languages:

- If the code should work before the language is built, such as if you need to represent the concepts under the structure aspect of another language before that language is built, replace the instance of `conceptNode<>` with `node<AbstractConcept Declaration>`.
- If the code needs to refer to a concept in a language implementation, and is not expected to build when the concept in the other language is not yet built (implementation does not exist), you should use `concept<>`.

> (R) Code using the deprecated `conceptNode<>` should continue to work in MPS 3.2, but plan to migrate as soon as possible because `conceptNode<>` is likely to be removed from the next major version of MPS.

model
A type to hold an instance of an MPS model. For instance:

```
model m=node.model;
```

> Note the `model//` syntax that makes it possible to refer to a model by name. A similar syntax makes it possible to refer to a language by name. For instance, you can type `language/jetbrains.mps.baseLanguage.logging/` to obtain a reference to the MPS logging language. In contrast to model, there is no *SModel* type to hold a reference to a language.

search scope
Represents the ISearchScope type. Please note that ISearchScope, and by extension the type search scope have been deprecated since MPS 3.0. It is not recommended to use search scope when writing new code.

reference
A type to hold a reference. A reference has a role and target. For instance, assume you have an AST with an `AuthorRef` node. You can locate the reference *r* that holds the link to the

Person node in the *author* role as shown in the following code fragment:

```
void process(node<AuthorRef> node) {
    reference r = node.reference<author>;
    assert r.role.equals("author");
    assert r.target instanceof node<Person>;
}
```

Note that in this case, it is easier to navigate the author reference directly, as in `node.author`, because we know that we need the author reference. The reference expression is really most useful only in some special cases. For instance, if you need to collect reference links and perform some calculation over them. Another case is when you need to calculate the name of the reference. For instance, assume that a concept has references whose name depend on some convention. You can calculate the name and use the reference query with an expression (#) to locate this reference, as shown in the following code snippet (notice that the author reference name is determined at runtime).

```
void process(node<AuthorRef> node) {
    string name="a"+"ut"+"thor";
    node<LinkDeclaration> decl = new node<LinkDeclaration>();
    decl.role = name;
    reference ref = this.reference<# decl>;
    assert r.role.equals("author");
    assert r.target instanceof node<Person>;
}
```

It is also possible to set the value of a reference in a generic way. The following code fragment demonstrates how. Note that you will need to import the *jetbrains.mps.smodel* *@java_stubs*.

```
((SNode) source).setReferenceTarget(link.role, destination);
```

enummember<Enum Data Type>
Represents an enumeration member. For instance, since Cardinality is an enumeration concept of *baseLanguage*, you can do:

```
enummember<Cardinality> card = enum/Cardinality/.<0..1>;
string value;
value = card.value;
// note the shorter version, using enum member value:
value = enum member value/Cardinality : 0..1/;
```

7.6 Learning more

The *SModel* primer included in this chapter is meant to help you get started with the *SModel* language. The language has various capabilities that are discussed in the MPS User

Guide, but not described here. You can learn more about the *SModel* language by visiting `http://confluence.jetbrains.com/display/MPSD30/SModel+language`.

The MPS platform also offer many examples of code written with *SModel*. You can find these examples under the Module Pool. Browse the various languages offered by the platform and open the Behavior Aspect. Most behavior methods and constructors take advantage of the *SModel* language. You can copy fragments of these code examples into your own projects and experiment with them. This should help you quickly become productive with the language.

7.7   The Quotation language

The *Quotation* language is useful when you need to create nodes of the Concepts of a target language. For this reason, you are likely to encounter usages of the *Quotation* language (called *quotations*) in the Behavior aspect of different languages.

Creating node instances is often needed in constructors. In a traditional programming language, you would assemble an instance of a concept by creating a new instance and setting the different attributes of the instance programmatically. While this is also possible with MPS with the *SModel* language, quotations provide a more convenient way.

To understand why, let's consider an example. We will assume that the language you are developing extends *baseLanguage*. You need a Concept C with a child of type `IfStatement`. We will further assume that instances of C must have the if statement initialized to the following AST fragment:

```
if (true) { return false; }
```

Without quotations, you could create the AST fragment with the code shown next to (1) in Figure 7.3. When using the *Quotation* language, you can simply enter the `IfStatement` as if you were editing such a statement in the MPS editor.

```
concept behavior C {

  constructor {
    // Using SModel to initialize the AST if fragment:
    this.ifStatement = new node<IfStatement>();
    node<BooleanConstant> constant = new node<BooleanConstant>();
(1) constant.value = true;
    this.ifStatement.condition = constant;
    this.ifStatement.ifTrue = new node<StatementList>();
    node<ReturnStatement> returnStatement = new node<ReturnStatement>();
    returnStatement.expression = new node<BooleanConstant>();
    this.ifStatement.ifTrue.children.add(returnStatement);

(2) // Using Quotations to initialize the AST if fragment:
    this.ifStatement = <if (true) { return false; }>;
  }
}
```

Figure 7.3: **Node Creation with *SModel* or *Quotation*.** This figure compares the construction of a node instance with (1) the *SModel* language or (2) the *Quotation* language. In (1) We use *SModel* to initialize an instance of `IfStatement`. The code is verbose and it is not immediately clear what is being done. In (2), we use a *Quotation* language. The quotation presents the *baseLanguage* editor for the `IfStatement` concept. As a result, it is immediately clear what statement is being constructed.

Figure 7.4 presents detailed instructions to create the quotation shown in (2). Follow similar steps to create nodes for different concepts by entering a different concept name in step 3.

Figure 7.4: **Using Quotations.** This figure illustrates how to initialize node instances with the *Quotation* language. Follow steps 1-4. In Step 3, note that auto-completion ctrl + SPACE is available to help you locate the relevant concept name.

```
this.ifStatement = krValue>;        (1) Type "<q"

this.ifStatement = <q|;             (2) Press Ctrl + SPACE

this.ifStatement = <      >;        (3) Enter "IfStatement"

this.ifStatement = <if (<condition>) {
    <no statements>                 (4) Configure the statement
}>;
```

Quotations are more convenient than using *SModel* directly because they let you configure a new AST node for a Concept by editing the properties, children and references of the concept using the editor associated with the concept. This is an advantage, but can also be a drawback. A potential problem is that the editor must be generated and compiled for a language before quotation can be used for concepts of that language. If you were to try using quotations in the behavior concept of a language to setup nodes of these same concepts, you would create a bootstrapping dependency condition. Bootstrapping dependencies occur when the compilation of a language requires two compilations to succeed. This is described in the MPS User guide at `http://confluence.jetbrains.com/display/MPSD30/` `Removing+bootstrapping+dependency+problems`. A simple solution to solve this problem is to convert the quotation to the *Light Quotation* language. *Light Quotation* does not introduce a dependency on the editor of the concept. However, light-quotation is not as intuitive a language as the *Quotation* language.

Fortunately, you can easily setup a node instance with the *Quotation* language, and then use an intention to convert it to Light Quotation. You do this by placing the cursor just before the opening bracket of the quotation, and invoking the "Convert to NodeBuilder" intention. If you prefer to edit nodes with the *Light Quotation* language directly, you can type "<" rather than "<q" in step 2 of Figure 7.4, and use ctrl + SPACE to find the light-quotation concept.

7.8 AntiQuotations

Antiquotations are used when you need quotations to include dynamic content. For instance, assume we needed the value of the condition determined dynamically, in the example shown in Figure 7.3 (i.e, instead of `true`, we need to calculate the boolean used in the condition of the IfStatement).

You can insert dynamic content in a quotation expression by typing the % character. This opens an anti-quotation expression. Be aware that the type of the expression you type as an anti-quotation must match the type of the node expected at the location where you enter the anti-quotation. In the example shown in Figure 7.5, the type of the anti-quotation is that of an expression from *baseLanguage*. We use a BooleanLiteral, which extends Expression

```
// expression is calculated dynamically;
boolean expression = true && false;
node<BooleanConstant> booleanLiteral = new node<BooleanConstant>();
booleanLiteral.value = expression;
node<> ifStatemnet = <if (%( booleanLiteral)%) { return false; }>;
```

Figure 7.5: **Using AntiQuotations.** This figure illustrates how to use an anti-quotation with the *quotations* language. The arrow points to the anti-quoted element (enclosed in %(and)%.).

to be able to dynamically set the boolean value for the `IfStatement` condition.

8 — Behavior In Practice

8.1 Example Concept

Since behavior nodes are attached to a Concept type, we create a concept to demonstrate how to attach a Behavior aspect to these concepts. Figure 8.1 presents this concept.

Figure 8.1: **Definition of ConceptWithBehavior.** The figure displays the structure of ConceptWithBehavior, a simple concept with three properties (*a,b,c*), two children roles (*aList, another*) and one optional reference (*aNeighbor*).

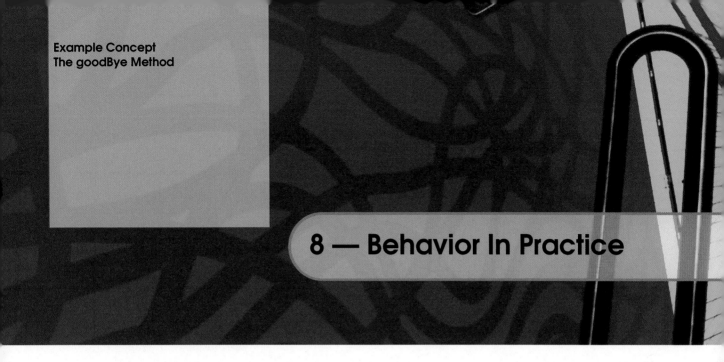

```
concept ConceptWithBehavior extends     BaseConcept
                             implements <none>

    instance can be root: false
    alias: <no alias>
    short description: <no short description>

    properties:
    a : integer
    b : string
    c : boolean

    children:
    aList   : ConceptWithBehavior[0..n]
    another : ConceptWithBehavior[0..1]

    references:
    aNeighbor : ConceptWithBehavior[0..1]
```

8.2 The goodBye Method

Let's attach a Behavior aspect to ConceptWithBehavior. Start by creating the Behavior node, as explained in Section 7. You should see the content shown in Figure 8.2. Continue by adding instructions inside the constructor body to initialize the properties with initial values. You could set a=2, b="hello" and c=true. Note the use of *this* to access the properties on the concept node.

After you have finished with the constructor, press ⏎ with the cursor within «concept methods». This should yield the view in Figure 8.3.

Figure 8.4 presents detailed instructions for adding new methods to the behavior.

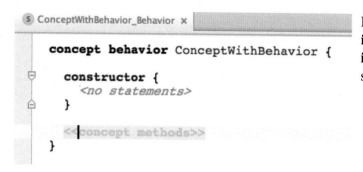

```
  ⓢ ConceptWithBehavior_Behavior  ×

    concept behavior ConceptWithBehavior {

      constructor {
        <no statements>
      }

      <<concept methods>>
    }
```

Figure 8.2: **Empty Behavior for ConceptWithBehavior.** The empty constructor should look like this.

```
    concept behavior ConceptWithBehavior {

      constructor {
        this.a = 1;
        this.b = "hello";
        this.c = true;
      }

  💡 public <type> <no name>() {
        <no statements>
      }

    }
```

Figure 8.3: **Behavior after completing the constructor.** The constructor is shown after adding property initialization code.

```
             (1) Type void
    public <type> <no name>() {
      <no statements>
    }
                     (2) Type goodBye
    public void <no name>() {
      <no statements>
    }

    public void goodBye() {
    (3) this.b = "goodbye";   Type this.b="goodBye"
    }
    (4) Invoke intention menu, select Make Virtual
    public void goodBye() {
    ┌─────────────────────────────────┐
    │            Intentions           │
    ├─────────────────────────────────┤
    │ 📄 Make Abstract              ▶ │
    │ 📄 Make Method Final          ▶ │
    │ 📄 Make Static                ▶ │
    │ ✏ Make Virtual                ▶ │
    │    Implement Behavior Method... │
    └─────────────────────────────────┘
```

Figure 8.4: **Steps to add a virtual method to Behavior.** Follow these steps to add a virtual method called good-Bye to ConceptWithBehavior. In step 1, you define the return type of the method to be void. In step 2, you name the method. In step 3 you create the method body. In step 4 you make the method virtual, allowing it to be overridden in the behavior of subconcepts. Following this exact sequence is not strictly necessary as long as you complete all steps.

9 — The Intentions Aspect

9.1 Overview

The Intentions Aspect is a component of a Language that makes it possible to define new intentions. The Intentions aspect is expressed with the MPS *jetbrains.mps.lang.intentions*. This language can be used to define intention AST Root nodes.

Figure 9.1: **AST Roots of the Intentions Aspect.** This figure presents the type of AST Roots that can be created under an Intentions Aspect. To test this, create a new MPS Language, right-click on language name, select `new ⟩ Intentions Aspect`. After the aspect is created, select it, right-click, browse over New. Selecting a type of AST Root node will create this root in the intentions aspect of the language.

Figure 9.1 presents the different AST Root nodes that can be defined in an Intentions Aspect. The following sections describe these types of Root Nodes in detail.

(R) Note that you could create intentions in any part of a language by importing the *jetbrains.mps.lang.intentions* language, however, only intentions inside the Intentions Aspect can be discovered by MPS to produce the intention menu. Make sure you create intentions in the Intentions aspect of your language if you want these intentions to be enabled in the MPS editor.

9.2 Intention

Definition 9.2.1 Intentions are the special user interface elements that are shown with the light-bulb symbol (💡). Clicking on the 💡 opens a menu where each item is called an intention (the intention menu was described in Section 2.10). Accepting the intention performs some modification of the AST in the context of the node selected when the intention menu was activated.

Figure 9.2 presents a freshly created Intention root node. The following sections describe the attributes of an Intention root node.

```
intention <no name> for concept <no forConcept> {
    error intention : false
    available in child nodes : false

    description(node, editorContext)->string {
        <no statements>
    }

    <isApplicable = true>

    execute(node, editorContext)->void {
        <no statements>
    }
}
```

Figure 9.2: **New Intention Root Node.** You should name the intention immediately after creating it. The attributes of the intention root node are described in the text.

9.2.1 For Concept

This is a reference to the concept that the intention is associated to. Intentions are only available when the cursor is on top of a node of the "for concept".

9.2.2 Error Intention

This boolean attribute determines whether this intention is meant to fix an error in the AST. If you set this attribute to true, you should implement the `isApplicable` concept function to detect the specific error condition that the intention is designed to fix.

9.2.3 Available in Child Nodes

This boolean attribute determines when the intention will be shown. Setting this attribute to true will make the intention visible over nodes that are children of the context node. Setting the value to false limits the intention to the be active only in the cells that render the context node. Consider the `IfStatement` concept for instance and the associated intention `UnwrapIfThenBlock`. The intention is marked as available in child-nodes because it is useful for the intention to be active when the cursor is positioned over the condition of the `IfStatement` concept, rather than just on the constant editor cell that renders the `if` keyword.

9.2.4 Description Concept Function

This concept function must return a string that will be displayed in the intention menu. Note that the string must follow a special capitalization, known as Title Case. To capitalize the description, you should capitalize a word unless it is a preposition, article or conjunction. For instance, you would type "Process this AST", and not "Process This AST" (MPS 3.1 conveniently offers an intention to convert a string to title case). MPS will check that you used Title Case and conveniently highlight deviations with a warning. Using Title Case for your intention descriptions help make the intention menu appear consistent when intentions from different languages are combined in a single menu.

> (R) Note that you should also prefer shorter descriptions to longer ones because only a few words can be shown in the intention menu.

9.2.5 Is Applicable

Pressing over this attribute will introduce a concept function whose value determines when the intention is active (return value true). The signature of the isApplicable concept function is as follows:

```
isApplicable(editorContext, node)->boolean {
}
```

9.2.6 Execute Concept Function

The execute concept function is where you can implement what the intention will do when it is activated by the end user. The signature of the concept function provides access to the node that the cursor is positioned on in the editor. You can use this node to walk the AST up or down and modify it.

The execute concept function is only called when isApplicable returned true and the node is compatible with the "for concept" and "available in child nodes" attributes.

9.3 Surround-With Intention

Surround-With Intentions are very similar to regular intentions, but are designed to surround a part of the AST with another construct (e.g., such as a node that represents parentheses). Creating a new Surround-With Intention creates an AST identical to that shown in Figure 9.2. Surround with intention differ from regular intentions in that they do not appear in the intention menu. Instead, surround-with intentions are shown in the surround-with intention menu which can be triggered with a keyboard shortcut (PC: ctrl + ⌥ + T or Mac: ⌘ + option + T). When the user invokes this key combination, the editor displays the menu shown in Figure 9.3.

Figure 9.3: **Activating the Surround-With Intention Menu.** Pressing ctrl + ⌥ + T on Windows or ⌘ + option + T on Mac OS will display the surround with intention menu. Note that the surround-with intention menu is context dependent. In the menu shown, the string literal can be surrounded with parentheses (choice 1) or cast to some type (choice 2).

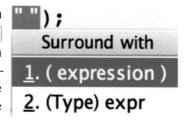

9.4   Parameterized Intention

Parameterized intentions are offered in the general intention menu with a description that depends on one parameter. Figure 9.4 presents a freshly created Parameterized Intention root node. The attributes of the parameterized intention are similar to those of general intentions, but also provide the `<add query>` attribute, which you can use to define a parameter (press ⏎) with the cursor over `<add query>` to define a parameter for the intention.

```
parameterized intention <no name> for concept <no forConcept> {
    error intention : false
    available in child nodes : false

    <add query>

    description(node, editorContext, parameter)->string {
      <no statements>
    }

    <isApplicable = true>

    execute(node, editorContext, parameter)->void {
      <no statements>
    }
}
```

Figure 9.4: **New Parameterized Intention Root Node.** The attributes of the parameterized intention root node are described in the text.

9.4.1   Adding a Parameter

After you have pressed return over the <add query> attribute, the editor changes to reveal the content of Figure 9.5. A new parameter has the following attributes:

Type

This attribute let's you define the type of the parameter. You can use either a primitive type or may prefer to return a generic concept type. In this later case, enter `concept<>` (use auto-completion after you typed the beginning of concept).

Parameter Concept Function

This concept function must return a list of parameter values to be displayed in the intention menu. As an example of parameter concept function, Figure 9.6 presents the parameterized intention that is defined in the MPS platform to let programmers switch between different kinds of loops (while, do while, for and foreach loops).

```
type: <no paramType>
parameter(node, editorContext)->list<?> {
  <no statements>
}
```

Figure 9.5: **New Intention Parameter.**

9.5   Universal Intention

Universal Intentions were introduced in MPS 3.3. This is an experimental feature that aimed to combine intention and parameterized intentions and was built with the light-DSL features (see Volume II). Being experimental, universal intentions may be removed from future versions of MPS. Since this feature does not add new functionality compared to the other inten-

```
parameterized intention AlterStatementListContainer for concept IContainsStatementList {
  error intention : false
  available in child nodes : false

  type: concept<>
  parameter(node, editorContext)->list<?> {
    list<concept<>> list = new arraylist<concept<>>{concept/IfStatement/, concept/WhileStatement/,
      concept/DoWhileStatement/, concept/ForStatement/, concept/ForeachStatement/};
    list.remove(node.concept);
    return list;
  }

  description(node, editorContext, parameter)->string {
    "Change to " + parameter.conceptAlias + (parameter.isExactly(ForeachStatement) ? "each" : "") +
      parameter.isExactly(DoWhileStatement) ? "-While" : "" + " statement";
  }

  isApplicable(editorContext, node)->boolean {
    true;
  }
}
```

Figure 9.6: **Parameterized Intention for Loops.** This parameterized intention lets the end-user switch to a different kind of loop using an intention when the cursor is already positioned on a loop. Shown is the Parameter section of the intention that provides a list of concepts to represent the different types of loops which a given loop can be converted to. Note that the list excludes the concept for the current kind of loop since this conversion would not be helpful.

tions, refer to Sections 9.4 and 9.2 for details about their attributes. Note that if you decide to try universal intentions, you will need to add jetbrains.mps.nodeEditor@java_stubs to the intentions aspect dependencies.

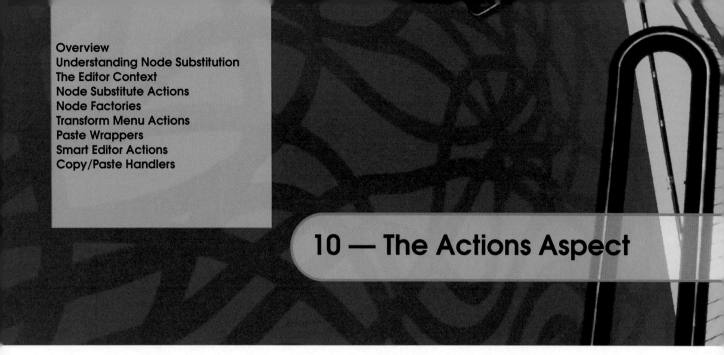

10 — The Actions Aspect

10.1 Overview

The Actions Aspect is a component of a Language that makes it possible to define actions that can modify the AST. The Actions aspect is expressed with the *jetbrains.mps.lang.actions* language. this language can be used to define action AST Root nodes. Figure 10.1 presents the different AST Root nodes that can be defined in an Actions Aspect. The following sections describe these types of Root Nodes in detail.

Figure 10.1: **AST Roots of the Actions Aspect.** This figure presents the type of AST Roots that can be created under an Actions Aspect. To test this, create a new MPS Language, right-click on language name, select new ⟩ Actions Aspect . After the aspect is created, select it, right-click, browse over New. Selecting a type of AST Root node will create this root in the actions aspect of the language.

10.2 Understanding Node Substitution

The MPS editor provides a default mechanism to substitute nodes of the AST with other nodes. The default mechanism works as follows. When the user presses ctrl + SPACE with the cursor positioned over a node (the *source node*), the editor will display an auto-completion menu with a set of choices that the user can accept. If the user accepts one of the choices, the editor will replace the node where the cursor is positioned with another node determined by the menu item that was selected. When the user presses ctrl + SPACE , we will say that he/she invokes the substitution menu.

In practice, a number of rules are used to determine which choices should be offered when invoking the substitution menu over a source node. The default rules are:

- If the source node is in an AST context where a concept *C* is allowed, any substitutions that would create a target node that is a subconcept of *C* are allowed, except when the concept:
  - Is abstract
  - Implements the *IDontSubstituteByDefault* interface concept
  - Has a constraint which indicates that the concept cannot be a child in the current AST context.[1]
  - Has a constraint which indicates that the concept cannot be a parent in the current AST context.[1]
  - Is involved in a reference with 1:1 cardinality. In this case, the smart reference behavior is implemented, which results in offering to substitute the source node with any instance of concept *C* visible in the scope. The name of each concept in scope is shown in the substitution menu.

These rules can be adjusted when they do not provide the substitution behavior that would be needed for a new language. Adjusting these rules consists in implementing Node Substitution Actions, described in Section 10.4.

It is often necessary to preserve information from the source node to the target node during a node substitution. For instance, it may be useful to preserve the statements in the body children of an `IfStatement` if the user needs to substitute the `IfStatement` with a `BlockStatement`. MPS provides a modular mechanism to transfer information from source node to target node. The mechanism has two parts:

- Node Substitute Actions determine which source nodes can be substituted by which target nodes.
- Node Factories determine how data is transferred from a source node to a target node.

Both parts are necessary for node substitutions to perform smoothly if information is to be preserved.

10.3   The Editor Context

Actions sometimes need to change the state of the editor. For instance, some actions need to select a specific node after the action has modified the AST. To this end, MPS offers the editorContext parameter in concept functions defined by many actions. The editorContext parameter provides access to an implementation of the *EditorContext* interface. This interface has a number of methods. We describe here some of the more frequently needed methods.

selectWRTFocusPolicy

These methods can select a node in the editor, taking into account the focus policy. Remember that the focus policy is set in the editor attached to a concept, and may be recursive, in which

---

[1] See Chapter 11 to learn how to define such constraints.

case calling selectWRTFocusPolicy may select a child of the node passed as parameter.

select

This method selects a node in the editor, but does not apply the focus policy defined by the editor of the node.

selectRange

This method selects a range of editor cells, delimited by the start node and end node given as parameters.

isInspector

This method returns `true` if the editor is displayed in the ![2: Inspector], and false otherwise.

openInspector

This method opens the ![2: Inspector] if it was not yet open.

executeCommand

This method will execute a command in an asynchronous manner. You may either provide a Runnable instance as a parameter, or a Computable instance.

With Runnable   If you provide a Runnable, the run method of the instance will be called at some future time. This approach is useful for commands that do not need to return a value.

With Computable   The Computable<T> interface has one method, called compute, that takes no parameter and returns a value of some type T. If you provide an implementation of this interface to the executeCommand method, the computable instance will be called at a later time.

runWithContextCell

Two commands are available to run commands that need access to a cell of the editor. These methods are called runWithContextCell and accept as first parameter an implementation of the *EditorCell* interface. The second parameter is similar to that described for the variants of `executeCommand()`.

isEditable

This method returns a boolean that is true if the cursor is within an editor cell with property editable set to true. False is returned otherwise.

10.4   Node Substitute Actions

You can create a new Node Substitute Action in an Actions aspect by following the direction given in the caption of Figure 10.1.

> **Definition 10.4.1 Node substitute actions** are used to substitute one node of the AST (source node) by another one (target node) when some user interaction occurs. Customizing the action that occurs when a node is substituted by another helps move data from the source node to the target node and makes for a smoother user experience.

Creating a new Node Substitute Action presents the content shown in Figure 10.2 in the editor. Immediately after creating the substitute action AST root, you should name it. The name will be used under the actions aspect in the Project Tab and can be used in large projects to locate the substitute node actions with Navigate ⟩ Go To Root Node [ctrl + N or ⌘ + N].

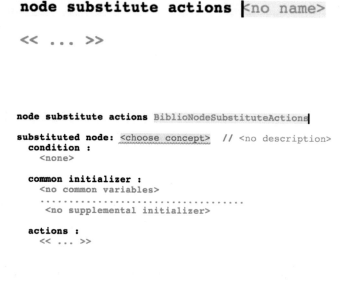

Figure 10.2: New Node Substitute Actions AST Root. Press ↵ with the cursor over « ... » to create a new node substitute action.

Figure 10.3: Freshly Created Node Substitute Action. After you press ↵ over the « ... », a new action is created, which updates the editor with the content shown in this figure. In the area in red <choose concept>, enter a reference to the concept of the original node that is to be substituted.

After you insert an action, a node substitute actions concept has several attributes that you can configure (shown in Figure 10.3). The following sections describe these attributes.

10.4.1 Substituted Node

This is the concept of the node to which the *node substitute actions* apply. If you wanted to substitute a node of concept `Person` with another node, you would enter a reference to the `Person` concept in this attribute.

10.4.2 Description

This is a comment string that can be used to briefly document the purpose of the substitution action.

10.4.3 Condition

Pressing ↵ over the <none> attribute will create a concept function.

```
(parentNode, currentTargetNode, childConcept, link,
 wrapped, model,
 operationContext, scope) -> boolean {
 ...
}
```

This concept function determines when the action can be performed. If the function returns true, the action is enabled and disabled when the function returns false. The parameters of this function are:

- **parentNode** The node that is the direct parent of the node to be substituted.
- **currentTargetNode** The node to be substituted.
- **childConcept** The target node must be an instance of this concept or one of this concept sub-concepts.
- **link** contains an instance of LinkDeclaration, or *null* if the link could not be determined. LinkDeclaration represents either aggregation or reference links and describes the context where the substitution occurs.
- **wrapped** True when the target node will be wrapped by another concept before being inserted in the AST in place of the source node.
- **model** The model that contains the node to be substituted.
- **operationContext** An instance of IOperationContext. The operationContext is marked as deprecated in MPS 3. The operation context provides access to the project and module.
- **scope** An instance of *IScope*. *IScope* is deprecacted since MPS 3. Avoid using this function parameter that may be removed in a future version of MPS.

10.4.4 Common Initializer

This attribute makes it possible to declare variables that are initialized with data from the source node, and will be available inside the concept function that create the target node. Pressing ⏎ over the <no common variables> attribute will create the code fragment shown here:

```
<no type> <no name> = (parentNode, currentTargetNode,
                       childConcept, model,
                       operationContext, scope)->void {
  <no statements>
}
```

To declare the common initializer, enter the type of the variable and the name you wish to use to refer to the data. You can add multiple common initializer variables by pressing ⏎ to insert new ones when the cursor is over the first or last line of one of them (pressing ⏎ will not create a new common initializer when the cursor is in the body of the concept function since this instead adds new lines to the function).

Common initializers that you have defined become visible in the substitute action code blocks where the target node is constructed.

10.4.5 Supplemental Initializer

This blocks allows to access common initializers and the source node. Pressing ⏎ over `<no supplemental initializer>` will create the concept function shown here:

```
(parentNode, currentTargetNode, childConcept, model,
 operationContext, scope)->void {
  <no statements>
}
```

> ⓡ In MPS 3, it is unclear where to put any data gathered by the supplemental initializer to impact the construction of the target node since there are no examples in the code base.

10.4.6 Actions

Pressing ctrl + SPACE over the « ... » will display the substitution menu shown in Figure 10.4.

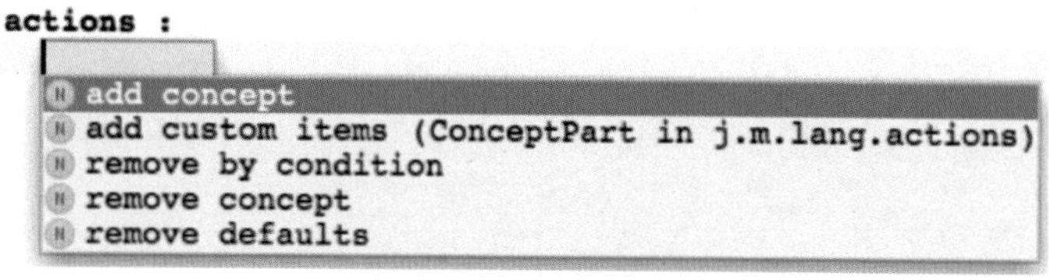

Figure 10.4: **Actions Substitution Menu.** The action substitution menu is displayed when you press ctrl + SPACE over the « ... » shown under **actions**.

Remove Defaults

This action type lets you remove all items that were provided by the substitution menu default construction mechanism.

Remove Concept

This action type lets you provide a reference to a concept that should be removed from the substitution menu. Removals are done from the list assembled by the substitution menu default construction mechanism.

Remove By Condition

This action type lets you define a concept function that controls when a substitution menu item is removed. The concept function has this signature:

```
(parentNode, currentTargetNode, concept, childConcept,
 model,
 operationContext, scope)->boolean {
```

```
  concept != concept/NullLiteral/
  && concept != concept/BooleanConstant/
  && concept != concept/StringLiteral/
  && concept != concept/IntegerConstant/
  && !(concept.isSubConceptOf(TemplateArgumentPatternRef))
  && concept != concept/TemplateArgumentParameterExpression/;
}
```

The parameter *concept* is often used to restrict the substitution to a subset of the concepts that would be allowed by the structure aspect. For instance, in the above listing, the substitution items are limited to the concepts listed and the ones that are sub-concepts of TemplateArgumentPatternRef. Note the use of `concept.isSubConceptOf` to test for sub-concepts. Concepts are removed from the substitution menu when the concept function returns `true`.

Add Concept

This action type lets you provide a reference to a concept that should be shown in the substitution menu. Note that the concept you indicate here must be a sub-concept of the source concept. If you need to add several concepts, it is possible to create several Substitute Node Actions, but in this case it is more convenient to use Add Custom Items (see Section 10.4.6).

Add Custom Items

This action type provides the most flexibility to modify the substitution menu. See Figure 10.5 for a list of the choices available when you pick this action type.

Figure 10.5: **Add Custom Items.** This substitution menu is displayed when you press ctrl + SPACE over the « ... » shown under **add custom items**.

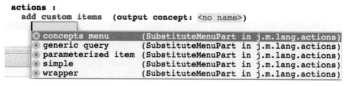

concepts menu

This choice provides a concept function with signature:

```
(parentNode, currentTargetNode, childConcept, model,
 operationContext, scope)->sequence<concept<A>> {

  if (parentNode.ancestor<concept = E> != null){
     return new arraylist<concept<A>>{concept/B/,
                                      concept/C/};
  } else {
     return new arraylist<concept<A>>{concept/B/};
  }
```

```
}
```

The function is used to return a list of the concepts to provide in the substitution menu. In the example provided, the target concept is *A*, and we return the *B* and *C* sub-concepts of *A* when the parent AST contains the *E* concept. If the *E* concept is not found among the ancestors of the node to be substituted, we only add the *B* concept to the substitution menu. This example illustrates how you can customize the concepts offered in the substitution menu according to the local AST context.

simple

A simple action type is shown in Figure 10.6. In this example, a LocalVariableDeclaration (source concept not shown) is substituted with another LocalVariableDeclaration when the text `final` is typed (matching text).

```
actions :
  add custom items  (output concept: LocalVariableDeclaration)
    simple item
      can substitute
        <default>
      matching text
        final
      description text
        final local variable
      icon node
        <default>
      type
        <default>
      create child node
        (pattern, parentNode, currentTargetNode, childConcept, model, operationContext, scope)->node<LocalVariableDeclaration> {
          node<LocalVariableDeclaration> result = model.new initialized node(LocalVariableDeclaration , );
          result.isFinal.set(true);
          return result;
        }
      selection handler
        <default>
```

Figure 10.6: **Simple Action Type.** This simple action example is part of the MPS platform and makes it possible to substitute a variable declaration for one that has the final modifier set to true. Note the use of `model.newInitializedNode`. Also notice that only the final modifier is set on the variable declaration that is returned. Other attributes that are not set on the result will be transferred from the source node to the target node by a node factory (not shown).

parameterized item

This action type is similar to the simple action type, but creates multiple substitution items, one for each value of a parameter. The following listing shows the query concept function which is used to calculate the values of the parameter. In this example, we use the type string for the parameter.

```
parameterized item
  parameter type = string
  query
    (parentNode, currentTargetNode, childConcept, model,
      operationContext, scope)->sequence<string> {
  <no statements>
}
```

An example of parameterized item is provided in the Kajak robot example shipped as a sample with the MPS platform. If you open this sample and navigate to the AndOrSubtitute action, you will see the content of Figure 10.7.

```
parameterized item
  parameter type = concept<LogicalOperator>
  query
    (parentNode, currentTargetNode, childConcept, model, operationContext, scope)->sequence<concept<LogicalOperator>> {
      concept/LogicalOperator/.sub-concepts(model, scope).where({~it => !(it.abstract); });
    }
  matching text
    (pattern, parameterObject, parentNode, currentTargetNode, childConcept, model, operationContext, scope)->string {
      parameterObject.conceptAlias;
    }
  description text
    (pattern, parameterObject, parentNode, currentTargetNode, childConcept, model, operationContext, scope)->string {
      parameterObject.name;
    }
  icon node
    <default>
  type
    <default>
  create child node
    (pattern, parameterObject, parentNode, currentTargetNode, childConcept, model, operationContext, scope)->node<Logical
      node<LogicalOperator> newInitializedInstance = parameterObject.new initialized instance();
      newInitializedInstance.left = currentTargetNode.left;
      newInitializedInstance.right = currentTargetNode.right;
      newInitializedInstance;
    }
```

Figure 10.7: **Parameterized Item Example from Kajak Sample Project.** In this example, the action collects all sub-classes of the concept LogicalOperator that are not abstract. These concepts are used as the parameters. Matching text is determined directly from the concept's alias and the description from the name of the concept. Create child node initializes an instance of the parameter concept and returns this instance.

wrapper

The wrapper action type can be used to substitute a source node with a target node that wraps the source node. Figure 10.8 presents a freshly created action type.

```
actions :
  add custom items  (output concept: Concept)
    wrap <no concept>
      wrapper block
        (nodeToWrap, parentNode, currentTargetNode, childConcept, model, operationContext, scope, editorContext)->node<Concept> {
          <no statements>
        }
      return small part
        <false>
      selection handler
        <default>
```

Figure 10.8: **Wrapper Action Type.** A freshly created wrapper action type is shown.

You can specify the node to *wrap* by entering a reference to the concept that you wish to wrap. The *wrapper block* offers a concept function to create the wrapper node. The *nodeToWrap* parameter is the node that is to be substituted by the wrapper (source node of the action). Figure 10.9 presents a wrapper that is part of the MPS platform and wraps a *baseLanguage* statement into a `StatementList`.

Wrappers may have a selection handler. Attaching a handler to the wrapper will create a concept function that needs to return the node to select in the editor after the substitution has occurred. Note that editor cell selection may also be done directly in the wrapper block using the editorContext. In this case, the handler should return *null* or be left undefined.

 Wrapper has one attributes that is not documented: *return small part*. You may need to experiment with changing the boolean *return small part* to see the effect of this value on the substitution.

```
actions :
  add custom items  (output concept: StatementList)
    wrap Statement
      wrapper block
        (nodeToWrap, parentNode, currentTargetNode, childConcept, model, operationContext, scope, editorContext)->node<StatementList>
          node<StatementList> statementList = new initialized node<StatementList>();
          statementList.statement.add(nodeToWrap);
          return statementList;
        }
```

Figure 10.9: **Statement to StatementList Wrapper.** The wrapper shown is part of the MPS platform and is used to wrap a *baseLanguage* `Statement` into a `StatementList`. In this handler's implementation, a new statement list is created. The nodeToWrap is of type `Statement` and is added to the list. The list is returned.

generic query

This action type returns a concept function that must return a sequence of implementations of the Java interface *SubstituteAction*.

 The MPS code base contains no example or documentation for this type of action. It is likely that this was useful in earlier versions of the MPS platform when less flexibility was available and implementations had to be written in Java.

10.5   Node Factories

You can create a new Node Factories in an Actions aspect by following the direction given in the caption of Figure 10.1.

> **Definition 10.5.1** Node Factories make it possible to customize the initialization of concept nodes at the time when the node is about to be added to the AST.

Figure 10.10 presents a freshly created Node Factories AST root node. Node factories are complementary to the node constructors offered by the Behavior aspect. In contrast to node constructors, a factory is aware of the context where the node will be inserted. The node factory setup code is called after the constructor code, just before the node is inserted into the AST.

10.5.1   Description

Use this attribute to describe the purpose of the Node Factory.

10.5.2   Setup Code

Implement the setup concept function to initialize the node before insertion in the AST. The concept function has the following parameters:

- sampleNode If not null, sampleNode contains the source node of a substitution. The factory is responsible for transferring any information from the source node that should be preserved during a node substitution.

- newNode This is the node that will be inserted into the AST. If the factory is invoked during a node substitution action, this is the target node of the substitution.
- model This is the model where the nodes are defined.
- enclosingNode This node will be the immediate parent of the targetNode. Use this node to learn about the AST context where newNode will be inserted.

Figure 10.10: **New Node Factories AST Root.** Press ⏎ with the cursor over « ... » to create a new node factory.

```
node factories <no name>

node concept: <choose concept>
    description : <none>
    set-up      : (sampleNode, newNode, model, enclosingNode)->void {
                    <no statements>
                  }
```

10.6 Transform Menu Actions

Transform Menu Actions make it possible to define node side transformations.

> **Definition 10.6.1** Side transformations are a mechanism to help end-users interact with the AST. It is often useful to transform a node into another node when a specific text is typed to the left, to the right, or either side of a node. Side transformations make it possible to implement this type of interaction with the AST.

You can create a new Transform Menu Actions root node in an Actions aspect by following the direction given in the caption of Figure 10.1. Figure 10.11 presents a freshly created Transform Menu Actions root node. You should name the actions root node after creating it. The name will help you locate the action under the Project Tab and with name lookups (⌘ + N).

Figure 10.11: **New Transform Menu Actions AST Root.** Press ⏎ with the cursor over « ... » to create a new side transform action.

side transform actions <no name>

<< ... >>

Pressing return over the « ... » will create a new action. Figure 10.12 presents a new side transform action.

By default, the side transform action is created as a right-transform action. You can change the direction of the side transform from right to left or two-sided by placing the cursor at the beginning of the right keyword and invoking the auto-completion menu option + ⏎ . Select the direction you require and press return. Side transform rules have the following attributes:

10.6.1 Concept

This is a reference to the concept that the side transform is attached to. Use auto-completion to locate a concept.

```
right transformed node: <choose concept> tag: default_    //<no description>
   condition :
     <none>

   common initializer :
     <no common variables>
     .....................................
     <no common initializer>

   actions :
     << ... >>
```

Figure 10.12: New Side Transform Action. This figure presents a freshly created Side Transform action. See the text for a description of the attributes of the action.

10.6.2 Tag

Side transform rules are active when the cursor is positioned over certain cells of an editor. If you leave the default tag (called `default_`), any cell that renders a separator (i.e., a space between two cells of an editor) can invoke the side-transform rule. You can override the default tag to make it more precise, for instance to enable side-action rules only on the separator spaces around some specific cells. To do this, you need to define the tag attribute.

The tag attribute determines which cells of the attribute are associated with the side-transform rule. You can select one of six pre-defined tags: `default_`, `ext_1`, `ext_2`, `ext_3`, `ext_4`, `ext_5`. To change the tag, position the cursor before the first character of the tag (i.e., before the d of `default_`) and invoke the auto-completion menu.

The tags have no particular meaning and are only used as far as determining which cells of an editor are associated with a side transform rule. To associate a cell of the editor to a specific side transform, open the editor for the concept associated to the side-transform rule, put the cursor over the cell where the side transform should be active, and add the `side-transform-anchor-tag` style. See Section 5.7.1 to learn more about editor styles. After you have entered the style, specify the same tag you have indicated in the side transform rule. Use auto-completion in the style issue to find the appropriate tag. Note that you may associate multiple tags to one cell of the editor. If this is required, instead of selecting a single tag by name (e.g., `default_`, `ext_1`), select the composite entry in the auto-completion menu. This provides a list of tags where you can enter multiple elements.

10.6.3 Condition

Condition lets you specify a predicate that determines when the side transform action is active. Press ⏎ over <none> to display the following concept function.

```
(operationContext, model, scope, sourceNode)->boolean {
}
```

The function has four parameters and must return a boolean. The action is active when the concept function returns `true`, and inactive otherwise.

10.6.4 Common Initializer

This attribute makes it possible to define common initializers for the side-transform action. See Section 10.4.4 for a description of how to configure new common initializers.

10.6.5 Actions

When invoked over a concept, side transform actions will typically modify the AST. You can implement AST modifying actions in one of four ways. See Figure 10.13 for the type of actions available. These choices are available when you invoke auto-completion over the pink editor cell below `actions:`.The following sub-section describe each type of action.

Figure 10.13: **Auto-completion Choices for Side Transform Actions.**

```
add concept
add custom items (ConceptPart in j.m.lang.actions)
include transform for
remove by condition
remove concept
```

Add Concept

Definition 10.6.2 Add Concept is a flexible side-transform action that you can use to replace the node on which the action was invoked (the `sourceNode`) with an instance of some concept.

See Figure 10.14 for a freshly created Add Concept Action.

Target Node

Pressing ⏎ over `<default>` creates the following concept function:

```
(sourceNode, operationContext, model)->node<> {
}
```

This function can be used to define the value of the targetNode parameter for the handler function. The function is invoked before the action and is useful to walk though the AST up or down from the source node.

```
actions :
  add concept <no concept>
    target node
      <default>
    handler
      (operationContext, pattern, sourceNode, targetNode, result, model, editorContext)->node<>
        <no statements>
      }
```

Figure 10.14: **Add Concept Action Type.** Use this action to add a concept.

Handler

The handler is a concept function that determines how the AST is modified when the side-transform rule is invoked. In the case of the Add Concept action, the concept function should substitute the sourceNode with another node, optionally insert the targetNode in this other node (i.e., when a part of the source node should be preserved by the side transformation) and return the other node.

Assume that you are creating a language to represent simple arithmetic expressions of the form 1+2+3. You can easily model such an expression with the structure aspect of the language, but how do you make the editor behave like a text editor when a user types the keys 1, +, 2, + , followed by the digit 3? You can do this by defining appropriate side transformation actions. See the side transform actions attached to BinaryOperation in *baseLanguage* for examples of handler implementation. Note that these implementations handle operator priorities and associativity.

Figure 10.15 and 10.16 present an editor and concept that you can use to play with side transform actions and start to understand them better. In the editor and in a sandbox solution, create a new root node of type ForSideTransformTest.

If you create this concept and editor, you can follow the steps described in Figure 10.17 and see how the add concept action is triggered in the editor.

> (R) The Add Concept action is limited to adding concepts when the user types the alias of the concept on the left, right or both sides of a node. If you find that you would like to to perform side transform actions that depend on other text that the alias of an existing concept, you should consider using the Add Custom Items action type, described in the next section.

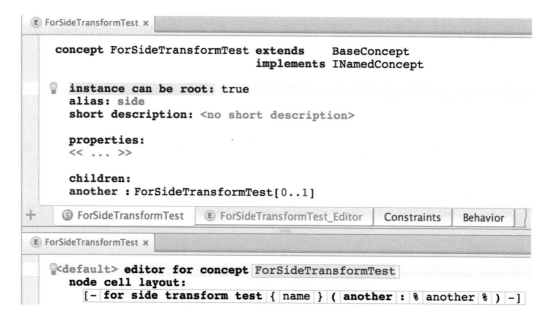

Figure 10.15: **Side Transform Toy Concept and Editor.** The structure and editor aspects are shown for a minimal concept. Try creating similarly simple concepts and editor to play with side transform actions. Understanding side-transform actions will often be easier when you can focus on just one or a few concepts.

```
side transform actions SideTransformTest

  both sides transformed node: ForSideTransformTest tag: default_  //<no description>
    condition :
      (operationContext, model, scope, sourceNode)->boolean {
        sourceNode.another.isNotNull;
      }

    common initializer :
      <no common variables>
      .....................................
      <no common initializer>

    actions :
      add concept ForSideTransformTest
        target node
          (sourceNode, operationContext, model)->node<> {
            sourceNode.another;
          }
        handler
          (operationContext, pattern, sourceNode, targetNode, result, model, editorContext)

            sourceNode.another = new node<ForSideTransformTest>();
            sourceNode.another.another = targetNode : ForSideTransformTest;
            sourceNode;
          }
```

Figure 10.16: **Side Transform Action Toy Example.** The action is only active when the node has another node as child. The targetNode is set to the child of the sourceNode. The handler creates a new instance of ForSideTransformTest and stores the targetNode at its child. The new node is returned.

(1) Create the root concept and add another node (press return after another)
(2) Rename the new concepts sourceNode and targetNode

```
for side transform test sourceNode(another: for side transform test targetNode(another: <no another>))
```

(3) Choose one side, left or right of the constant cell "for side transform test".
(4) Type "side" immediately next to the constant cell, on the right, here:

```
for side transform testsidsourceNode(another: for side transform test targetNode(another: <no another>
```

```
for side transform test sourceNode(another:
    for side transform test <no name>(another: for side transform test targetNode(another: <no another:
```

Figure 10.17: **Add Concept Toy Example In the Editor.** Follow these instructions to experiment with the add concept side transform with the toy example. After you follow these steps, a new node is added between sourceNode and targetNode.

Add Custom Items

The action Add Custom Items is useful when you need flexibility for the text that will trigger a side transformation. Add Custom Items actions make it possible to define a custom matching text, which when typed next to an editor cell will trigger the action. After creating a new Add Custom Items node, you need to define the type of the output concept. Enter a reference to the concept that this side transform action will produce. Adding a type here is useful, because side-transform rules may transform the type of the node, for instance going side-ways in the concept hierarchy, to return a sibling of the concept on which the side transform was invoked. MPS will check that the output concept is a valid concept in the context where the source node can be present. When you have configured the output concept, you should use the auto-completion menu over the « ... » to set the type of custom item. There are two types of custom items: simple custom items (see Figure 10.18) and parameterized item (see Figure 10.19). These types share several attributes which are described in the following sections.

simple custom items

Figure 10.18 presents a side-transform with a simple custom item.

Matching Text   This attribute lets you specify the text that an end-user must type next to a node to invoke a side-transform action. Two choices are available here, `simple text` and `get text`. The first lets you enter a constant string, while the second provides a concept function to calculate the matching text value.

Description Text   This attribute lets you specify a description text that an end-user may see in the auto-completion menu when they type a prefix of the matching text next to the node. Options for configuration are the same as for matching text.

```
actions :
  add custom items   (output concept: <no concept>)
    simple item
      matching text
        <default>
      description text
        <default>
      icon node
        <default>
      type
        <default>
      do transform
        (model, operationContext, sourceNode, pattern, scope, editorContext)->node<> {
          <no statements>
        }
```

Figure 10.18: **Side Transform Simple Custom Item.** The attributes of Simple Custom Items are described in the text.

Icon Node   This attribute should return a concept (i.e., `concept/C/` if C is a concept) of a node of this concept. It is not clear how the icon will be located from the concept reference or the node and how to provide new icons.

Type   Using this attribute, you may define a concept function that returns a node. The function has the following signature:

```
(pattern, parentNode, currentTargetNode, childConcept,
 model, operationContext, scope)->node<> {
}
```

MPS documentation indicates that the type node is useful to implement smart-completion.

Do Transform   This attribute is used to implement the action of the side-transform. The function should return the node that will replace the sourceNode.

parameterized item

Figure 10.19 presents a side-transform with a parameterized item. In addition to the attributes described for simple custom item, you can define the type of a parameter and provide a concept function that returns a sequence of values of this type. The parameter is available in the do transform concept function, which now has the following signature:

```
(scope, operationContext, sourceNode, parameterObject,
 pattern, model, editorContext)->node<> {

}
```

```
actions :
  add custom items  (output concept: <no concept>)
    parameterized item
      parameter type = <type>
      query
        (scope, model, operationContext, sourceNode)->list<Type> {
          <no statements>
        }
      matching text
        <default>
      description text
        <default>
      icon node
        <default>
      type
        <default>
      do transform
        (scope, operationContext, sourceNode, parameterObject, pattern, model, editorContext)->node<> {
          <no statements>
        }
```

Figure 10.19: **Side Transform Parameterized Item.** The attributes of Parameterized Items are described in the text.

Include Transform For

This side-transform type make it possible to query for a node to which side-transformations are already attached. All side-transform actions attached to the node returned by the query are included in the substitution menu. The query concept function has the following signature:

```
(sourceNode, operationContext, model)->node<> {
  <no statements>
}
```

Remove Concept

This side-transform type accepts a reference to a concept. Source node will be removed if its type matches that of the concept provided.

10.7 Paste Wrappers

You can create a new Paste Wrapper in an Actions aspect by following the directions given in the caption of Figure 10.1. Figure 10.20 presents a freshly created paste wrapper.

Definition 10.7.1 Paste wrappers make it possible to handle paste events and adjust the pasted AST fragments. Adjusting pasted AST fragments is necessary to provide a more flexible copy/paste experience. Indeed, without paste wrappers, users would only be able to paste AST fragments whose type match the AST concepts expected at the insertion point. Paste wrapper can modify the AST according to (*i*) the type of the pasted AST fragment and (*ii*) the type allowed in the local AST context where the fragment is pasted.

paste wrappers <no name>

<< ... >>

Figure 10.20:   **New Paste Wrappers AST Root.** Press ⏎ with the cursor over « ... » to create a new paste wrapper.

Figure 10.21 provides an example Paste wrapper from the MPS platform. This wrapper makes it possible to paste an expression into an AST context where Statement instances are expected. For instance, consider the following while statement:

```
while ((line=reader.readLine())!=null) { // << (1) copy
                                          // an expression
    // do something
}
line=reader.readLine(); // << (2) paste as a statement
}
```

It would be natural for a Java programmer to want to copy the AST fragment `line = reader.readLine()` and paste it into another part of the program as a statement. However, because the type of this AST fragment is an expression, it is necessary to wrap the expression into an ExpressionStatement before this can be accomplished. The paste wrapper implementation shown in Figure 10.21 does just this.

```
paste wrapper Expression -> Statement
  (sourceNode)->node<Statement> {
    node<ExpressionStatement> result = new initialized node<ExpressionStatement>();
    result.expression.set(sourceNode);
    return result;
  }
```

Figure 10.21: **Expression to Statement Paste Wrapper.** This figure presents a Paste Wrapper that converts Expression nodes to Statement nodes by wrapping them in an ExpressionStatement.

10.8 Smart Editor Actions

These actions are not used in the platform at least since MPS 3.0. They will be marked as deprecated in a future release and should not be used.

10.8.1 Generate Code Actions

These actions are not used in the platform at least since MPS 3.0. They will be marked as deprecated in a future release and should not be used.

10.8.2 Surround Code Actions

These actions are not used in the platform at least since MPS 3.0. They will be marked as deprecated in a future release and should not be used.

10.9 Copy/Paste Handlers

You can create a new Copy/Paste Handlers Action in an Actions aspect by following the directions given in the caption of Figure 10.1. Figure 10.22 presents a freshly created Copy/Paste Handlers node.

> **Definition 10.9.1** Copy/Paste Handlers make it possible to define copy and/or paste handlers for a language. A copy handler is invoked when the user copies a fragment of the AST to give your language a chance to prepare an AST fragment before it is copied to the clipboard. A paste handler is invoked immediately after an AST fragment has been pasted from the clipboard into an AST. Paste handler make it possible to adjust the AST immediately after paste, for instance to rebuild references between the pasted fragment and the rest of the AST.

Figure 10.22: **Copy Paste Handlers AST Root.** Press ⏎ with the cursor over the top « ... » to create a new Paste handler, or over the bottom « ... » to create a new Copy handler.

```
copy paste handlers <no name>

<< ... >>

<< ... >>
```

When you insert a copy handler into the Copy/Paste Handlers root node, you will be presented with a concept function as shown in Figure 10.23. The `copy preprocessor` concept function has two arguments: `copy` and `original`. The `copy` argument contains a copy of the AST fragment that will be copied to the clipboard. The `original` argument contains a reference to the fragment of the AST that was copied, but is still in the original AST context.

 Note that access to the parent of original will return the parent node from the source AST, but calling parent on the copy will return null because copy is not part of the original AST.

When you insert a paste handler into the Copy/Paste Handlers root node, you will be presented with a concept function as shown in Figure 10.23. The `paste post processor` concept function has one argument: `pastedNode`. This argument is a reference to the `pastedNode` that was inserted in the destination AST. You can use this reference to adjust the node that was just pasted, or the rest of the AST to accommodate the pasted content.

```
copy paste handlers MyCopyPasteHandlers

paste post processor BiblioRecord
  (pastedNode)->void {
    <no statements>
  }

copy pre processor BiblioRecord
  (copy, original)->void {
    <no statements>
  }
```

Figure 10.23: **Copy Paste Concept Functions.** This figure presents the paste and copy concept functions that become available after you insert a paste and a copy handler.

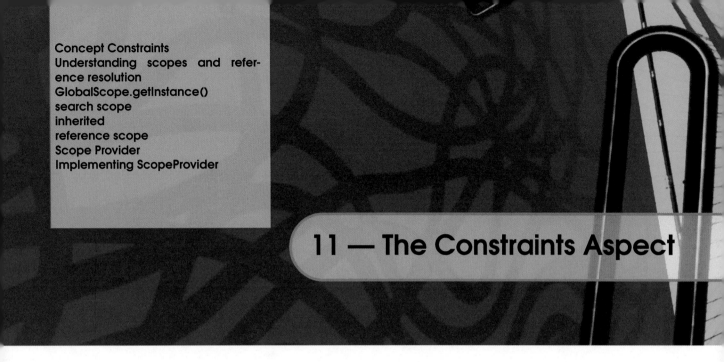

11 — The Constraints Aspect

The Constraints aspect is expressed with the *jetbrains.mps.lang.constraints* language.

> **Definition 11.0.2** The Constraints aspect lets you declare constraints that help you control where nodes of a language are allowed. The constraints created in this aspect complement and restrict the concept relationships that you can declare in the Structure aspect of the language.

Figure 11.1: **AST Roots of the Constraints Aspect.** This figure presents the single AST Root that can be created under a Constraint Aspect. You can create this root node by right-clicking on language name, and selecting `new` `Constraints Aspect`. After the aspect is created, select it, right-click, browse over New. Select the Concept Constraints node to create this root in the constraints aspect of the language.

Figure 11.1 shows that you can only create one type of AST Root node in a constraint aspect: the Concept Constraint Root node. The next section describe this root node in detail.

11.1 Concept Constraints

Figure 11.2 shows a newly created Constraints root node. Constraints node have several attributes that are described in the following subsections.

11.1.1 can be child

Pressing ⏎ over <none> will create a concept function as shown in this listing:

```
(childConcept, node, link, parentNode, operationContext,
 scope)->boolean {
```

```
concepts constraints <no concept> {
   can be child <none>

   can be parent <none>

   can be ancestor <none>


   <<property constraints>>

   <<referent constraints>>

   default scope
      <no default scope>


}
```

Figure 11.2: **New Concept Constraints Node.** This figure presents a freshly created Concept Constraints root node. Press ⏎ with the cursor over property constraints or referent constraints to add a new property constraint, or referent constraint, respectively.

```
      parentNode.isInstanceOf(A);
}
```

The can be child concept function returns a boolean that indicates if the concept can be a child in the specific AST context. A typical implementation tests the type of parentNode (as shown in the fragment above), or tests variables in the parent node or ancestors to determine if the child is suitable in the context.

11.1.2 can be parent

Pressing ⏎ over <none> will create a concept function as shown in this listing:

```
(childConcept, scope, node, childNode, operationContext, link)
   ->boolean {
}
```

The can be parent concept function returns a boolean that indicates if the concept can be a parent in the specific AST context. A typical implementation tests the type of childNode, or tests variables in the childNode or descendants to determine if the child is suitable in the context. The constraint can be parent is most useful to restrict the type of nodes shown in the auto-completion menu when substituting nodes for other nodes, because the node substituted has a child node at that time and it is sometimes necessary to restrict possible substitutions.

11.1.3 can be ancestor

Pressing ⏎ over <none> will create a concept function as shown in this listing:

```
(childConcept, node, childNode, scope,
 operationContext)->boolean {
}
```

The `can be ancestor` concept function returns a boolean that indicates if the concept can be an ancestor in the specific AST context. The `can be ancestor` constraint is also most useful to restrict the set of nodes offered for substitutions.

11.1.4 Property constraint

Definition 11.1.1 A property constraint makes it possible to restrict the values of a specific property of a concept.

Figure 11.3 presents a freshly created property constraint. You can add constraints on the getter, the setter or define a custom validation code.

Figure 11.3: **Property Constraint.** This figure presents a freshly created property constraint. Press ⏎ with the cursor over one of the `<default>` attributes to add a constraint on the setter, getter, or to add validation code.

```
property {<choose property>}
    get:<default>
    set:<default>
    is valid:<default>
```

get

If defined, this concept function calculates the string that is returned when the property is queried.

```
(scope, node)->string {
  <no statements>
}
```

set

If defined, this concept function parses the string propertyValue and sets the value on the node.

```
(propertyValue, node, scope)->void {
  <no statements>
}
```

is valid

If defined, this concept function returns a boolean which indicates if the value of the property is valid for the given node. If both `is valid` and `set` are defined, `set` will only be called if `is valid` returned true for the propertyValue.

```
(propertyValue, node, scope)->boolean {
  <no statements>
}
```

11.1.5 Referent Constraint

> **Definition 11.1.2** A referent constraint makes it possible to restrict how references are established to nodes of the concept.

Figure 11.4 presents a freshly created referent constraint.

```
link {<choose reference>}
  referent set handler:<none>
  scope:
    <default>
  presentation :
    <no presentation>
;
```

Figure 11.4: **Referent Constraint.** This figure presents a freshly created referent constraint.

reference

This attribute will auto-complete to show the set of references available in the concept. Pick one to attach the constraint to the reference link. The following listing shows an example of referent set handler from the MPS platform (from the typesystem language for ConceptReference). The example illustrates that the handler decides in which cases to update the reference, and can perform complex transformations.

referent set handler

```
(referenceNode, oldReferentNode, scope,
 newReferentNode)->void {

  if (newReferentNode.isNotNull
      && newReferentNode != oldReferentNode) {

    referenceNode.name.set(
      NameUtil.decapitalize(newReferentNode.name));
    if (referenceNode.parent.isInstanceOf(InferenceRule)) {
      referenceNode.parent :
        InferenceRule.name.set("typeof_"
        + newReferentNode.name);
    }
  }
}
```

presentation

Determines how the reference is shown in the auto-completion menu.

scope

> **Definition 11.1.3** Scope define a way to locate suitable targets for a reference that the user is editing. To this end, a Scope implementation determines the set of node instances that are allowed as reference targets for a given concept. Scopes determine the visibility of nodes that can participate in references. You will need to understand how MPS defines scopes to take full advantages of references in your languages.

presentation

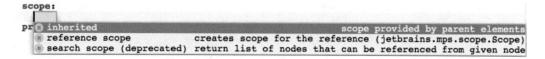

Figure 11.5: **Scope Auto Completion Menu.** This figure presents the auto-completion choices available for the scope attribute.

The scope attribute offers three auto-completion options, shown in in Figure 11.5.

11.2 Understanding scopes and reference resolution

When MPS encounters the need to set a reference on a node, it looks up the scope constraint assigned to the concept reference. For instance, assume concept A has a reference called myRef to a concept of type B. When an end-user needs to set the myRef reference to a concept instance somewhere else in the AST, MPS will try to locate the scope constraint associated with myRef in concept A. If none is found, it considers that all nodes compatible with the target B concept are valid targets of the reference. If a scope is found, the scope is used to restrict, and sometimes expand the set of references available to set myRef. Note that scopes cannot change the type of the reference, they only help language designer implement policies about which concept nodes are valid targets of specific references. The following sections describe the types of scope resolution strategies available since MPS 3.

 Scope are also used when MPS needs to validate references. This could happen for instance after an AST fragment has been pasted into a new AST. In this case, MPS will perform scope resolution for each reference, find those existing references that are not in the set returned by the calculated scope, and mark them as errors.

11.3 GlobalScope.getInstance()

In some cases, you may find that you need to use a method that requires scope, but you are in the context of a concept function that does not expose a scope parameter. In such cases, you can still obtain a scope instance by using the expression `GlobalScope.getInstance()`. For instance, in a node factory, the setup concept function does not expose a scope parameter. If you need to locate a root of a specific type in the model, you might need to do:

```
node<A> a = enclosingNode.model.nodesIncludingImported(
    GlobalScope.getInstance() , A).first;
```

This code fragment will locate the first instance of the A concept available in the model and place it in the a variable.

11.4   search scope

The simplest type of custom scope, search scope, makes it possible to implement code that locates all visible potential targets for a reference. Note that this approach does not scale well to large ASTs because such code may have to be duplicated for each reference where the scope constraint is needed. For this reason, search scope was marked as deprecated since MPS 3.0 and it is not recommended to use this approach. The next two approaches are recommended if you are developing new languages with MPS.

 Note that you can construct the equivalent of a search scope with the reference scope approach, if you use the ListScope helper.

11.5   inherited

The inherited scope uses scope resolution mechanisms implemented by other Concepts. These other concepts are known to MPS because they are declared to implement the *Scope-Provider* interface concept. An inherited scope delegates to a chain of *ScopeProvider* implementations to resolve the scope for a particular concept target. The inherited scope has a single attribute: search for which must be set to indicate the allowed targets of the reference. The value of the search for attribute determines the value of the *kind* parameter discussed in the next sections.

11.6   reference scope

This creates a concept function that must return a Scope implementation (see Paragraph 11.7).

```
(exists, referenceNode, contextNode, containingLink,
 linkTarget, operationContext, enclosingNode, model,
  position, scope, contextRole)->Scope {
}
```

exists
This boolean parameter is true when the reference target already exists, and false otherwise. The attribute can be false when creating smart-references.

model
The model that contains the node that will contain the reference.

contextRole

Role of the reference that is being created.

contextNode

Node with the reference, or closest, non-null context node.

position

The index of the reference to be created in the role that contains it. Can only be different from zero if the reference is created inside a children role with [1..n] or [0..n] multiplicity.

operationContext

The operation context.

Deprecated parameters

In addition to the above parameters, a reference scope concept function defines a set of parameters that have been marked as deprecated. These parameters are not defined here because they are not useful and should not be used since they will be removed in some future MPS release. The parameters include: referenceNode, containingLink, linkTarget, enclosingNode, scope.

11.7 Scope Provider

This interface concept needs to be implemented by concepts that modify the scope. It declares two abstract virtual behavior methods:

```
public virtual Scope getScope(concept<> kind, node<> child) {
  return null;
}

public virtual Scope getScope(concept<> kind, string role,
                              int index) {
  return this.getScope(kind, null);
}
```

Concepts that implement ScopeProvider must provide implementation for these two methods. The first method returns a scope constructed from nodes that have already been defined in the AST. The second method is used when trying to build smart references that are applicable in a given role. The parameters of these methods are described below.

kind argument   The `kind` argument indicates the type of the nodes we need a scope for. This is typically the concept of the target of a reference. Assume concept A has a reference *bRef* to concept B, and the scope needs to be built to set *bRef*. In this case, the editor will call one of the getScope methods with the kind argument set to the B concept.

child argument   The `child` argument contains the node that contains the reference. This argument is null is MPS is trying to build a scope for a smart reference (the wrapper node does not yet exist in this case). Assuming the previous example and that A is not a smart-reference to B, then the child argument will be set to the node of A where the user is trying to set *bRef*.

role argument   The `role` argument contains the role of the reference link that the scope is built for. Assuming the previous example, the role argument will have value "bRef".

index argument   The `index` argument contains the index of the reference in the node that contains it. This is used with smart references when a concept has 0..n or 1..n smart references as children. When the editor needs to populate the auto-completion menu with smart-references, it invokes a suitable ScopeProvider by calling the second getScope() method and provides the index of the child for which the reference is sought.

Scope return type   The Scope return type is an abstract Java class provided with the MPS platform. You can navigate to the implementation by pressing ⌘ + N . When the dialog appears, press ⌘ + N again to include concepts and classes beyond those in your language, then type Scope. Locate the class in package *jetbrains.mps.scope*. MPS ships with several helper classes that simplify the creation of scopes for scoping rules of many languages. See Section 11.8 for details about how to implement the ScopeProvider methods with these helper classes.

11.8   Implementing ScopeProvider

11.8.1   Scope Helper Classes

The MPS platform offers several helper classes to help implement ScopeProvider getScope methods. These classes are useful when you need to calculate scopes for *baseLanguage* extensions[1]. These helper classes include:

EmptyScope

The *FilteringByNameScope* helper class implements an empty scope, that is a scope with no nodes.

ListScope

The *ListScope* helper class constructs a scope using a list of nodes passed into the constructor of the helper. For instance, assume you need to return a scope where exactly two nodes a and b are visible. You can create such a scope with ListScope as follows:

---

[1]The Scope helper classes described in this section would be awkward to use with languages that do not extend *baseLanguage* because (1) they rely on the *jetbrains.mps.baselanguage.scopes* runtime solution and (2) they use interface concepts defined in *baseLanguage*, such as IVariableDeclaration or BaseMethodDeclaration.

```
nlist<> list = new nlist<>;
list.add(a);
list.add(b);
return ListScope.forNamedElements(list);
```

SimpleRoleScope

The *SimpleRoleScope* helper class is useful when possible references for a scope are stored in a children association link and all implement the *INamedConcept* interface. The MPS Calculator Sample provides an example. In this example, a calculator concept has input and output fields. Output fields are defined with expressions using input fields as variables. The scope of output fields must show the names of input fields defined in the calculator, when the reference originates from an output field.

Retrieving a scope for the list of inputFields defined in the calculator is done with the `SimpleRoleScope.forNamedElements(this, link/Calculator : inputField/)` expression. Providing the inputField link allows the helper class to restrict references to fields defined as input fields (thus excluding output fields).

DelegatingScope

The *DelegatingScope* helper class constructs a scope that delegates to another scope instance provided to the constructor of the helper.

CompositeScope

The *CompositeScope* helper class constructs a scope by adding all nodes visible in a set of scopes provided to the constructor of the helper. Assuming you have two scopes a and b, you can combine these scopes in the following manner:

```
return CompositeScope.createComposite(scope1, scope2);
```

FilteringScope

The *FilteringScope* helper class delegates scope construction, but filters nodes in the delegate scope using some predicate. Assume you would like to return the same scope as another scope implementation called `delegate`, but need to remove references to nodes that start with the letter "a". You can do this with the following code:

```
return new FilteringScope(delegate) {
  @Override
  public boolean isExcluded(node<> node) {
    if (node instanceof node<INamedConcept>) { return false; }
    node : INamedConcept.name.startsWith("a");
  }
};
```

Note that this code fragment depends on the *SModel* language.

FilteringByNameScope

The *FilteringByNameScope* helper class delegates scope construction, but filters nodes in the delegate scope by removing nodes if their name is in some exclusion list. Assume we need to remove all nodes from a delegate scope if the names of the nodes are either "Bob" or "Bill". We can do the following:

```
return set<string> exclusionList =
        new hashset<string>{"Bob", "Bill"};
new FilteringByNameScope(exclusionList, delegate);
```

ModelsScope

The *ModelsScope* helper class returns a scope for all nodes of a given concept if they are contained in a set of models.

```
list<model> models = new arraylist<model>{referenceNode.model};
return new ModelsScope(models, false, "A");
```

In the above code fragment, the second parameter to the constructor of `ModelsScope` indicates whether the scope should match only root nodes (true) or all nodes (false). ModelsScope—a scope containing all nodes of a given concept contained in the supplied set of models

ModelPlusImportedScope

The *ModelPlusImportedScope* helper class is similar to ModelsScope, but includes all models also imported by the specified models.

Scopes

The Scopes class defines several static helper methods. These methods are useful with languages that have similar visibility rules to *baseLanguage*. They include:

```
public static Scope forVariables(concept<> kind,
        sequence<node<IVariableDeclaration>> variables,
        Scope parentScope);
```

```
public static Scope forMethods(concept<> kind,
                              Scope methodsScope,
                              @Nullable() Scope parentScope);
```

```
public static Scope forLoopLabels(
        sequence<node<LoopLabel>> labels,
        Scope parentScope);
```

```
public static Scope forTypeVariables(
        sequence<node<TypeVariableDeclaration>> variables,
        Scope parentScope) ;
```

You would use these helper static methods with an expression like the following:

```
Scopes.forMethods(kind, newMethods, parent scope)
```

See the MPS code base for examples of using these helper methods. You can find these examples by navigating to the Scopes class, selecting the method of interest and looking for usages (select Global to search the entire platform).

11.8.2 parent scope

This expression represents the scope visible to the parent node. Scopes are often built recursively by traversing the AST, from the node where the source of a reference is needed, going up until no parent is available. The parent scope expression makes it possible to add new references to the parent scope or simply return it as is.

11.8.3 come from

This expression makes it possible to test that the reference comes from a given fragment of the AST. The expression comes from node will return true only if the source of the reference is contained in the AST fragment that starts with node. The comes from expression is useful in cases where it is necessary to restrict references to a sub-part of the AST. For instance, consider the following program fragment:

```
int a=3;
for (int b=0;b<10;b++) {
  if (b>a) {
    ..
  }
}
```

In such a program, the variable *b* is defined in the for language statement and should be visible only in the body of the for block. This means that when a user tries to create a reference to a variable somewhere in the program, a reference to *b* must be available only if the source of the reference is in the part of the AST that corresponds to the for block statement.

Assuming that the ForStatement concept represents the for statement in the language, that the VariableDeclaration concept declares variables, and that the ForStatement has a child body of type BlockStatement, you can achieve this behavior by making ForStatement implement ScopeProvider and defining the following getScope method:

```
public Scope getScope(concept<> kind, node<> child)
  overrides ScopeProvider.getScope {
  if (kind.isExactly(VariableDeclaration)) {
    if (come from body) {
      return Scopes.forVariables(kind, this.variable,
                                parent scope);
    } else {
      return parent scope;
    }
  }
  super.getScope(kind, child);
}
```

In the above fragment, the getScope method checks that MPS needs to obtain a reference for *VariableDeclaration*. If this is not the case, it delegates to the super getScope method. This method would typically return null and cause MPS to continue looking for a suitable ScopeProvider by walking up the AST.

If the kind matches *VariableDeclaration*, the getScope method determines if the reference originates within the body of the for loop (i.e., come from body). When this is the case, the helper method Scopes.forVariables is used to add the for loop variable (this.variable) to the parent scope. The for loop variable is the b variable defined in condition of the for loop in the previous example. If the reference did not originate within the body of the loop, the getScope method simply returns the parent scope.

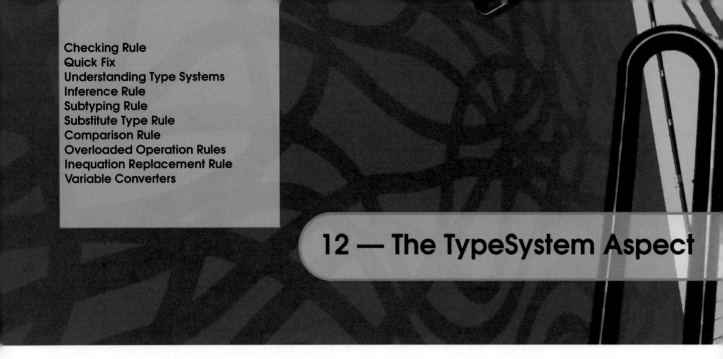

12 — The TypeSystem Aspect

The TypeSystem Aspect is a component of a language that makes it possible to calculate types of AST fragments and to define and report semantic errors to the user of the language. The Type System Aspect is expressed with the MPS *jetbrains.mps.lang.typesystem* language. Figure 12.1 presents the different AST Root nodes that can be defined in a Type System Aspect.

The Type System aspect contains nodes with different functions. Most of the AST root nodes are used to define the type system for a language. These include Inference, Subtyping, Comparison, InequationReplacement and OverloadedOperation Rules. In addition to this role, the TypeSystem aspect makes it possible to implement semantic error detection for a language. This is done with the Checking Rule AST Root node. When an error is detected, MPS makes it possible to define a Quick Fix, which is code that can modify the AST and resolve the error. The following sections will first describe the semantic error capabilities, and will continue with a description of the TypeSystem capability.

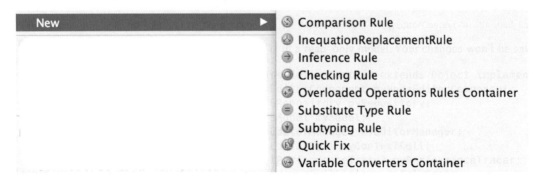

Figure 12.1: **AST Roots of the Type System Aspect.** This figure presents the type of AST Roots that can be created under a Type System Aspect (typesystem for short). To test this, create a new MPS Language, right-click on the Type System Aspect, browse over New. Selecting a type of AST Root node will create this root in the typesystem of the language.

12.1 Checking Rule

Checking Rules implement semantic error detection for a language.

> **Definition 12.1.1** Semantic error detection is often needed to detect errors that cannot be prevented only by defining the language structure and constraints (these aspects define the language syntax).

An example of semantic error that you may want to enforce in a new language is to prevent nodes of the same name to exist in a specific scope. For example, in the Bibliography example introduced in Chapter 4, we prefer not to have bibliographical records with the same name. By default, this is allowed by the structure of the *Bibliography* language, and we cannot use the constraint aspect because names can be edited at any time after nodes have been added to their parents. The Checking Rule provides a mechanism to detect such a condition and inform the user that this is an error in this language.

To add semantic error detection to a language, create a new Checking Rule node in the TypeSystem aspect of this language [Typesystem Aspect⟩ New ⟩ Checking Rule]. Figure 12.2 presents a new Checking Rule. You should name the rule as soon as possible since the name can be used to locate it under the aspect in the Project Tab and with [⌘]+[N] for name lookups. A Checking Rule has several attributes which are described in the following sections.

```
checking rule <no name> {
  applicable for <condition>
  overrides false

  do {
    <no statements>
  }
}
```

Figure 12.2: **New Checking Rule.** This figure presents a freshly created Checking Rule.

12.1.1 Applicable for

This attribute lets you define what the rule applies to. You can enter a reference to a concept, or provide a pattern that will match fragments of the AST.

concept

If you select to create a rule applicable to a concept, you need to enter a reference to a Concept in this attribute. Once you have entered the concept name, a variable is created to let you refer to an instance of the concept. The name of the variable follows the "as" keyword, shown in Figure 12.3.

pattern condition

With `pattern condition`, it is possible to match nodes with the MPS *pattern* language. The *pattern* language can match fragments of an AST. Those nodes that match the pattern become selected to execute the statements in the do section of the rule. The *pattern* language

```
checking rule CheckConceptB {
    applicable for concept = B as b
```

Figure 12.3: **Applicable For.** The applicable for attribute can be specified with a concept and associated variable name. The concept name is entered before the "as" keyword. The variable name after the "as" keyword helps refer to an instance of the concept. The rule will run as many times as needed to check each instance of the concept found in an AST.

is clearly described in the MPS online user guide [GP15]. Here, we provide an example to illustrate how to use patterns to detect semantic errors.

Figure 12.4 presents a Checking Rule that uses a pattern to find articles with a title and two authors and any number of other elements. The do statements check that the first author has name Simi, or report an error in the editor, highlighting the bibliography record that does not comply with the detection rule.

```
checking rule CheckBiblioForNYoShAuthors {
    applicable for > @item{ $ itemName ,                                                  < as myItem
                      authors = { $ firstName   $ lastName ($ key1), Fabien   Campagne ($ key2) }
                      title = "$ title"
                    }
                                  _
    overrides false

    do {
      if ($title.contains("NYoSh")) {
        if (!($lastName.equals("Simi"))) {
          error "The last name of the first author of the NYoSh article must be Simi" -> myItem;
        }
      }
    }
}
```

Figure 12.4: **Example of Pattern for Checking Rule.** Note the green brackets that indicate that the content in between these brackets is an expression of the *pattern* language. In this case, the pattern matches any BiblioRecord with an itemName, one title, and two authors. The underscore character (_) is a wildcard that matches any other element, making it possible for the pattern to match articles that have publication years, for instance. In the do statements, notice how $title is used to obtain the title of the BiblioRecord from the item the pattern matched. Parts of the pattern that are needed to write the rule can be marked in the pattern using the appropriate intention.

12.1.2 Overrides

The overrides attributes determines whether the rule overrides rules of super-concepts (that replaces rules associated with super-concepts when overrides is true), or if the rule adds to those rules of the super-concepts (when overrides is false).

12.1.3 Do

The do attribute let's you enter a block of statements to check error conditions and report errors. You check error conditions with statements from *baseLanguage* such as if statements and conditions which use the attributes of the node selected by the `applicable for` attribute. When using patterns in the `applicable for`, you can also access value of property names with the $ prefix. You can access nodes with the # prefix and lists of nodes with the * prefix. Typical `do` blocks check for specific condition of the values of the node and its context which constitute semantic errors. When the condition is detected, it can be reported to the editor with the `error` statement.

The error statement

The `error` statement takes two arguments: an expression of type string which is the error message that you wish to display to the end user, and a reference to the node that should be highlighted as the source of the error. The error node does not have to be the same as the `applicable for` node. An example of using the error statement is shown in Figure 12.4.

(R)   Open the `2: Inspector` to see which inspected attributes are available when you place the cursor over the error keyword.

In addition to sending an error message to the editor and highlighting the node that caused the error, the error statement can provides a way to configure a Quick Fix for the error. To link an error to a Quick Fix, you need to open the `2: Inspector` and configure the attributes of the inspected cell. You can see these attributes in Figure 12.5.

node feature to highlight   This attribute is optional and configures a feature of the selected node to highlight as responsible for the error. A node feature in this context refers to either a property, children or reference of the node. Use auto-completion to select the node feature.

intention to fix an error   This attribute makes it possible to link the error to a Quick Fix. Press `↵` over the « ... » to add a Quick Fix configuration node. See section 12.2 for details.

foreign message source   The foreign message source must be an expression that evaluates to a node. When provided, the node will be linked to from the error message, so that the end-user will be taken to the message upon clicking on the link (or activating the link with `ctrl` + `⌥` + `click` on Windows, or Mac OS: `⌘` + `option` + `click`).

The ensure statement

The `ensure` statement makes it possible to define assertions. The statement has the same attributes as those described for the error statement in Section 12.1.3.

The info statement

The `info` statement makes it possible to provide information messages to the end-user of the language, without triggering an error condition.

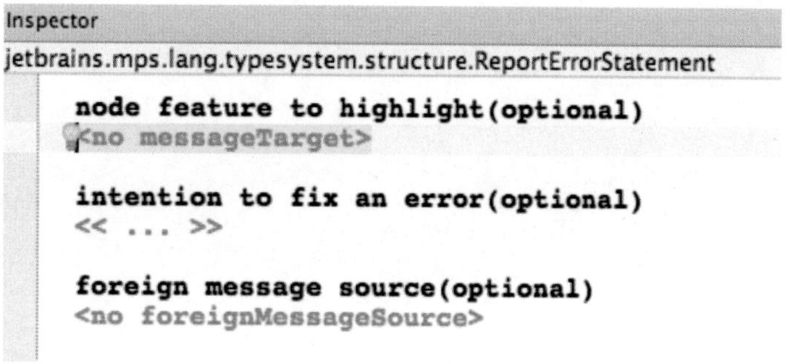

Figure 12.5: **Inspected Cell for the** error **Statement.** This figure presents the content shown in the inspector tab when the error statement is selected in the editor. You can use the inspected attributes to configure Quick Fix.

```
Inspector
jetbrains.mps.lang.typesystem.structure.ReportErrorStatement

   node feature to highlight(optional)
   <no messageTarget>

   intention to fix an error(optional)
   << ... >>

   foreign message source(optional)
   <no foreignMessageSource>
```

The warning statement

The warning statement makes it possible to define warnings. The statement has the same attributes as those described for the error statement in Section 12.1.3.

12.2 Quick Fix

Quick Fix implement corrections for errors that you may set to run automatically when the associated error is detected. You can create a Quick Fix AST Root node by right-clicking on the TypeSystem aspect and selecting New Quick-Fix. You should see the editor content shown in Figure 12.6. Figure 12.7 provides a listing for a QuickFix that resets the name of an author to the string "Simi". This Quick Fix can be associated with the semantic error described in the previous section to automatically reset the last name of the first author of the NYoSh article. Figure 12.8 shows how to connect the semantic error to the Quick Fix.

Figure 12.6: **Freshly Created Quick Fix AST Root Node.** This figure presents the content of the editor after creating a new Quick Fix. See text for description of the node attributes.

```
quick fix <no name>

arguments:
<< ... >>

fields:
<< ... >>

<no descriptionBlock>

execute(node)->void {
   <no statements>
}
```

12.3 Understanding Type Systems

Many programming languages have the notion of types. Most languages support primitive types, and make it possible to define new custom types. While the structure aspect makes it possible to define a concept hierarchy for type definition and for the expressions that are compatible with each type, language designers often need the ability to check and enforce compatibility between types and expressions of the language.

```
quick fix FixSimiLastName

arguments:
node<Person>   author

fields:
<< ... >>

<no descriptionBlock>

execute(node)->void {
   author.lastName.set("Simi");
}
```

Figure 12.7: **Quick Fix to Reset Author Name.** The Quick Fix shown resets the last name of an author parameter to the string "Simi".

```
intention to fix an error(optional)
FixSimiLastName (author = myItem.descendants<concept = Person>.first)
apply immediately:
true
```

Figure 12.8: **Associating a Quick Fix to an error statement.** You can attach a Quick Fix to an error statement by entering binding information in the inspector tab when the error statement is selected in the editor. Shown is a binding that connects the error described in the previous section with the fix implemented in Figure 12.7

Indeed, while the type of variable declarations is clearly defined by the structure of the language (i.e., an `int var;` declaration has type the primitive integer type), the type of expressions must often be calculated from the specific nodes that are composed to yield a specific expression (e.g., the type of the expression `(1+2/3)` is a float even though all of the AST nodes are IntegerConstant). The MPS TypeSystem aspect has been designed to offer a declarative way to express rules that support type calculations. When an appropriate set of type system rules are defined for a language, the MPS runtime will be able to solve a system of inequalities derived from the rules, and provide the calculated type for expression nodes of the language.

Weak and Strong Sub-typing

MPS supports weak and strong sub-typing relations. Note that when we do not explicitly specify whether a sub-typing relation is weak or strong, we imply that it is weak.

Definition 12.3.1 A weak sub-type relation $t_a :< t_b$ implies that expression of types t_a and t_b can be used interchangeably in special cases only (e.g., for *baseLanguage*, weak sub-typing implies that t_a and t_b can be used interchangeably as parameters of methods or as right-hand side of an assignment).

Definition 12.3.2 A strong sub-type relation $t_a :<< t_b$ implies that (1) the weak sub-typing relation holds: $t_a :< t_b$ and (2) expressions of type t_a and t_b can be used interchangeably in all situations where expressions of either t_a or t_b can be used.

It is worth noting that the above definitions leave it to a language designer to define the specific circumstances in which weak and strong sub-typing are needed. You can think as weak and strong sub-typing as two levels of sub-typing relations.

 If your language does not seem to require two levels of sub-typing relations, I suggest to use strong sub-typing. Use the Liskov substitution principle [LW94] to determine if $t_a :<< t_b$ holds for two concepts. If you find that the principle does not hold in some circumstances, you can then start to use weak sub-typing and detect such cases as needed.

Weak and Strong Type Coercion

Definition 12.3.3 Type coercion refers to the implicit conversion of a type to another type. A classical example of type coercion is the coercion of the integer type to the float type, which is necessary to make it possible to evaluate expression that mix integers and floats.

A type can be coerced into another type only under certain circumstances. Such circumstances often have to do with the location of the type in a type hierarchy. The MPS typesystem provides operators to determine whether a type can be coerced into another type. As for sub-typing, MPS offers two levels of type coercion: weak and strong.

Coerce expression

The coerce expression determines if weak type coercion is possible between two types. The coerce expression has the following form:

```
coerce( type :< condition )
```

The parameter type is the type that would be coerced. The parameter condition has two forms: you can specify a concept as in:

```
node<C> coerced = coerce(e :< concept = C as c);
```

The result will be `null` if the type e cannot be coerced to the type represented by concept C. If the result is not `null`, it contains the type e coerced to C;

You can also specify a pattern as a condition. In this case, only each type that the argument can be coerced to will be tested for pattern match. The result of the expression will be not null only when a type is found that can be coerced to and that matches the pattern.

You can test strong coercion with the `coerceStrong` expression, which follows the same syntax as the weak coerce expression.

Coerce Statement

MPS offers a coerce statement. The coerce statement acts as an if statement that checks if a type can be coerced to another type. In contrast to an if statement, the coerce statement declares a local variable with the coerced type. For instance, in the following code fragment:

```
coerce (operandType :< concept = BaseClassifierType
                          as baseClassifierType) {
  if (!(baseClassifierType.getMembers(nodeToCheck)
            .contains(nodeToCheck.member))) {
     error "Declaration is out of scope" -> nodeToCheck;
  }
} else {
}
```

The baseClassifierType variable is declared by the coerce statement, and set to the type that operandType was coerced to. Note that baseClassifierType is visible inside the first block statement, where the coercion condition holds.

Accessing Calculated Types

To access the calculated type of an expression (or any node for that matter), you can use expr.type. This will yield an object of type node<>.

 The type expression returns an already calculated type. It should not be used inside inference rules because the purpose of these rules is to support the calculation of the value that will be retrieved by .type. However, you can access calculated types in the Generator or TextGen aspects and change generated output according to the type.

Comparing Types

It is often useful to compare types. For instance, you may need to determine if type t_a is a (weak or strong) subtype of type t_b. To this end, MPS provides the isSubtype($t_a :< t_b$) and isStrongSubtype($t_a :<< t_b$) expressions. Figure 12.9 illustrates how these expressions are used in practice.

```
node<> exprType = node.type;
if (isSubtype(<int> :< exprType)) {
    // do something when IntegerType is a sub-type
    // of exprType
}
if (isStrongSubtype(<int> :<< exprType)) {
    // do something when IntegerType is a strong
    // sub-type of exprType
}
```

Figure 12.9:   **Comparing Types.** You can retrieve the type of an expression using the type attribute on the expression node. The two if statements indicate how to compare types to determine weak or strong sub-typing.

The following sections describe how typesystem rules are defined in MPS.

12.4   Inference Rule

Inference rules calculate the type of nodes of a concept. For this reason, most inference rules in the MPS platform are named with the pattern typeof_ConceptName. I suggest to use the same rule naming convention in your languages. Figure 12.10 show a freshly created Inference Rule. The following sections describe the attributes of this type of rule.

Figure 12.10: **New Inference Rule.** This figure presents a freshly created Inference Rule.

```
inference rule <no name> {
    applicable for <condition>
    applicable always
    overrides false

    do {
        <no statements>
    }
}
```

12.4.1 Applicable for

This attribute determines the condition when the inference rule is active. You can bind the rule to a concept, or define a pattern. When you enter a concept name, a variable name is updated to the right of the `as` keyword. You may accept the automatic name or edit the name to make it more readable. You can also specify the applicability condition with a pattern. See the Checking Rule description of pattern for more information (Section 12.1.1).

12.4.2 Applicable

By default this attribute shows `always`, but pressing ⏎ over this keyword will change `always` to `if` and offer a *baselanguage* query. Use the query block to calculate a boolean. Returning true will indicate that the inference rule is active.

12.4.3 Overrides

The overrides attributes determines whether the rule overrides the rules of super-concepts. Pressing ⏎ over the `false` value will create a *baselanguage* query block. When the query returns true, the inference rule will replace the rules associated with super-concepts. When overrides is set to false the rule adds to the rules defined by the super-concepts, but does not replace them.

12.4.4 Do

This block statement lets you define the actions that make up the rule. Statements in this block can be expressed with *baseLanguage* that is extended with the concepts of *jetbrains .mps.lang.typesystem*. The following instructions are commonly used in the `do` block of Type System rules.

The Inequality Operators

Operators support two modes: *infer* and *check*. In the default *infer* mode, the operator add a type equality or inequality rule that will be used in the system of inequalities by the type system solver. An intention on the operator makes it possible to turn the operator into the check only mode[1]. In this mode, the keyword `check` is shown instead of `infer`. Operators

---

[1] The mode can also be edited in the 🔧 2: Inspector

in check mode will verify that the calculated type of the operands satisfies the inequalities, but will not attempt to calculate these types. Available operators include:

:==:

This operator expresses that the type on the left-hand side must be the same as the type on the right-hand side.

:<=:

This operator expresses that the type on the left-hand side is a weak sub-type of the type on the right-hand side.

:<<=:

This operator expresses that the type on the left-hand side is a strong sub-type of the type on the right-hand side.

:>=:

This operator expresses that the type on the left-hand side is a weak super-type of the type on the right-hand side.

:>>=:

This operator expresses that the type on the left-hand side is a strong super-type of the type on the right-hand side.

:~:

This operator expresses that the operands on either side of the operator are weakly comparable.

:~~:

This operator expresses that the operands on either side of the operator are strongly comparable.

Other Operators and Statements
typeof

This operator returns the type of its argument. In contrast to the `.type` expression, `typeof` is designed to be used safely inside inference rules.

when concrete

This operator delays the evaluation of a block of typesystem statements until the time the type of its argument has been calculated (i.e., made concrete).

ensure

This statement ensures that a condition is true. The statement does nothing is the condition is true, but reports an error message and highlights a node in the editor if the condition is false. The ensure statement has the same attributes as the error and warning statements, described in Section 12.1.3.

```
ensure <condition> reportError <message> -> <nodeToReport>;
```

operation type

This operator returns the type of an operation, as calculated by an Overloaded Operation Rule (see Section 12.8). The `operation type` operator takes three arguments: the concept that represents the operation, the left operand and the right operand. The return value of operation type is either the type of the operation, or null when the type could not be determined. Here's a code fragment showing how to call `operation type`:

```
node<> opType = operation type(operation, leftType, rightType);
```

 It is a good idea to enclose the uses of `operation type` in blocks that ensure the left and right arguments are concrete.

12.5 Subtyping Rule

Subtyping rules are used to define sub-typing relations between types. Figure 12.11 presents a freshly created sub-typing rule. You should name the rule immediately after creating it. Sub-typing rules have the following attributes:

Figure 12.11: **New Sub-typing Rule.** This figure presents a freshly created sub-typing rule.

```
subtyping rule <no name> {
    weak = false
    applicable for <condition>

    supertypes {
        <no statements>
    }
}
```

Weak

This attribute is a boolean value that should be true when the rule indicates weak sub-typing, and false if the relation indicates strong sub-typing.

Applicable For

This attribute lets you specify either a concept or pattern condition for the type that is a sub-type in the relation. If you mean to describe the relation $T_a :<=: T_b$, you should specify a reference to concept T_a in this attribute (remember that types are simply concepts that extend the Type interface concept). Patterns may also be used to indicate a structural condition on the node whose type T_a is sought.

Super-types

Use this attribute to return the type(s) of a super-type. You may return a single type, or an `nlist<>` with several types. Figure 12.12 presents how sub-typing rules are used in MPS to implement char type boxing and unboxing in *baseLanguage*.

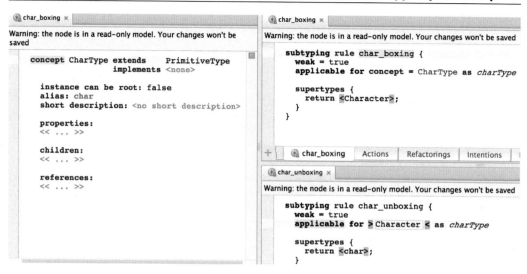

Figure 12.12: **Character Type Boxing Unboxing.** This example presents the CharType on the left panel, and the boxing (top right) and unboxing (bottom right) sub-typing relations. Note the use of a pattern when unboxing to match the Character Java object implementation, while the boxing sub-typing rule matches the CharType concept.

12.6 Substitute Type Rule

Substitute Type rules make it possible to substitute a type for another one. They were introduced in MPS 3.3. In contrast to other rules described in this Chapter, the concept bound to the rule should be one that represents a type. Figure 12.13 presents a freshly created Substitute Type Rule. The substitute block must return either `null`, if no substitution is to occur with the rule, or another type that will replace the type attached in `applicable for`.

Applicable For

This attribute must identify the concept for the type that will be substituted by the rule.

Supertypes

This *baselanguage* block can implement logic to check if the `applicable for` type can be substituted by the rule. If the conditions are met and type substitution should occur, the block must return the new type. If no substitution is needed, the block must return `null`.

Note that you can use Substitute Type to override the type of a node using annotations (annotations are described in Section 17.1). Assume concept A has an annotation B, such that you can annotate nodes of A with instances of B. The editor makes it possible to configure the presentation of the annotated node. Similarly, defining a Substitute Type rule for concept B will make sure the substitution type rule is considered whenever an instance of A has an annotation of type B.

Figure 12.13: **New Substitute Type Rule.** This figure presents a freshly created Substitute Type rule.

```
substitute type rule <no name> {
    applicable for <condition>

    substitute {
        <no statements>
    }
}
```

12.7 Comparison Rule

Comparison rules are used to help the typesystem establish when two types are weakly or strongly comparable. While you can describe straightforward type comparison rules inside Inference rules with the :~: and :~~: operators, defining a Comparison Rule makes it possible to perform additional tests to determine where or when two types should be comparable.

Figure 12.14: **New Comparison Rule.** This figure presents a freshly created comparison rule.

```
comparison rule <no name>

applicable for <condition> , <condition>

rule{
    <no statements>
}
weak= false
```

Figure 12.14 presents a freshly created Comparison Rule. You should name the rule immediately after creating it. The rule has the following attributes:

Applicable For

This attribute accepts two conditions. Each condition can match a type that is a candidate for the comparison rule. Use the auto-completion menu to select either a concept condition or a pattern condition and enter either the concept reference or the pattern instance that each type should match.

Rule

Rule is a *baseLanguage* statement block that should return a boolean. The boolean indicates whether the types matched by the conditions are comparable (`true` must be returned), or not (`false` is returned).

Figure 12.15 presents an example of Comparison Rule taken from the MPS platform (*baseLanguage*). This rule declares that any *baseLanguage* type, excluding primitive types is comparable to the null type.

```
comparison rule  any_type_comparable_with_nulltype

applicable for  concept = BaseConcept as baseConcept , concept = NullType as nullType

rule{
   if (baseConcept.isInstanceOf(PrimitiveType) || baseConcept.isInstanceOf(PrimitiveTypeDescriptor))
   return true;
}
weak= false
```

Figure 12.15: **Any Type Comparable to Null.** Any type that is not a primitive type is strongly comparable to null.

Weak

This boolean attribute determines whether the rule describes weak comparability (boolean is true) or strong comparability (boolean is false).

12.8 Overloaded Operation Rules

These rules are used to calculate the type of an operation, giving the type of the operands (operation arguments). Languages that support operator overloading make it possible to use the same operator with different types as arguments. For instance, in *baseLanguage* it is possible to write either "a"+"b" or 1+2, where the arguments to the + operator are either strings or primitive integer types.

Designers of such languages need a way to determine the type of the operation according to the type of the operands. In MPS, such type calculations can be expressed inside Overloaded Operation Rules.

Once you have created a new Overloaded Operation Rules container, you can name the container, and insert new rules into it. Two types of rules can be added to the container: `OverloadedOpTypeRule_OneTypeSpecified`, or `OverloadedOperatorTypeRule`.

12.8.1 OverloadedOpTypeRule_OneTypeSpecified

You can use this type of rule when knowing the type of a single operand completely determines the type of the operation. Figure 12.16 presents a freshly created `Overloaded OpTypeRule_OneTypeSpecified`

```
operation concepts: <choose concept>
one operand type: <operandType> is exact: false use strong subtyping false
is applicable:
<no isApplicable>
operation type:
(operation, leftOperandType, rightOperandType)->node<> {
   <no statements>
}
```

Figure 12.16: New **OverloadedOpTypeRule_OneTypeSpecified.**

Operation Concepts

Use this attribute to define the set of operation concepts that you wish to describe overloading rules for. Use auto-completion to locate the operation concept reference, and press ⏎ to add a new concept reference. It is useful to enter several operators in this list when the rest of the rule is the same for several operations (e.g., operators == and != would behave similarly and could be entered together in this attribute).

One Operand Type

You can use this attribute to describe the type of the operand that triggers this rule. The attribute accepts an expression, but you would typically use the quotation language to enter a type here. For instance, to match operations where one of the operands is a string, you would enter[2]:

```
one operand type: <string>
```

Is Exact   This boolean attribute determines whether the operand type must be matched exactly, or if sub-types of the indicated operand type will be considered.

Use Strong Subtyping   When exact is false, this boolean attribute indicates whether a strong subtyping relation must hold between the type indicated in the operand type attribute and the type estimated for the operand. When exact is true, this attribute is not displayed.

Is Applicable

Pressing ⏎ in this attribute creates a concept function that must return a boolean. When the concept function returns `true`, the rule is active, and inactive when the function returns `false`. The function has this signature:

```
(leftOperandType, rightOperandType, operation)->boolean {
}
```

Operation Type

This concept function must return the calculated type of the operation, given the left and right operand types. The concept function has the following signature:

```
(operation, leftOperandType, rightOperandType)->node<> {
}
```

If the operation type is constant, remember that it is convenient to use the quotation language to return the type (e.g., as <string>).

---

[2]Remember that StringType is the name of the concept for the *baseLanguage* string type.

12.8.2 OverloadedOperatorTypeRule

This rule is very similar to the one operand rule, but considers the type of the two operands to determine the type of the operation. Figure 12.17 presents a freshly created `Overloaded OperatorTypeRule`. The attributes of this rule have been described in the previous section (see Section 12.8.1).

```
operation concepts: <choose concept>
left operand type: <leftOperandType> is exact: false use strong subtyping false
right operand type: <rightOperandType> is exact: false use strong subtyping false
is applicable:
<no isApplicable>
operation type:
(operation, leftOperandType, rightOperandType)->node<> {
    <no statements>
}
```

Figure 12.17: **New Two Operands Overloading Operation Rule.** A freshly created OverloadedOperatorTypeRule rule is shown. The rule is similar to `OverloadedOpTypeRule_OneTypeSpecified`, but considers the type of two operands to calculate the type of the operation.

Figure 12.18 presents a rule from the MPS platform (*baseLanguage*) that determines the type of the unary minus operation (e.g., -a, -1).

```
operation concepts: UnaryMinus
left operand type: <Numeric>.descriptor is exact: false use strong subtyping false
right operand type: <Object> is exact: false use strong subtyping false
is applicable:
<no isApplicable>
operation type:
(operation, leftOperandType, rightOperandType)->node<> {
    coerce (leftOperandType :< concept = PrimitiveType as primitiveType) {
      return primitiveType;
    } else {
      return leftOperandType;
    }
}
```

Figure 12.18: **Unary Overloaded Operation Rule.** The rule determines whether the left operand can be coerced to a primitive type. In this case, the type of the operation becomes the type of the primitive type. In the other case, the type of the operation is the type of the left operand.

12.9 Inequation Replacement Rule

Inequation Replacement Rules are described in the MPS Online Manual. See `http://confluence.jetbrains.com/display/MPSD31/Typesystem`.

Figure 12.19 presents a freshly created Inequation Replacement Rule. This rule has the following attributes:

Figure 12.19: **New Inequa-**
tion Replacement Rule.

```
replacement rule <no name>

applicable for   <condition> <: <condition>

custom condition: true

rule{
    <no statements>
}
```

12.9.1 Builtins

EquationInfo

If an error is detected within an Inequation Replacement Rule, it is useful to be able to locate the node that generated the error. This is not immediately possible since nodes are not given as parameters of a replacement rule. To help in this situation, you can access the built-in `equationInfo` variable and retrieve the node with error. The following statement demonstrates how to do this:

```
equationInfo.getNodeWithError()
```

12.10 Variable Converters

These rules can be used to provide custom code to the typesystem engine. This is a low-level mechanism that should be avoided, and is likely to be deprecated and replaced with a new mechanism in a future release of MPS. If you find that none of the typesystem declarative features make it possible to express a type calculation (this should be really exceptional), a variable converter can be defined. The typesystem will call variable converters as a last resort if it is unable to calculate the type of a node. The variable converter implementation must return the type of the node as determined by *baseLanguage* statements.

 Do not rely on Variable Converters for new code as they are likely to be removed from the platform in a future release.

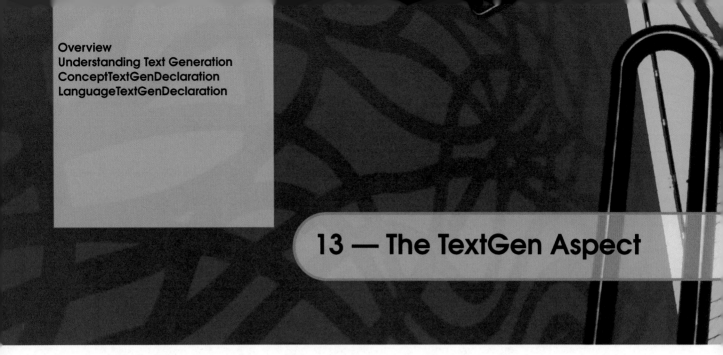

13 — The TextGen Aspect

13.1 Overview

The TextGen Aspect is an optional component of a language that makes it possible to define a mapping from the nodes of the concepts of the language to text. The TextGen Aspect is expressed with the *jetbrains.mps.lang.textGen* language. This language can be used to transform ASTs to text.

Figure 13.1: **AST Roots of the TextGen Aspect.** This figure presents the type of AST Roots that can be created under a TextGen Aspect. To test this, create a new MPS Language, right-click on the language name, select New ⟩ TextGen Aspect . When you have created the aspect, select it, right click, browse over New. Selecting a type of AST Root node will create this root in the TextGen aspect of the language.

Figure 13.1 presents the different AST Root nodes that can be defined in a TextGen Aspect. The following sections describe these types of Root Nodes in detail.

13.2 Understanding Text Generation

The TextGen aspect makes it easy to generate text from AST Root nodes. Each AST Root node in the source AST will be written to an individual file. The name of the file is taken to be the name of the root node by default (i.e., such as defined in INamedConcept). Since MPS 3.3, you may override this choice using the file name attribute of concept TextGen nodes.

 In the absence of a suitable generator, each concept of a language must be transformed to text. MPS will generate an error if you build an AST where some nodes have no associated transformation. You can prevent errors by marking a solution with such models with Do not generate (under Module Properties, Advanced Tab).

13.3   ConceptTextGenDeclaration

A ConceptTextGenDeclaration root node (concept textgen for short) will transform nodes of one concept to text. Figure 13.2 presents a freshly created concept textgen.

```
text gen component for concept <no name> {
    use textgen of ancestor
}
```

Figure 13.2: **New Concept Textgen.** This figure presents a freshly created concept textgen (ConceptTextGenDeclaration). You should bind the textgen to a concept immediately after creating the root node because some attributes depend on what concept is bound to the node. A name is automatically generated following the pattern ConceptName_TextGen.

Note that if you bind a concept textgen to a root node, several attributes will be displayed for editing: *file name*, *extension*, *encoding*, and *text layout*.

file name
The *file name* attribute provides the name of the file that will be written by TextGen. If the attribute is left in default state, the value of node's name property will be used.

extension
The *extension* attribute makes it possible to specify the extension of the filename that will be generated (note that you should not include a dot (.) as part of the extension or it will generate files with two dots).

encoding
The *encoding* attribute allows to specify the file encoding (encoding is a categorical attribute that provides common encodings, including UTF-8 and US-ASCII).

layout
Since MPS 3.3, this attribute makes it possible to declare a file layout. A file layout consists of distinct locations where text can be written inside a file. You can define a hierarchical layout where one location contains other locations, as well as define a default location. The default location is indicated immediately after the keyword `Initial text area`. The default location will be used when appending text without specifying a location (a location can be configured on each append statement, under the 2: Inspector).

Text locations are useful to handle situations where a file has a header and a body, and you need to generate both to the header and body when generating a node. For instance, in Java, if using a node requires declaring an import statement, it is convenient to specify an IMPORTS location in the file layout and use the location in the append statement that writes the import directive.

13.3.1 Use textgen of ancestor

By default, the concept delegates textgen to the first ancestor that provides a textgen concept. If you press ⏎ over this attribute, you can override the textgen output. This is done by defining the body of a concept function. This concept function has three parameters:

context

This parameter is deprecated and should no longer be used.

buffer

This is a buffer where text can be written. The buffer has several methods that can be used directly (i.e., append, foundError(), getLineSeparator(), etc). However, it is more convenient to use special textgen statements to interact with the buffer. These commands include:

error   Indicates that an error occurred during text generation. You can provide an error message.

append   Append text to the output buffer. After typing the append statement, invoke auto-completion to select an operation or element to output. Figure 13.3 presents the elements available when no language operations have been defined.

Figure 13.3: **New Concept Textgen.** Auto-completion following the append keyword provides a number of elements that can be output to the buffer. Note that this concept textgen was bound to a root node and displays the root node attributes.

```
text gen component for concept B {
  file name : <Node.name>
  extension : <no extension>
  encoding : utf-8
  text layout : <no layout>

  (context, buffer, node)->void {
    append [    ];
  }
}
```

ⓝ $list{	collection
ⓝ $ref{	reference
ⓝ ${	node or property
ⓝ \n	new line
ⓝ constant	constant string
ⓝ indent	append indentation

The append statement supports the following elements:
- **$list** This element formats a collection to text. You can specify a string as a separator (via an intention attached to the element). Each element of the collection will be written in turn, with any two elements separated by the string separator.
- **$ref** This element is used to write references. You must pass a node of type reference (use the syntax node.reference<refName>). Note that both the inspector and an intention let you indicate if the name of the referenced object must be unique in the output file.
- **${}** This element is used to write nodes or a property of a node to the buffer. Properties are written to text and nodes are written by delegating to the appropriate concept

textgen (this is equivalent to using a visitor pattern). Note that auto-completion can be used to locate the node or node property to output (syntax: node.property for a property, or node to output the node).

- **\n** This element writes a newline to the buffer.
- **constant** This element writes a constant string to the buffer. You can introduce a constant element by typing a double quote instead of invoking the auto-completion menu.
- **indent** This element inserts an indentation in the buffer.
- **$attributed node$** This element is only available when the concept associated with the concept TextGen is an annotation (i.e., extends `NodeAttribute`). In this case, `$attributed node$` refers to the node that the annotation is attached to.

increase depth   This statement increases the indentation depth. Useful after an opening bracket (i.e., { in Java-like languages).

decrease depth   This statement decreases the indentation depth. Useful after a closing bracket (i.e., } in Java-like languages).

with indent   The `with indent` statement increases the indent at the start of the block, and reduces the indent at the end of the block. Note that you are responsible for setting the `with indent` property (visible with the [2: Inspector]) on each `append` statement inside the block. For instance, in the following listing:

```
append {not indented} \n
with indent {
    append {now indented} \n
    append {also indented} \n
    append {NOT indented (see inspector)} \n
}
```

If you set the `with indent` attribute only on the first and second append statements, the output will look like:

```
not indented
    now indented
    also indented
NOT indented (see inspector)
```

indent buffer   Manually append the indentation characters to the output buffer. This statement can be used when the following buffer output should be indented.

> (R) Note that the with indent attribute is only visible if you open the [2: Inspector] when the cursor is on top of the append keyword. No visual cue is be given in the editor that could help you differentiate append statements `with indent` true or false.

node

This is the node that needs to be transformed to text.

13.4 LanguageTextGenDeclaration

A LanguageTextGenDeclaration root node (language textgen for short) provides a way to group text generation code into one place. Figure 13.4 presents a freshly created language textgen.

```
base text gen component <no name> extends <no baseTextGen> {
    << ... >>

    << ... >>
}
```

Figure 13.4: **New Language Textgen.** This figure presents a freshly created concept textgen (ConceptTextGenDeclaration). You should name the language textgen to help you find it under the TextGen aspect or by text lookups. A language textgen has two « ... ». Pressing ⏎ over the first placeholder will create a textgen operation. Pressing ⏎ over the second will create a private textgen function. You can create more of each kind by pressing ⏎ in each section between operations or functions.

13.4.1 Operations

An operation has a name, and zero, one or more parameters. After an operation has been named in a language textgen, the operation becomes available in the auto-completion menu of the concept textgen. This makes it convenient to delegate from a concept textgen to language textgen operation.

It is common for a language textgen operation to have one parameter of type node< conceptName>. Such operations are used to append one concept node to the output buffer.

 Auto-completion in the concept textgen is aware of the types and number of parameters of a language textgen operation. This facilitates entering append statements in textgen concepts when operations are reusable across different concepts.

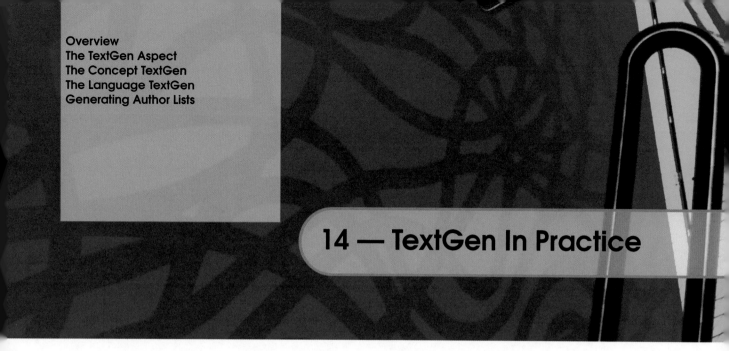

14 — TextGen In Practice

14.1 Overview

This chapter illustrate how to use the TextGen aspect to transform nodes of the *Bibliography* language to text.[1]

In the following sections, we describe the different TextGen Root nodes needed to transform nodes of concepts from the *Bibliography* language to text. In this example, we target the BɪʙTᴇX format. This is useful if you need to maintain a bilbiography with MPS, and then need to transform it to text to provide it to the BɪʙTᴇX and LᴬTᴇX tools. This means that the text output will look very similar to the editor.

14.2 The TextGen Aspect

Let's start by creating the TextGen aspect. Remember that the TextGen aspect is optional, so you need to follow the instructions in 13.1 to create it.

14.3 The Concept TextGen

Create a concept textgen for the Bibliography concept. Figure 14.1 shows the configured concept textgen.

14.4 The Language TextGen

The first node that we create in the TextGen aspect is the language textgen. Create this AST root node and call it BibliographyToBibTeX. Note that you do not need to include TextGen in the name because when you look for this aspect MPS includes an icon to remind you of the type of each result element that matched your query.

---

[1] The definition of the Bibiography language was presented in Chapter 4.

```
text gen component for concept Bibliography {
  file name : <Node.name>
  extension : (node)->string {
    "bib";
  }
  encoding : utf-8
  text layout : <no layout>

  (context, buffer, node)->void {
    // the following line can only be entered after
    // you have defined a bibliography operation in
    // the Language TexGen
    append bibliography   ${node};
  }
}
```

Figure 14.1:   **Concept TextGen for the Bibliography Concept.** This figure presents a configured concept text gen for the Bibliography concept. Note that the append statement cannot yet be typed at this point. You need to first create the bibliography operation as described in the next section.

14.4.1   A Node for Each Language Concept

Add an operation to the language textgen called bibliography. This operation will transform Bibliography nodes to text. Add a parameter to the operation with type `node<Biblio graphy>`. Leave the body empty for now, you should have entered the following:

```
operation bibliography(node<Bibliography> biblio) {
}
```

Create one operation for each concrete concept of the *Bibliography* language: `Biblio Record`, `TitleElement`, `PublicationYear`, etc. You don't need to create an operation for nodes of an abstract Concept. Figure 14.2 presents the empty operations that you should have when you are done.

 Note that it can be easier to copy the first operation, then paste it and modify its name and type of node (you can also press `ctrl` + `D` over an operation to duplicate it). This saves time because the AST fragment that you copy already has the node<> type setup and you just need to change a few elements.

14.4.2   Bibliography Operation Implementation

The implementation of `operation bibliography` is responsible for writing an entire bibliography to BIBTEXformat. Since a bibliography is made up of BiblioRecords, the text generation implementation is straightforward. We can simply do:

```
foreach r in biblio.records {
  append record r;
  append \n ;
}
```

This code iterates through each bibliographical record of the bibliography node and delegates the texgen of each record to the `operation record`. After this it prints a new line.

```
base text gen component BibliographyToBibTeX extends <no baseTextGen> {
  operation bibliography(node<Bibliography> biblio) {
    <no statements>
  }

  operation title(node<TitleElement> title) {
    <no statements>
  }

  operation publicationYear(node<PublicationYear> year) {
    <no statements>
  }

  operation record(node<BiblioRecord> record) {
    <no statements>
  }

  operation person(node<Person> person) {
    <no statements>
  }

  operation authors(node<AuthorsElement> authors) {
    <no statements>
  }

  operation author(node<Author> author) {
    <no statements>
  }

  operation authorRef(node<AuthorRef> authorRef) {
    <no statements>
```

Figure 14.2: **Empty Operations for Bibliography.** This figures shows the empty operations that you should create for the *Bibliography* language. There is one operation for each concept of the *Bibliography* language that is not abstract.

You could also append with the $list element, but this would require that you define a concept textgen for the `BiblioRecord` concept.

Let's append something to the output for each record written. Change the `operation record` implementation to write the name of the record, as shown in Figure 14.3.

```
operation record(node<BiblioRecord> record) {
    append ${record.name};
}
```

Figure 14.3: **Simple Record TextGen Implementation.** An implementation of the record textgen that writes the name of the record.

After you have done this, recompile the *Bibliography* language. Verify that you get no errors in the log. If all is correct, you should be able to preview the text output of any `Bibliography` node. You can use the solution created in Chapter 4 to preview the text output. Open the Biblio node, right-click ⟩ Preview Generated Text . This menu will allow you to visualize the output that the textgen aspect generates. Remember to rebuild the language in order to get the text output that corresponds to the code in the textgen aspect. Previewing should give you a list of record names, one per line in the text output. Let's now make the output more similar to the BıBTEXformat. Change the operation record to match the content shown in Figure 14.4.

```
operation record(node<BiblioRecord> record) {
  append {@item} {{} ${record.name} {,} \n;
  increase depth;
  with indent {
    int index = 0;
    int last = record.elements.size - 1;
    foreach element in record.elements {
      append ${element};
      if (index++ != last) {
        append {,} \n;
      }
    }
  }
  decrease depth;
  append {,} \n;
}
```

Figure 14.4: **Operation Record.** This operation appends a `BiblioRecord` to the output buffer. Note the use of the textgen elements described in section 13.3.

This implementation starts by writing the constant string @item to the output, then it prints an opening bracket, followed by the record name. Note that the constant elements for @item and { could be merged into one constant cell. The name is followed with a comma and a new line (the new line is the reason we cannot use $list, since this element cannot use newline as separator). The next statement increases the depth of indentation before opening the `with indent` block. This will result in a double indentation being written because the `with indent` block also increases indentation level inside the block. However, remember that you must set the `with indent` attribute for the first statement inside the block (open the ⊕ 2: Inspector to see the attribute), because the indent must be written before $element. Inside the block, we keep track of the index of the element and compare with the last element, making sure we append the comma to separate elements, but not after the last element. Finally, the append element takes care of delegating to the appropriate textgen operation. The specific operation is chosen according to the type of the node in element (i.e., the operation with the more specific type will be called).

14.5 Generating Author Lists

Figure 14.5 presents the textgen operations that we use to format author lists to the output. Note that we do not define an operation for AuthorRef nodes because the AuthorRef concept textgen delegates directly to the Person textgen (see Figure 14.6).

Figure 14.5: **Operations for Authors and Person.** These textgen operations take care of formatting authors in the BIBTEXformat. Note the use of $list with the keyword with, that separates individual authors with the keyword *and*.

```
operation authors(node<AuthorsElement> authors) {
  indent buffer;
  append {Authors = "} $list{authors.authors with  and } {"};
}

operation person(node<Person> person) {
  append ${person.lastName} {,};
  if (person.middleName.isNotEmpty) {
    append { } ${person.middleName} {,};
  }
  append { } ${person.firstName};
}
```

Figure 14.6:   **AuthorRef Concept TextGen.** The AuthorRef concept textgen delegates to the Person texgen operation.

```
text gen component for concept AuthorRef {
  (context, buffer, node)->void {
    append person node.author;
  }
}
```

Finally, we write the operations shown in Figure 14.7 to format title and publication year elements.

Figure 14.7: **Title and Year TextGen Operations.** Note the use of Integer.toString to convert the year integer to a String.

```
operation title(node<TitleElement> title) {
  indent buffer;
  append {Title = "} ${title.value} {"};
}

operation publicationYear(node<PublicationYear> year) {
  indent buffer;
  append {Year = "} ${Integer.toString(year.value)} {"};
}
```

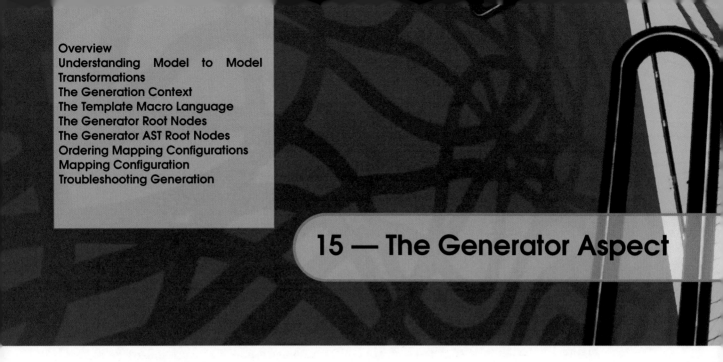

15 — The Generator Aspect

15.1 Overview

The Generator Aspect is used to perform model to model transformations. In contrast to the TextGen aspect (see Chapter 13), which converted models to text, a Generator converts a model (i.e., ASTs or AST fragments) into another AST or AST fragment. Generators are often used to define a transformation from one language to another language. However, they can also be used to convert parts of one language into other constructs of this same language. This last type of transformation is particularly useful when higher level statements of a language can be expressed with several lower-level AST concepts of the same language.

15.2 Understanding Model to Model Transformations

In the previous two chapters, we described how the TextGen aspect can be used to transform an AST (model) to a text. Text generation should be thought of as an export step, useful to interface with legacy systems that depend on lexer and parser technology, but that bring back all the drawbacks of these technologies. Transforming a model (i.e., an AST) from one language to another can be done in a more natural way in MPS. The approach is one of model to model transformation. Model to model transformation consists of converting an AST in some language, either the entire AST or parts of it, to an AST whose nodes belong to concepts of another language. As an example, consider the parallel foreach language. This language is an MPS Sample project. Parallel foreach provide a foreach statement that extends the *baseLanguage* statement, and can execute loop iterations in parallel. Because a parallel foreach statement can be translated to pure *baseLanguage*, it is convenient to transform the parallel foreach AST fragment into *baseLanguage* AST fragments. The transformation introduces all the statements and variables needed to implement the logic of the parallel foreach statement.

Figure 15.1 illustrates the concept of model to model transformation using a different example.

There are several types of model to model transformations (MMT):

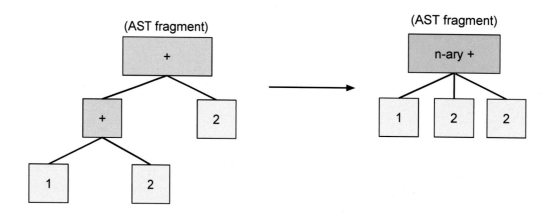

Figure 15.1: **Example of Model to Model Transformation.** This figure illustrates the process of model to model transformation. On the left, an AST fragment that describes the expression $1+2+2$ is shown encoded in a language that offers only binary $+$ operators. On the right, the same expression is shown expressed as an AST in a language that offers a n-ary $+$ operator. The arrow is an example of model to model transformation. Note that the arrow points from left to right, implying that the unary transformation is being converted to the n-ary operator, but in this case, because the two ASTs are semantically equivalent, the transformation from right to left would also be possible.

- MMTs that fully preserve the semantic of the input AST fragment into the output AST fragment. The MMT shown in Figure 15.1 belongs to this type. If we write $i \overset{t}{\mapsto} o$, where t is the MMT, i the input AST fragment and o the output AST fragment, then there exists a reverse MMT r such that $i \overset{t}{\mapsto} o \overset{r}{\mapsto} i$.
- MMTs that simplify the input AST fragment by removing parts that are not needed for some activity. Since these transformations remove information, they are not reversible.

15.3 The Generation Context

The generation context offers a number of capabilities useful when you need to implement concept functions in the Generator Aspect. The following capabilities are offered:

Unique Name Generation The expression `genContext.unique name from x in context C` will yield a unique name derived from the name of the node x. You can specify a node C to indicate the context in which uniqueness must be guaranteed.

Access to Template Variables It is possible to associate values to variables inside a template and pass these variables from template to template. You can access the value of a variable in the context where it is defined by using the expression `genContext.varName` where `varName` is the name of the variable.

Access to the Input or Output Models   The generation context provides access to nodes of the input or output models. These nodes are returned by expressions of the form `genContext.get something`, where `something` is one of the get method variants.

Particularly useful is the method called `get original copied input for (<outputNode>))`.   You can use this method to retrieve the original input node corresponding to the argument node. This method is useful when some other generator may transform the input model before your generator has a chance to look at it. This can happen because MPS generators are executed in distinct steps, and later steps may work on an input model that substantially differs from the original input model. For instance, assume that you wish to retrieve the parameters of a closure literal, defined in *baseLanguage* in order to expose these parameters in a method that you generate. The *baseLanguage* closure generator may run before your generator has a chance to inspect the closure parameters. In this case, you would need to retrieve the parameters from the input model, using the closure, or a parent of the closure in the current AST.

> (R)   Do not confuse `genContext.get original copied input for (<outputNode>))` with `genContext.inputModel`.   The method called `inputModel` returns the input model of the current generation step, not the original input model (unless the generation step when the method is called happens to be the first generation step).

15.4 The Template Macro Language

The template macro language makes it possible to identify parts of the target AST and to substitute them with AST fragments derived from the input model. It is important to understand that there are two parts to a template macro (macro for short):

where: the part that identifies which node of the output AST is to be changed.

value: the part that calculates the value that the where node will take.

To fulfill the where part, macros are tied to nodes of the output AST in the projectional editor. This is done by selecting one AST node and invoking an intention to tag the node with a specific macro. The type of the macro needs to match the type of the node. This is enforced in MPS because only the macros compatible with a node are shown as intentions when the node is selected. This means that if you do not see the macro that you are looking for offered as an intention, you probably selected the wrong kind of node in the editor. This problem can be relatively common when you first use the template macro language, so do not hesitate to check the type of the node that you are trying to attach a macro to (use `right-click` ⟩ `Go To` ⟩ `Editor Declaration` and see which kind of node, property or reference you had selected).

> (R)   If you have checked that the cursor is placed inside the appropriate location for the type of property macro you need to use, but do not see the correct macro intention, make sure that the editor of the output concept has been compiled and is up to date.

Because the template macro language is used directly in the editor of the target concept(s), it provides a convenient way to transfer information from the input models into the output models. While this may sound abstract, a few examples will help illustrate what can be achieved with this language.

15.4.1 Property Macros

Property macros are used to set the value of properties in the output AST. Assume an output node of type *A*, where *A* has the `text` property. If you create a template that outputs an instance of *A*, you can use a property macro to set the value of `text` in the output AST.

Assume that the template input is set to an instance of concept *I*, and that this concept has a string property called `source`. To set a property macro on the `text` property of the output node, you need to put the cursor inside the string of the `text` property value (typically between the double quotes that delimit the value). After you have done this, press `option` + `↵` to display the intention menu. In the list of choices displayed, select "Add Property Macro: node.source (property)". The special symbol $[] should appear around the initial value of the element. Figure 15.2 provides detailed instructions for setting a property macro. Note that the templates shown in this figure are inline-templates: they are designated with the `<T` and `T>` symbols.

(R) To edit the concept function associated with the property macro, make sure you position the cursor immediately in front of the $ sign before you open the `2: Inspector`.

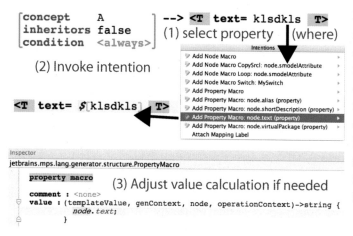

Figure 15.2: **Setting a Property Macro.** Follow these directions to set a property macro on any property of the output node. Note that in this example, we use the same concept as input and output, but this is not required. In step 3, we use the `2: Inspector` to edit the value that will be set in the output property.

15.4.2 Reference Macros

Reference macros are used to change an output reference with a value that points to a different node. Remember that references point to nodes across the AST. Reference macros work in a similar way to property macros. You first indicate which reference of the output you need to modify, by placing the cursor inside the display of the reference. You then invoke the intention menu and choose "Add Reference Macro". Several intention choices may be offered, one for each reference in the input node, but you don't need to select any if the reference is to be calculated. You then specify the value that needs to be put at this position in the output node by entering a *referent* concept function in the inspector. The signature of this function is:

```
(outputNode, genContext, operationContext, node)->node<X> {
}
```

The value of the X type will match the type of the reference that you have selected before invoking the reference macro intention.

15.4.3 Node Macros

Node macros are used to replace an entire node of the output with a different value of the same node type. In order to use a node macro, you need to select a single node of the output concept in a template or template fragment. Once you have selected the where, use the intention menu to locate the choice "Add Node Macro". Selecting this choice will prefix the node with the $$ symbol.

There are several concrete types of node macros, and you can choose a specific type in one of two ways:

- Selecting a more specific node macro intention (this may be easier because the set of node macros is prefiltered to show only those macros compatible with the node context (*where*) already selected).
- Inserting the cursor between the two $$ signs and invoking the auto-completion menu. This will provide a list of all the concrete node property macros that can be used. The symbol is red because the node macro is still abstract. You need to identify a concrete node macro to remove this error.

The following paragraphs present a description of the different concrete node macros that MPS provides.

$COPY_SRC$

The $COPY_SRC$ node macro will copy the input (source or SRC) node to the output, apply any template that can be applied to the node, and leave the output of the template in the output model. This macro is very useful to insert transformed parts of the input AST into a template. Importantly, you do not need to figure out the exact sequence of transformations that the input node will need to go though. This is specified declaratively in the mapping configuration (see Section 15.8).

You need to specify how to obtain the SRC of the template by using the 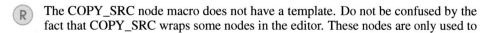. The concept function called *mapped node* must return the input node, and has the following signature:

```
(genContext, node, operationContext)->node<> {
}
```

> (R) The COPY_SRC node macro does not have a template. Do not be confused by the fact that COPY_SRC wraps some nodes in the editor. These nodes are only used to

visually indicate the type of the node that will be copied by the macro. The nodes below the COPY_SRC macro are in no way a template, and their content is discarded. If you see yourself changing the nodes below COPY_SRC and hoping to see the output altered, you probably need to use the MAP_SRC node macro instead.

$COPY_SRCL$

The $COPY_SRCL$ node macro is similar to the $COPY_SRC$ macro, but works with lists of nodes. Use it when you need to transform a sequence of nodes. The concept function called *mapped nodes* must return a sequence of input nodes, and has the following signature:

```
(genContext, node, operationContext)->sequence<node<>> {
}
```

$CALL$

The $CALL$ node macro is used to call a specific template. The output of the template will be used instead of the content of the macro (i.e., the selection around which the macro is set will be discarded and the template output that result from the CALL will be substituted). Template calls may provide parameter values when the template was defined with parameters.

$EXPORT$

The $EXPORT$ node macro is used to annotate a template fragment and associate it with an export label. See Section 15.8.2 for a description of export labels.

IF

The IF node macro evaluates a condition (defined by a concept function under the [2: Inspector]). When the condition evaluates to true, the content under the IF macro, in the editor, in used in the output model. When the condition is false, the content of the alternative element (specified in the [2: Inspector]) is used instead.

$INCLUDE$

The $INCLUDE$ node macro is used to include a template defined elsewhere in the output AST. You can use the INCLUDE macro to avoid repeating fragments of templates in different locations of a larger template. Use the *include template* attribute under [2: Inspector] to specify the template to include. Note that the editor content inside the INCLUDE macro is discarded.

$INSERT$

The $INSERT$ macro can be used to execute a query and replace the template node wrapped by this macro with the result of the query execution. The query of the $INSERT$ macro can be defined in the [2: Inspector]. Open the inspector and provide an implementation for the following concept function (called "output node"):

```
(genContext, node)->node<> {
}
```

The method should return the node that will be substituted for the node immediately below the $INSERT$ macro.

$LABEL$

The $LABEL$ node macro can be used to attach a Mapping Label to an output node. The LABEL macro does not change the output nodes that it wraps, but associate it to a mapping label. Open the ⏻ 2: Inspector and set the label in the attribute called *mapping label*.

$LOOP$

The $LOOP$ node macro calculates a list of input nodes and applies the template that the macro wraps to each of the input nodes in sequence. The difference between LOOP and $COPY_SRCL$ is that $LOOP$ provides an explicit template (the node attached to the macro being the root of this template), while $COPY_SRCL$ delegates the choice of the template to the mapping configuration.

Since MPS 3.2, the LOOP macro makes it possible to define a variable name, into which a counter value will be written for each iteration of the loop. To define the variable name, select the $LOOP$ macro and open the inspector. Enter a suitable name after "Variable Name". This variable will be available in the generator context. To access it, type genContext., then locate the #Context Variable# auto-completion choice. Accept this choice and type the name of the variable that you have defined under the inspector of the LOOP macro. Note that LOOP counter variables start at zero.

MAP_SRC

The MAP_SRC node macro wraps a template and has several capabilities:
- You can use it to assign a label to a part of the output AST. If this is the only thing that you need to do, consider using a LABEL instead.
- You can use it to specify how to map an input node to an output node, using the wrapped nodes as template. In this case, you specify a concept function to locate the input and use the wrapped nodes as template.
- Need to output nothing when some input attribute is missing. When the concept function returns null, the MAP_SRC macro is ignored and does not contribute to the output. If you need to specify an alternative output, consider using the IF node macro.

MAP_SRCL

The MAP_SRCL node macro is similar to MAP_SRC, but will work with sequences of input nodes. The wrapped nodes act as a template that is applied in sequence to each of the input nodes.

$SWITCH$

The $SWITCH$ node macro provides a way to switch the template according to some condition. Open the ⏻ 2: Inspector and enter a reference to a template switch (see Section 15.7.4) in the *template switch* attribute. Note that if the selected template switch has no default template, then the wrapped template is used, otherwise, priority is given to the default template in the referenced switch.

$TRACE$

The MPS documentation indicates that the $TRACE$ node macro is used to associate an input node to the generated code. This is useful to map generated code back to input AST when debugging, as is done with `trace.info` files. A default mechanism is often sufficient to maintain this association (see Debugger section of the MPS reference manual), but the $TRACE$ macro can be used to capture additional associations.

VAR

The VAR node macro gives a value to a variable. The variable then has a value inside the node to which VAR is attached (and its descendants). You must specify a variable name (which is displayed to the right of VAR in the editor, and a concept function to calculate the value of the variable (see ⬛ 2: Inspector).

You can access a variable in the contexts where it is defined with the expression `genContext.varName`. Auto-completion will show all the variables defined in the generationContext when you type `genContext.` ctrl + SPACE .

$WEAVE$

The $WEAVE$ macro makes it possible to append child nodes returned by a query concept function with a template. Both query and template are defined in the ⬛ 2: Inspector . If the template provided in the inspector has some children, the nodes returned by the query are appended to the list of children provided by the template. An optional query anchor can be defined in the inspector to indicate where to weave in a list of children (see Section 15.8.7).

15.5 The Generator Root Nodes

In contrast to most other aspects, an AST Root Node is already available under the Generator aspect. This Root Node is called a Mapping Configuration (see Figure 15.3 to learn how to locate it). The Mapping Configuration is presented in Figure 15.4.

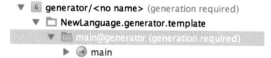

Figure 15.3: **Inside a Generator Aspect.** Click on `main` to edit the Generator's Mapping Configuration.

15.6 The Generator AST Root Nodes

While a mapping configuration already exists by default in a Generator aspect, it is possible to define additional AST Root nodes under these aspects. For instance, you can define additional mapping configurations, something that is useful when you need to define more control over the order in which transformations are applied. Section 15.7 describes how you can controls in which order mapping configurations are processed in this way. Figure 15.5 presents the other generator AST Root nodes that can be created in a Generator aspect. The following sections describe these root nodes in detail.

Figure 15.4: **The Generator Mapping Configuration.** The figure shows a freshly created Generator Mapping Configuration Root Node. The generator has several attributes. Press ⏎ over the « ... » below each attribute to insert an element in this attribute. When pressing ⏎ over <always>, you can insert a concept function. The attributes of a Mapping Configuration are described in detail in Section 15.8. Note that you can rename the mapping configuration. This is particularly useful in languages that need to define several of them. Section 15.7 describes how you can specify the order in which different mapping configurations are invoked.

```
mapping configuration main
top-priority group      false

mapping labels:
  << ... >>

exports:
  << ... >>

parameters:
  << ... >>

is applicable:
  <always>

conditional root rules:
  << ... >>

root mapping rules:
  << ... >>

weaving rules:
  << ... >>

reduction rules:
  << ... >>

pattern rules:
  << ... >>

abandon roots:
  << ... >>

drop attributes:
  << ... >>

pre-processing scripts:
  << ... >>

post-processing scripts:
  << ... >>
```

Figure 15.5: **The Other Generator Root Nodes.** Include various templates, additional mapping configuration root nodes, and generator descriptor.

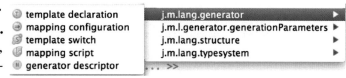

15.7   Ordering Mapping Configurations

Straightforward generator aspects can often be implemented with a single mapping configurations. In some cases, however, it can be useful to split down transformations into separate groups, that will be applied one after another in a certain order. For this reason, you can define multiple Mapping Configuration root nodes in a Generator aspect. You should name each mapping configuration according to the general step of transformation that this mapping configuration implements. You can define ordering relationships to control in which order mapping configurations will be invoked. MPS calls these relationships generator priority rules.

> (R) If you had developed generators with MPS 3.1 and migrate to MPS 3.2, you may experience problems with the generator. This is because 3.2 generation is more strict than 3.1, and some mapping configurations that happened to work in 3.1 may now fail to yield the desired generation results. These rare cases can be solved by entering explicit ordering relationships between mapping configurations.

> (R) Note that since MPS 3.2, you need to define a "Design" dependency from language A to language B when you need to specify priority rules between these languages. You can create "Design" dependencies in the Module property dialog, Dependencies tab, choose "Design" for the type of dependency. If you use "Design" dependencies in the generator aspect, you should also add a dependency for the module that contains the generator. Note that MPS 3.2 now distinguishes between "extends" dependencies (that you need to use when concepts of your language extend concepts of the other language) and "Generates into" dependencies (that you need to use if the generator of your language generates to the other language).

Defining priority rules between generators is done by specifying inequalities such as: $M_a = M_b$ To indicate that mapping configuration M_a should be processed together with M_b, or

$M_a < M_b$ To indicate that mapping configuration M_a should be processed before M_b

$M_a > M_b$ To indicate that mapping configuration M_a should be processed after M_b.

The operator $<=$ mean before or together and the operator $>=$ mean after or together.

These ordering inequalities can be defined by right-clicking on the Generator aspect in the Project Tab, opening Module Properties, and selecting the Generator Priorities Tab. Use the + button to insert a new priority rule, click on each generator part in turn to locate the mapping configuration of interest, select the checkbox of those mapping configurations you want to put on either side of the inequality. Finally, choose the priority rule operator as one of $=, >, <, <=, >=$. Figure 15.6 presents the dialog used to define generator ordering inequalities.

> (R) It is sometimes useful to define ordering rules that cross language boundaries. If you make a generator aspect depend on generator aspects of other languages, you will be able to define priority rules across all visible generators.

Figure 15.6: **Ordering Mapping Configura-tions.** This dialog is used to define relative priority rules between mapping configurations. The priority rule shown at the bottom is as shown after you press the + button. The red highlights are there to remind you to configure each generator (double click each to choose the generator name).

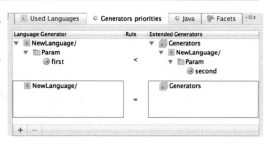

15.7.1 Mapping Configuration Parameters

If a mapping configuration requires parameters, you need to define each parameter as a new root node under the mapping configuration. To do this, select the `main@generator` model and do right-click ⟩ New ⟩ Generator j.m.l. ⟩ generationParameters ⟩ Generator Parameters

15.7.2 Other Generator AST Root Nodes

Figure 15.5 presents additional AST Root Nodes that can be created in the Generator aspect. To create these root nodes, select the `main@generator` model and do right-click ⟩ New ⟩ Generator j.m.lang.generator and select one of the node types shown in Figure 15.5. Note that all these root nodes belong to the *jetbrains.mps.lang.generator* language.

15.7.3 Template Declaration

A template declaration defines the transformation from an input node to an output node. Input and output nodes do not have to belong to the same language. Template declarations are identified in the Project Tab with this icon: ⓣ Figure 15.7 presents a freshly created template declaration. A new template declaration should be named immediately so that it is possible to refer to the template in the mapping configuration. It is often convenient to name the template with respect to the part of the AST that the template will generate.

  Input   This attribute defines the type of the input node that the template accepts. Set the input to refer to a concept that you wish to transform with the template.

  Parameters   You can define template parameters using this attribute (press ⏎ to insert a new parameter). Each parameter has a type and a name. Note that the order in which you define the parameters is also the order in which the parameters must be provided when you call the template in a mapping configuration. Calling the template with parameters consists in typing the name of the template. When the template has parameters, this will display `templateName()`. You can type literal inside the parentheses to provide parameter values, pressing return or comma will introduce new parameters. Note that type mismatches will be highlighted as errors. If you need to pass a value that depends on the generation context, you can introduce a *query* instead of a parameter literal. You do this by using the auto-completion menu at the position where you would type a value for the parameter. The auto-completion menu also provides access to the `null` value and some literals, but typing these values directly also works.

Content Node   The content node attribute is where the template transformation rules are encoded. Before you can edit the transformation, you need to specify the output node type. In its initial state, the `content node` attribute accepts a reference to a concept. Enter the name of the concept that you want the template to output. As soon as you have specified a concept reference, `content node` switches to display the editor for the output node. The editor is where the transformation rules can be specified. If you delete the root node in this editor, you will again have the ability to select the type of output node for the template.

It is important to understand that seeing the whole editor under content node does not mean that the entire node being edited will end up in the output. You must select precisely which part of the node displayed by the editor will end up being the template output. You do this by selecting a part of the tree that consists of exactly one node and using the intention called "Create Template Fragment". The part of the node that makes the template output is shown enclosed in **<TF** [and] **TF>** symbols. Note that a template can only have one output node, and therefore only one Template Fragment.

> (R) Note that a Template Fragment exist in a specific role of the source Concept (the source concept is the concept that contributes the editor used to edit the Template Fragment). A Template Fragment that was defined in a given role in the source node can only be inserted reliably in the same role in a destination node. Trying to insert the Template Fragment into a different role is not supported, even when the type of the roles would be compatible.

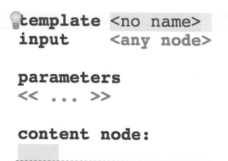

Figure 15.7:   **New Template Declaration.** You can declare that the template uses parameters, or specify the type of the output node under `content node`. After specifying the output type, the `content node` will switch to display an editor for the node whose context you specified.

Figure 15.8 presents a detailed walk-through that shows how to define a template fragment in the content node of a template declaration. This template takes a `BiblioRecord` as input and outputs another `BiblioRecord`. Note that the template shown is not particularly useful since it outputs constant output nodes. We will describe how to customize the output using information from the input node when we discuss the Template Macro language.

Figure 15.8: **Template Fragment Walk-through.** Follow these detailed instructions to learn how to setup the content node attribute of a template declaration. In Step (4), the error indicates that the template declaration is lacking a template fragment. Following Step 5 will resolve this error. You can invoke the intention menu with option + ↵ . You can deselect the item after step 5 since selection is only used to identify the node that should become the template fragment (template output).

```
template BiblioRecord
input    BiblioRecord

parameters
<< ... >>

content node:
<no content node>          (1) Press Control + SPACE
  Author
  AuthorRef
  AuthorsElement
  BiblioElement
  BiblioRecord      ◀── (2) Select BiblioRecord
  Bibliography              as the type of the content
  Person                    node
  PublicationYear
  TitleElement
  AbandonInput_RuleConsequence
  AbstractCheckingRule

content node:
@item{ <no name> ,         (3) The content node
                            attribute presents the
}                           BiblioRecord editor.
                            Change the record as
                            needed.
                              (4) We have customized
content node:                 the record in the editor.
@item{ theItemKey ,
   title = "someTitle"
   publication year = "2014"
}

                             (4) Select the entire
content node:                BiblioRecord. Try
@item{ theItemKey ,          using  Shift + Left
   title = "someTitle"       or Shift + Right
   publication year = "2014"
}        (5) Invoke the Intention Create Template Fragment
content node:
<TF @item{ theItemKey ,                          TF>
       title = "someTitle"
       publication year = "2014"
    }
```

15.7.4 **Template Switch**

A Template Switch makes it easier to handle cases when different outputs must be generated according to some condition, usally defined by some property of an input node (e.g., data contained in properties or fields, or state of references of the node). Follow the directions of Section 15.7.2 to create a new Template Switch. Figure 15.9 presents a freshly created template switch. When you press ⏎ over the « ... » below `cases`, you can create a new Template Switch Case (switch case for short). Each switch case has the following attributes:

concept   Indicate the name of the concept or interface concept that the case should match. Concepts that are not (exactly when inheritors is false) of this type will not be considered.

inheritors   When false, the concept must match exactly the concept attribute. When true, sub-concepts or concepts that implement an interface are accepted.

condition   A concept function can be defined to determine when the case is applicable (must return `true`). The function has the following signature:

```
(genContext, node, operationContext)->boolean {
}
```

consequence   Assign a suitable template to generate the output (any template defined in the generator will be available for completion), or choose one of the pre-defined choices below:

- `abandon input` This will produce no output. The input is discarded.
- `dismiss top rule` It is not clear what this option will do.
- `inline switch` This will create an inline template switch that you can edit to further handle more cases.
- `inline template with context` Specify an inline template to perform the transformation of the switch input. The output will be inserted in the context of the input node (i.e., in the output node transformed from the input node, at the position where the switch input would have been if it had not been transformed).
- `inline template` Specify an inline template.

```
template switch <no name> extends <none>

   null-input message: info : <no text>

 cases:|

      << ... >>

   default: <ignore switch>
```

Figure 15.9: **New Template Switch.** The template switch lets you output different output for a number of distinct cases. Press ⏎ over the « ... » to insert new cases. You can also specify a default output that will be generated when none of the cases defined in the switch can handle the input node.

15.7.5 Mapping Script

Mapping Scripts are used to perform operations that do not nicely fit the declarative style of the Mapping Configuration. You can define pre-processing or post-processing scripts and register them with the mapping configuration. A pre-processing script will be executed before the rules of the mapping configuration, while a post-processing script will be executed after rules of the mapping configuration. To create a new Mapping Script, select the generator model in the project tab and do `right-click` ⟩ `New` ⟩ `j.m.lang.generator` ⟩ `Mapping Script`. Figure 15.10 presents a freshly created Mapping Script. Name the script so that you can set a reference to it in the mapping configuration (see Sections 15.8.12 and 15.8.13).

```
mapping script <no name>

script kind : post-process output model

(genContext, model, operationContext)->void {
  <no statements>
}
```

Figure 15.10: **New Mapping Script.** Mapping Scripts are created with kind post-processing by default. You can switch to a pre-processing kind by completely deleting the text "post-process output model" and invoking the auto-completion menu.

15.7.6 Generator Descriptor

This AST Root node is marked as deprecated in MPS 3.0 and should not be used.

15.7.7 Root Nodes from Other Languages

You can create Root nodes that belong to other languages in a generator aspect. When you do so, MPS will consider these root nodes to be root templates for generation. This means that these root nodes will be generated in the output model when the generator is executed.

15.8 Mapping Configuration

A freshly created Mapping Configuration was shown in Figure 15.4. The attributes of a Mapping Configuration are described in the following sections.

15.8.1 Mapping Labels

Mapping labels associate a name to a fragment of the output AST. As generation proceeds, it is not unusual to need to refer to a part of the AST that was generated by another template. Mapping labels make it possible to identify such AST fragments, given that they have been associated with a mapping label when they were created.

In addition to providing a label to an output AST fragment, mapping labels can optionally record the type of the input AST fragment, as well as the type of the output AST fragment attached to the name. This is useful to check that the correct AST fragment is bound to each label (an error is reported by MPS if this condition does not hold for any defined mapping label). Figure 15.11 presents a new mapping label.

```
mapping labels:
   label <no name> : |<no input concept> -> <no output concept>
```

Figure 15.11: **New Mapping Label.** Enter a name for the label, and specify input and output type (enter a reference to a concept in each attribute). Press ⏎ over the label to add another one. You should name the mapping label immediately after creating it.

Attaching Output Fragments to a Mapping Label

You can attach a mapping label to a generator transformation by invoking the "Attach Mapping Label" to the output concept.

 In MPS 3.03, the intention will fail with an exception if any mapping label has an undefined name. Make sure all mapping labels have been named before using this intention.

Retrieving the Output AST Fragment for a Mapping Label

You can retrieve an output AST fragment bound to a mapping label with the expression:

```
genContext.get output label_name
```

When the mapping label is be applied to multiple input elements, you can retrieve a specific output with the expression:

```
genContext.get output label_name for (input_node);
```

15.8.2 Exports

Exports have been introduced in MPS 3.2 to make it possible to generate output from input nodes contained across several MPS models. The exports section of the mapping configuration is used to define export labels. Each export label describes how a node of an input language maps to a node of an output language. Figure 15.12 presents a freshly created export label definition (you can create a new export label by pressing ⏎ when the cursor is over the « ... » below exports:).

The export label definition has several attributes:

1. A name. The name is used to refer to the output fragment annotated with the export label. The name will be used with the $EXPORT$ node macro, see Section 15.4.3.
2. Input concept. The type of the input node that will be mapped during generation.

```
label <no name> : <no input concept> -> <no output concept>
   keep in:  <no dataHolder>
   marshal    : (inputNode, outputNode, keeper)->void  {
                   <no statements>
                }
   unmarshal : (inputNode, keeper, outputNode)->void  {
                   <no statements>
                }
```

Figure 15.12: **New Export Label.** Export Labels help to maintain mappings between input and output nodes of a generator transformation when inputs are defined in more than one model. See main text for description of each attribute.

3. Output concept. The type of the output node that will be created during generation.
4. Data Holder. This attribute should contain a reference to a concept that will be used to keep/hold information about the mapping of input to output nodes. The Data Holder is also called the Data Keeper. The concept of the Data Holder must be defined in the language that the generator generates to. Transient data holder instances will be created during a generation process. You can inspect these transient instances under Transient models (see Section 15.9 to learn how to visualize transient models).
5. Marshal concept function. This function must marshal an association between an input and output node into the data holder/keeper.
6. Unmarshal concept function. This function must unmarshal from the data holder/keeper, possibly using information from the input node, to establish a new connection from the input node to the output node. The unmarshal function should modify the output node to re-establish the connection across models.

Attaching Output Fragments to an Export Label

After defining an export label, a template that generates the output of an export can be annotated with the $EXPORT$ macro. Associating an $EXPORT$ macro to a template fragment is similar to associating a mapping label, but in the case of $EXPORT$, the output fragment becomes visible across models.

Retrieving the Output AST Fragment for an Export Label

You can retrieve an output AST fragment bound to an export label with the expression:

```
genContext.get exported label_name for node
```

For examples of using exports, see the Cross-Model Generation Cook-Book (https://confluence.jetbrains.com/display/MPSD32/Cross-model+generation+cookbook).

15.8.3 Parameters

You can declare that the mapping configuration requires some parameters. Note that the parameters must have been defined previously to link to them in this section. See Section 15.7.1 to learn how to define a new parameter.

15.8.4 Is Applicable

This attribute provides a simple way to disable a mapping configuration. Press ⏎ over `<always>`, in this attribute to insert a concept function with the following signature:

```
(genContext)->boolean {
}
```

The function must return a boolean. Return `true` in this function if the mapping configuration is applicable in a given context. Return `false` if the mapping configuration should not be used.

15.8.5 Conditional Root Rules

These generator rule can create a new output AST Root node without any input. The rule is called conditional because you can define the condition when the rule is active. You can see a new Conditional Root Rule in Figure 15.13.

```
conditional root rules:
  condition <always> --> : <no template>
```

Figure 15.13: **New Conditional Root Rule.** You can add a reference to an AST Root Node template. Note that the template must already have been created, or that you can use an intention to create a new one. Follow instructions in Section 15.7.7 to learn how to create other AST Root nodes in the generator that you can reference here.

15.8.6 Root Mapping Rules

A Root Mapping Rule can be used to transform a root node of the input model into a root node of the output model. See Figure 15.14 for a new root mapping rule. Root mapping rules have several attributes, described below:

Concept

The AST Root concept that this rule can transform. Enter a reference to the input Concept.

inheritors

A boolean, when true, sub-concepts of the Concept are also transformed by the rule. When false, sub-concepts will not be processed by the rule.

Condition

Pressing ⏎ over `<always>` will create a concept function with the following signature:

```
(genContext, node, operationContext)->boolean {
}
```

The method has access to the generator context (genContext), the input node and the operation context. It must return a boolean. Returning `true` activates the rule while returning `false` deactivates the rule.

Keep Input Root

A boolean, when true, keep the input AST Root node in the output model. When false (the default), the input AST root is consumed by the rule and removed from the model.

> (R) Note that if one of your AST Root nodes has Keep Input Root to true, the root node will need to be consumed by another rule, or be abandoned or it will preserved in the final output model.

Figure 15.14: **New Root Mapping Rule.**
```
root mapping rules:
 ┌concept         <choose applicable concept>┐ --> <no template>
 │inheritors      false                       │
 │condition       <always>                    │
 └keep input root default                     ┘
```

Template

The template attribute must point to an AST Root node template. You can either set the reference to an existing template (previously created in the generator), or use an intention to create a new one. Follow instructions in Section 15.7.7 to learn how to create other AST Root nodes in the generator that you can reference here.

15.8.7 Weaving Rules

A Weaving Rule makes it possible to insert an AST fragment into a specific location of an already generated AST. The rule has the inheritors and condition attribute that we have already described for Root Mapping Rules (see Section 15.8.6). The consequence attribute defines what AST fragment will be inserted (weaved), while the context attribute defines the location where the AST fragment will be inserted.

```
weaving rules:
 ┌concept     <choose applicable concept>┐ --> ┌choose consequence
 │inheritors  false                       │    │context : (genContext, operationContext, node)->node<> {
 │condition   <always>                    │    │              <no statements>
 └                                        ┘    └          }
```

Figure 15.15: **New Weaving Rule.** Weaving rules are used to insert an AST fragment into some specific location of an already generated AST.

Consequence

Invoking the auto-completion menu over `<choose consequence>` will present one or more choices. If several choices are shown in addition to <weave each>, they include the names of templates defined in the generator. You can select one of these templates to process input nodes and generate output nodes to be inserted in the destination context. If you do not see a template, but would like to use one, you can invoke the Intention menu (press ⌜option⌝ + ⌜⏎⌝ and should be offered the option "New Template"). Invoke this intention to create a template for this weaving rule.

One of the choices available in the consequence auto-completion menu is <weave each>. Accept this choice to introduce the attributes shown in Figure 15.16. Weave each makes it possible to generate input nodes that do not exist in the input model.

Inspector

When you select a weaving rule and open the ⌜⚙ 2: Inspector⌝, you will be able to configure three additional attributes:

mapping label

You can define a mapping label for the weaved content. The mapping label must be defined in the generator configuration.

description

Enter a description for this rule.

anchor

Press ⌜⏎⌝ over `<no anchorQuery>` to define a query function. The body of the function must return one node. This node will serve as an anchor and the weaved content inserted in front of this anchor. This feature was introduced in MPS 3.3.

Foreach/Weave Each

The `foreach` attribute let's you return a sequence of node<> that will be used as input to the weaving template. In the concept function, you typically use the generationContext (genContext parameter) to iterate through nodes of the input model. For this purpose, the useful genContext methods are named `get *`. Figure 15.17 provides a list of these methods. It is also possible to use the Weave Each attribute to create a custom set of nodes, even if they do not exist explicitly in the input model.

Apply

The `apply` attribute is where you specify a template to transform the input nodes. Select a template with auto-completion or create a new one with the "New Template" intention.

Context

Context specifies the location where the transformed AST will be inserted in the output AST. The concept function has three parameters (see Figure 15.15) and returns a node<>. The returned node must be the parent of where the transformed AST will be inserted. In this

```
foreach : (genContext, node, operationContext)->sequence<node<>> {
              <no statements>
          }
apply   : <choose template>
```

Figure 15.16: **Consequence Weave For Each.** Use the `foreach` attribute to construct a sequence of input node. The nodes do not have to exist in the input model.

```
                         genContext.get        ;
  get copied output by input                              search output node
  get original copied input by output  original input node copied to output
  get output by label                                     search output node
  get output by label and input                           search output node
  get output list by label and input                     search output nodes
  get prev input by label                        search preceding input node
```

Figure 15.17: **Generation Context Get Methods.**

function, you will often retrieve a node from the generation context using a mapping label set by some prior AST transformation.

15.8.8 Reduction Rules

Reduction Rules transform nodes of the input model into nodes of the output model. Reduction rules are similar to root mapping rules but are designed to transform nodes that are not root of their AST. Figure 15.18 presents a freshly created Reduction Rule. Reduction rules have the following attributes:

concept The Concept of the node that should be reduced (type of the source node in the input model).

inheritors When true, sub-concepts of Concept are reduced as well as exact type matches.

condition A concept function that returns `true` when the rule is active, and `false` otherwise.

consequence An attribute similar to the custom consequence types described in Section 15.7.4.

Figure 15.18: **New Reduction Rule.**

```
reduction rules:
  [concept    <choose applicable concept>]  --> choose consequence
   inheritors false
   condition  <always>
```

15.8.9   Drop Attributes

Prior to MPS 3.3, annotations used to be removed from the model before generation (or not propagated after transforming nodes in the generator). Since MPS 3.3, support has been added for annotations in TextGen and automatic annotation removal is no longer done before generation. In order to drop annotations which you do not want to generate, you can enter one or more Drop Attribute rules in the mapping configuration. Annotations that are not dropped will be propagated through each iteration of the generator and be available in the last model when TextGen is invoked.

Each Drop Attribute rule has two attributes: the concept of the annotation (i.e., attribute, must extend `NodeAttribute`) that you wish to remove. The second attribute is an optional concept function, which must return true when the annotation should be dropped.

15.8.10   Pattern Rules

Pattern Rules are activated when a fragment of the input model matches a pattern. See the description of the *pattern* language in Section 12.1.1. In addition to a pattern, Pattern Rules have a `condition` attribute. By default, the rule that match a pattern is always executed, but you can define a concept function to return `false` when the pattern rule should not be active despite matching the pattern. See Figure 15.19 for a freshly created Pattern Rule.

Figure 15.19: **New Pattern Rule.**

15.8.11   Abandon Rules

Abdandon Rules are used to indicate that an input node should be abandoned, that is should not produce an output. You can create an abandon rule by invoking the auto-completion menu with the cursor over the « ... » inside the Abandon Rule attribute. This will let you select a concept name. The rule is then configured with the appropriate concept. Pressing ⏎ over the « ... » will also create an abandon rule, but you will then need to bind a concept. Abandon rule have an optional condition, described here:

condition   By default, abandon rules are always executed (the condition attribute is rendered as "<none>"). Pressing ⏎ over none will introduce a concept function with the following signature:

```
(operationContext, genContext, node)->boolean {
}
```

This function must return a boolean with value `true` when the rule should abandon the node, or `false` otherwise.

15.8.12 **Pre-Processing Scripts**

Use this attribute to indicate that one or more pre-processing scripts (see Section 15.7.5) must be executed before the rules described in this Mapping Configuration. Note that using pre-processing scripts is discouraged and should be limited to rare situations where the declarative features of Mapping Configuration are unable to transform the models.

15.8.13 **Post-Processing Scripts**

Use this attribute to indicate that one or more post-processing scripts (see Section 15.7.5) must be executed after the rules described in this Mapping Configuration. Note that using post-processing scripts is discouraged and should be limited to rare situations where the declarative features of Mapping Configuration are unable to transform the models.

15.9   Troubleshooting Generation

When using model to model transformations with the generator aspect you may find yourself in a situation when you do not fully understand why a template matches or does not match some input models. MPS provides a feature that makes it easier to troubleshoot model-to-model transformations. To troubleshoot, turn on the feature that preserves transient models. You can do this by clicking on the T symbol at the lower right of the MPS workbench window, i.e.: 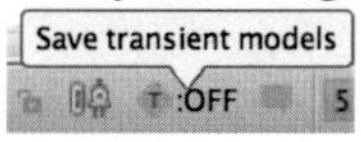 After you have enabled "Save Transient Models", each time you generate a model, such as when rebuilding a solution, a set of transient models will be shown at the bottom of the Project Tab. For instance, Figure 15.20 presents a set of transient models displayed in the Project Tab after rebuilding a solution in the NYoSh Workbench.

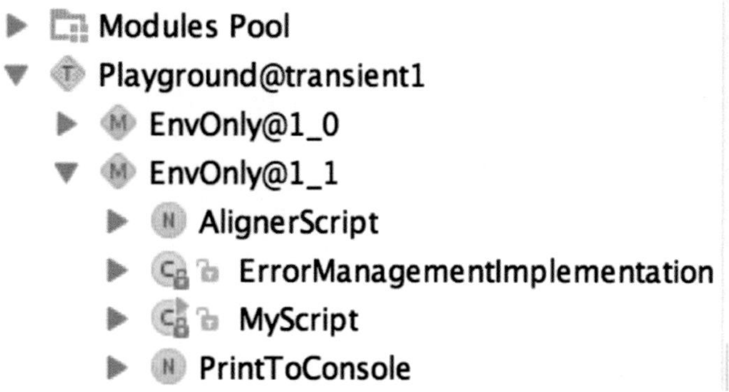

Figure 15.20: **Viewing Transient Models.** When "Save Transient Models" is active, MPS stores models generated during intermediate transformation steps under the Project Tab, below Modules Pool. The models are numbered in the order they are transformed and can be inspected to help troubleshoot model transformations.

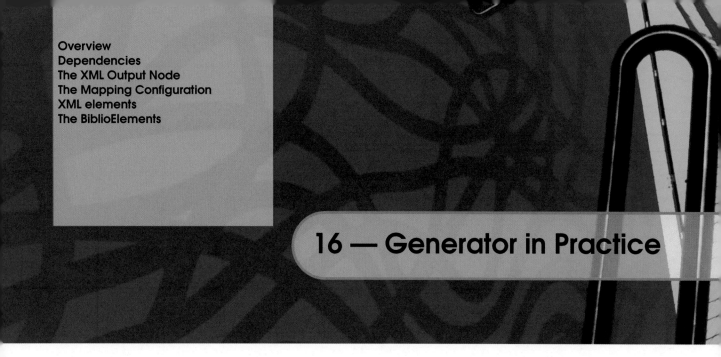

16 — Generator in Practice

16.1 Overview

This chapter illustrates how to use the generator aspect to transform ASTs expressed in the *Bibliography* language into an XML-based Bibliography language. While XML could be generated as text with a TextGen aspect, it is simpler to transform the AST with the model to model capabilities of the Generator aspect.

XML is a popular format for representing and exchanging bibliographies, as exemplified by the development of the Citation Style Sheet (CSL) [Cit] and the Meta Data Object Description Schema [Sta] (MODS) format. In the context of this chapter, and for the sake of simplicity, we will not target the MODS standard, but instead output a simple output format. Let's see how to do this.

16.2 Dependencies

In order to generate XML models, the generator aspect needs to depend on the *jetbrains .mps.core.xml* language. You can add a dependency on this language by opening the Project Tab, selecting the generator aspect of the Bibliography language and right-clicking to open the module properties dialog. In this dialog, select the dependency tab and locate the *xml* language (hint: xml is a good keyword). While you are in the generator Modules Properties dialog, add the *xml* language to the Used Languages tab.

Next, select the main@generator under the Generator aspect and add the *xml* language to the Used Languages tab. After you have done this, if you right-click on `main@generator`, you should have an option to do New ⟩ j.m.c.xml ⟩ xml file . Do this to create an AST root of Type xml file under the generator model. This AST Root will represent the XML file that will contain the bibliography.

16.3 The XML Output Node

After you have completed the last step, you should see the content of Figure 16.1. It is important to realize that you are seeing the editor of an XML Root node, decorated with a root template annotation on top. The root template annotation let's you specify the type of the concept that can be used as input. Let's enter a reference to the Bibliography concept in the input attribute since we aim to convert an entire bibliography node to one XML file node.

Enter "filename" immediately after xml, in place of <no name>. This will make it possible to refer to this root template from the mapping configuration.

```
root template
input <unspecified>

xml <no name>


<no prolog>
<no element>
```

Figure 16.1: **New XML Root Node.** This XML Root node is created under the main@generator model. We will use it to convert the bibliography content to XML.

16.4 The Mapping Configuration

Now that we have defined a root template, we can add a root mapping rule to the generator's Mapping Configuration node. Open the main@generator node, locate the root mapping rules: section and press ⏎. This will create a new root mapping rule. See section 15.8.6 for details about root mapping rules. Configure the input of the rule to be the Bibliography concept, and the output of the rule to be the filename template root node that we have already created (use auto-completion to locate it). Figure 16.2 presents the completed root mapping rule.

```
root mapping rules:
concept          Bibliography  --> filename
inheritors       false
condition        <always>
keep input root  default
```

Figure 16.2: **Completed Root Mapping Rule.** This rule declares that any Bibliography root node should be transformed using the filename XML root template that we have defined.

16.4.1 Changing the XML filename

Since we would like to generate one XML file for each Bibliography node, we need to replace the constant "filename" string with a value that depends on the name of the bibliography. We can do this by using a property macro. Put the cursor anywhere inside the filename string that you have typed, and invoke the intention menu (option + ⏎). Select the "Add Property Macro node.name". Figure 16.3 presents the root template editor after you have attached the name of the input node to the filename string.

Figure 16.3: **XML Root Template After Setting the XML Filename.** After using the property macro, the filename attribute is shown surrounded with the $[ ] signs. You can open the to verify the macro is bound to node.name, the name of the bibliography input node (place the cursor immediately before the $ character to set the context for the inspector).

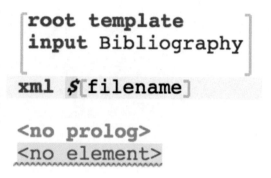

We can now use the editor of the XML file concept to describe the output that should go into the output XML node.

16.5 XML elements

Place the cursor over the `<no element>` attribute and use auto-completion (option + ↵). This offers one choice: the creation of a new XML element. Accept this choice. The editor presents a new XML element <<no tagName>></> with no name. You can type the name of the tag directly into the `no tagName` space. Call the tag "records". Notice that as you type the tag in the opening element, the closing element is also renamed.

> (R) The common error of using one tag for an opening element and introducing a typo in the tag for the closing element is eliminated because the projectional editor calculates the presentation from a node where tagName is stored only once. Matching element errors can be difficult to debug in text-based editors, especially when the elements are brackets or parentheses that do not have a name. These errors are eliminated by the use of a projectional editor to configure the output of the template.

We called the first element `records` because we need to store several `BiblioRecords` below the root of the XML file. Let's now translate each input `BiblioRecord` child of the input node to XML.

To do this, we will start by mocking a single new record inside the records element. Place the cursor between the opening and closing elements for records, and invoke the auto-completion menu. The choices presented in Figure 16.4 should be available. Accept the `<element/>` choice. Change the tagName of the new element to "record". If you continue typing or place the cursor at the end of record and press SPACE, you will get the option of entering an attribute name (see the auto-completion menu). Create a new attribute and rename it to the name "key". The value of the `key` attribute will hold the record name. Before we can set this value, we need to describe how each record element is created.

Place the cursor over the `record` element, and invoke the intention menu. Choose the "Add Node Macro Loop: node.records" choice. This will enclose the `record` element in a LOOP macro. Figure 16.5 presents the result of applying the node macro.

```
<records></records>
```
```
 &                                              entity reference
 &#                                             single character
 <!--                       (XmlContent in j.m.core.xml)
 <![CDATA                    (XmlContent in j.m.core.xml)
 <?                                      processing instruction
 <element/> (XmlBaseElement in j.m.core.xml)
 text                                                plain text
```

Figure 16.4: **Choices Available Inside the records Element.** These choices should be available when you invoke auto-completion inside the records element. You can create new elements, comments, text, an entity reference or a single character. Choose <element/>.

```
<records>
  $LOOP$[<record key=" "></record> ]
</records>
```

Figure 16.5: **Result After Applying LOOP Node Macro.** The LOOP macro instructs the generator to create one record element for each node.records input node.

Let's proceed by configuring the key of each record. To this end, type some text inside the key attribute (e.g., aKey) and apply a property macro to replace this string with node.name. Since the record is now inside a LOOP macro, the type of node is no longer Bibliography, but instead is BiblioRecord. Mapping the attribute value to node.name will replace the key attribute value with the name of each BiblioRecord node in the bibliography.

16.6   The BiblioElements

Now that we have translated the BiblioRecord to an XML element, we should translate the BibioElement nodes that each record contains.

A first thought is to use the LOOP macro again, to iterate through each of the elements. While this is possible, it is not optimal because the LOOP macro applies the same template to each node that it iterates over, and we need to generate different xml elements depending on the type of BiblioElement. We could work around this by using a template switch inside the $LOOP$ macro, but there is a simpler way. Rather than performing pattern matching with a template switch, we will delegate to the Mapping Configuration that will determine the appropriate template for each BiblioElement node. Delegating template resolution is done with the $COPY_SRC$ or $COPY_SRCL$ macros. Here, because we need to process a list of BiblioElement, we use the $COPY_SRCL$ macro.

Start by creating a new element as a direct child of the <record> element. You can call this element anything because it will be discarded by the $COPY_SRC$ macro, but assume you call it <myElement></myElement>. Now, position the cursor before the element that you have just created and invoke the intention menu. Select the macro called "Add Node Macro: CopySrcl node.elements". This will produce the template shown in Figure 16.6. You can open the inspector and verify that the source of the nodes to transform has been set to `node.elements` (note that you can change the source of the nodes directly in the inspector without having to change the template in the editor).

Figure 16.6: **Result After Applying COPY_SRCL Node Macro.**

```
<records>
  $LOOP$<record key="$[aKey]">
      $COPY_SRCL$<myElement></myElement>
    </record>
</records>
```

We are not done yet. What is left to do is to associate a template to each sub-concept of `BiblioElement`. We do this by navigating to the Mapping Configuration node, locating the Reduction Rule attribute, and adding one reduction rule for each sub-concept of `BibioElement`. Let's start with the `TitleElement` concept. Try to enter the reduction rule shown in Figure 16.7. Note the use of an inline template in this case, because the title element is simple and fits on one line. it is recommended to avoid using inline templates for complex template declarations. The property macro that is set on the text element contained in the `<Title>` element refers to the value property of the `TitleElement` concept.

```
reduction rules:
  concept      TitleElement  --> <T <Title>$[The Title of the Work]</Title> T>
  inheritors false
  condition   <always>
```

Figure 16.7: **Reduction Rule for TitleElement.**

Let's proceed and add a reduction rule for the `PublicationYear` subconcept of `BiblioElement`. The process is almost the same as for the `TitleElement`, but here we cannot find a property macro for the value property of `PublicationYear`. The reason is that the property has type integer, which does not match the string type of the text that can be stored in the `XmlElement` target concept. The solution is to select the intention called "Add Property Macro". This unspecified macro is available even when no property matches the type of the selected target element. You then open the [2: Inspector] and enter the conversion code manually in the value concept function:

```
(templateValue, genContext, node, operationContext)->string {
  Integer.toString(node.value);
}
```

Exercise 16.1 Complete the reduction rules for the `BiblioElement` sub-concepts. Refer to the previous chapter for information about the different generator mechanisms and macros that you can use.   ∎

The MPS online manual includes a detailed Generator tutorial that together with this book can help you learn more about the Generator Aspect. See `http://tinyurl.com/np7zleg` for the online tutorial.

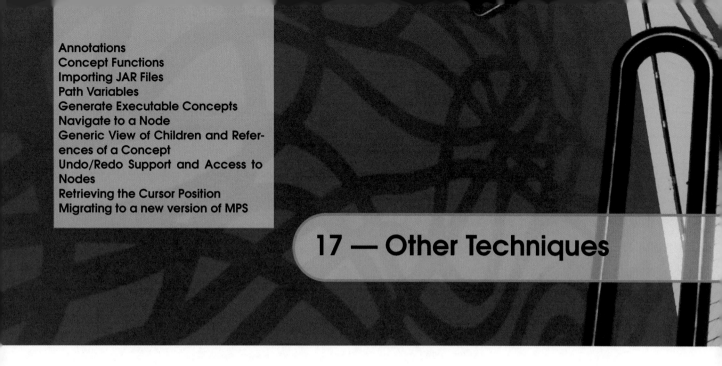

17 — Other Techniques

This chapter presents some techniques that you may find useful, but that do not easily fit into any of the other chapters.

17.1 Annotations

Node annotations attach information to nodes expressed in the AST of another language. Anotations are designed to facilitate the extension of individual nodes of another language. In MPS 3+, annotations are expressed using a combination of MPS aspects: Structure, Intentions and Editor.

This section explains how to create an annotation. Let's assume we need the annotation to extend a root node of type `Root` and that the annotation should have a string property called *email* that makes it possible to attach an email to the `Root` node.

17.1.1 Define the Annotation Concept

Let's define an annotation concept in the structure aspect of some language. We call the annotation concept `RootToEmail`. Create a new concept (see Section 3.2) as shown in Figure 17.1 (top left).

Multiple

A boolean that indicates if there can be more than one annotation per attributed concept. When false, only one annotation can be attached per concept. When true, a collection of annotations is attached to the concept.

Role

The role is the name associated with the attribute. In the *SModel* language, you can access an annotation with the syntax: `node.@role`. For instance, in the example shown in 17.1, the intention (top-right) accesses the email annotation with `node.@email` since the role name was `email` in the annotation structure concept (structure aspect, top right of the figure).

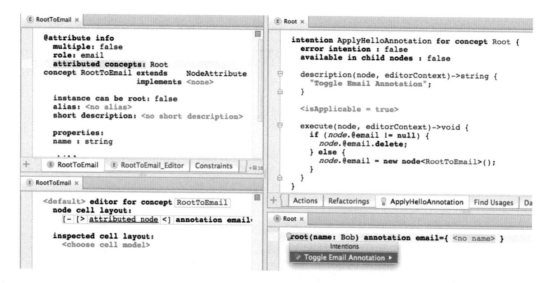

Figure 17.1: **The Completed Annotation Concept.** This figure presents a completed annotation concept, with one email property and a Root target node. When creating the new annotation concept, start by naming the annotation, then change the extends clause to make the annotation extend `NodeAttribute` (from language *jetbrains.mps.structure.core*). The annotation concept must extend `NodeAttribute` to be endowed with the attributes shown at the top of the editor. The top-right corner shows the structure definition of the annotation concept. The top-right shows the definition of the intention, the bottom left the editor for the annotation concept, and the bottom-right shows how the annotation can be used to annotate Root nodes.

Attributed Concept

This is the concept(s) to which the annotation can be attached. In Figure 17.1, this attribute contains a reference to the Root concept because we wish to add email annotations only to this concept. Press ⏎ over the attribute to add more than one attributed concept.

17.1.2 Define an Intention To Toggle the Annotation

To attach an annotation to a Root node, we need to create an intention that we can use in the editor to add or remove annotations to Root node instances. A suitable intention is shown in Figure 17.1 (top-right). Note that the intention toggles the annotation: it adds an annotation when none was present, or delete an existing annotation associated with a root node. Also note the syntax to access the annotation attribute: node.@<role>, where role is the role name defined for the NodeAttribute attributes of RootToEmail.

17.1.3 Define an Annotation Editor

The role of the annotation editor is to display the information associated with the annotation alongside the annotated node. In Figure 17.1 (bottom-left), we use the [>attributed node<] component to embed the original Root editor in the editor of the annotated node and display the email field of the annotation to the right of the original Root editor. The result is shown in the bottom-right corner of figure 17.1 (after the intention toggled the email annotation).

17.2 Concept Functions

Concept functions are useful to make it possible for end-users of a language to plugin-in domain or application specific logic. You have seen many examples of concept functions throughout this book, which are used judiciously by the MPS platform to customize its languages. Here we describe how to define custom concept functions and insert them into your own languages.

17.2.1 Function Concept

Defining a concept function consists in deciding on the signature of the method. A signature has parameters in a specific order and returns values of some type (functions that return no values are declared to return type void). Once you have decided on the signature of the function, you should create a new concept and extend ConceptFunction. For the purpose of illustration, let's assume you called the concept that will represent your new concept function AFunction. AFunction should extend ConceptFunction. Your concept does not need to provide an editor because the ConceptFunction editor will handle the rendering of sub-concepts. As soon as you extend ConceptFunction, AFunction will endowed with a few new attributes, called concept properties and concept links. You should ignore these, because these attributes are marked as deprecated.

In order to define the signature of the new concept function AFunction, you need to override behavior methods defined in ConceptFunction. To this end, you first associate a behavior to AFunction. You can do this by selecting the AFunction concept in the editor, placing the cursor over the Behavior tab, and clicking in the empty editor tab. Accept the suggestion to create a "Concept Behavior". Place the cursor anywhere inside the behavior associated with AFunction and invoke the menu Code 〉 Override Behavior Methods, or press ⌘ + O . This will open a dialog with the content shown in Figure 17.2.

Figure 17.2: **Override Behavior Methods Dialog.** You open this dialog by invoking the menu Code 〉 Override Behavior Methods, or pressing ⌘ + O when the cursor is inside a Behavior root node. In order to define parameters of the concept function, you need to override the getParameters() method (highlighted in blue in this snapshot). Select the method name in the dialog and press ↵ (or click OK). This will create a method stub in the behavior aspect that was active in the editor.

17.2.2 Function Parameters

The behavior method stub that was just created must return a list of elements with type node<ConceptFunctionParameter>. Each of the elements in the list will represent a parameter of the function. For each parameter of the function, you will define a new concept. Here, we assume that AFunction will have two parameters: id, of type string and input, of the Java type InputStream.

You define the first parameter by creating a new concept called ConceptFunction Parameter_id. Make this concept extend ConceptFunctionParameter and define its alias to be "id". Repeat the process of the second parameter, but set alias to be "input". To prevent the end-user from being able to remove the parameters or change their name in the places where the concept function will be used, you need to mark each of these parameter concepts with the interface conceptIDontSubstituteByDefault.

The parameter definition is almost complete. To finish, we need to define the type of each parameter. We do this with the typesystem aspect. Associate a typesystem inference rule to each parameter concept, and enter the following in the rule section: For `ConceptFunctionParameter_id`:

```
typeof(conceptFunctionParameter_id) :==: <string>;
```

When using the quotation language, remember that the concept name for the string type is `StringType`.
For `ConceptFunctionParameter_input`:

```
typeof(conceptFunctionParameter_input) :==: <InputStream>;
```

> (R) Note that in order to quote InputStream as shown above, you need to: (1) add java.io@java_stubs to the dependencies of the typesystem aspect for the language that contains the concept function parameter and (2) use the `ClassifierType` concept before you can enter InputStream.

Now that the parameters of the concept function are defined, we simply need to assemble and return the list of parameters in the behavior method of `AFunction`. To this end, we implement the `getParameters()` method with the following code fragment:

```
list<concept<ConceptFunctionParameter>> result =
  new arraylist<concept<ConceptFunctionParameter>>;
result.add(concept/ConceptFunctionParameter_id/);
result.add(concept/ConceptFunctionParameter_input/);
return result;
```

Briefly, this implementation creates a result variable of type `list<concept<Concept FunctionParameter>>`. It adds references to the concepts representing the parameters to this list, and returns the list. This defines the parameter part of the signature of the new concept function. In the next section, we look at how to define the return type.

17.2.3 Function Return Type

To define the return type of the concept function, you need to override the `AFunction` behavior method `getExpectedReturnType()`. To this end, navigate to the behavior aspect of `AFunction`, and press ⌘ + O to open the override dialog. Select the method called `getExpectedReturnType()` and press return.

Since return types have no names, the process is simpler than to define a function parameter. In this case, you just need to return a node that represents the return type of the function. You can do this with the quotation language. Assume we need to return an integer. You would implement the method `getExpectedReturnType()` as follows:

```
return <int>;
```

Figure 17.3 presents a complete behavior aspect of the `AFunction` concept.

```
concept behavior AFunction {

  constructor {
    <no statements>
  }

  public list<concept<ConceptFunctionParameter>> getParameters()
    overrides ConceptFunction.getParameters {
    list<concept<ConceptFunctionParameter>> result = new arraylist<concept<ConceptFunctionParameter>>;
    result.add(concept/ConceptFunctionParameter_id/);
    result.add(concept/ConceptFunctionParameter_input/);
    return result;
  }

  public node<> getExpectedReturnType()
    overrides ConceptFunction.getExpectedReturnType {
    return <int>;
  }

}
```

Figure 17.3: **Behavior Aspect of the AFunction Concept.** These method definitions declare two parameters to the function: an `id` and an `input` parameter. The return type is integer.

17.3 Importing JAR Files

MPS makes it possible to import JAR files that contain Java compiled classes. This is useful to reuse the vast amount of Java libraries that have been developed by the Java community. Two levels of interoperability with Java are supported: first class models (also called stubs) and libraries.

17.3.1 First Class MPS Models

In MPS releases prior to 3.0, MPS would create stubs to act as proxies for Java classes, methods and fields. Since MPS 3.0, JAR files can be imported as first class models without the need to create stubs. The distinction between stubs and models is a technicality that has only historical interest. The name stubs remains in use in part of the MPS user interface, but consider it as a synonym for a first class MPS model stored in a JAR file[1].

If you are using MPS 3+, you will find that you can import full models of the classes in a JAR file. When you import a JAR file as a set of models, you are able to directly refer to the models in MPS languages. This means that you can refer to a class by name, access static or instance methods, access fields of the class, etc., as you would access *baseLanguage* classes, methods and fields. To import a JAR file as a first class MPS model, you need to follow these steps:

1. From the project tab, create a new solution. You could call the solution *some.package .lib*. If the solution will contain JAR files with several top level packages, use a solution name that reflects the purpose of the combined JAR file. The name lib at the end will indicate that the solution contains one or more JAR files. Leave this solution empty.

2. Copy the JAR files that you would like to import into the solution folder, next to the

---

[1]This functionality is implemented with the custom persistence functionality of MPS, which will be described in volume II of this series.

file called `some.package.lib.msd`. Note that JAR files can reside elsewhere in the project directory, but moving them here will make it easier to locate in the next step because the model root will point to the correct location already.

3. Select the new solution in the Project Tab and do: `some.package.lib` `right-click` `Module Properties`. When the dialog opens, select the Common tab. See Figure 17.4 for an illustration of the steps up to this point.

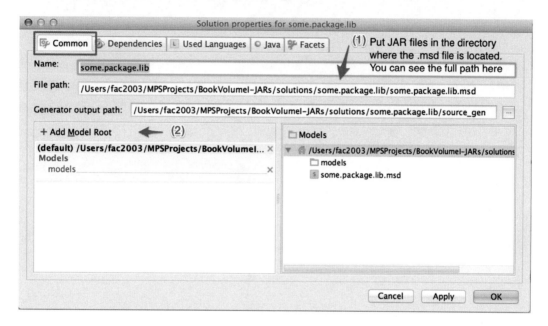

Figure 17.4: **Import JAR Files as Models, Step 1.** Follow these steps to start importing JAR files as first class MPS models. Open the Module Properties, make sure the Common tab is selected. Put the JAR files you wish to import in the directory where the File path points to. If `dir/*.msd` matches, `dir/*.jar` should find the JAR files. When prompted for a type of root, choose `java_classes`.

4. Click the +**Add Model Root** in this tab to add a new model root. Pick *java_classes* in the dialog that pops up. The type *java_classes* should be used if you only need to expose the signature of the methods and fields. If you need the source code of methods to be imported as well, pick *java_source_stubs*.

5. You will be presented with a file selection dialog. Navigate to the folder that contains the jar files you wish to import. Note that all the JAR files must exist into one folder. If you need several distinct folders, you can create several model roots. After you have clicked open, the dialog closes and the folder you selected is added as a new model root of type *java_classes*. If you have followed the earlier steps, you should see the JAR files directly under the model root that you have selected. You can adjust which JAR files are imported as models or excluded from the import by selecting the specific JAR files and pressing Models or Excluded at the top of the right panel. See Figure 17.5 for an illustration of the steps up to this point.

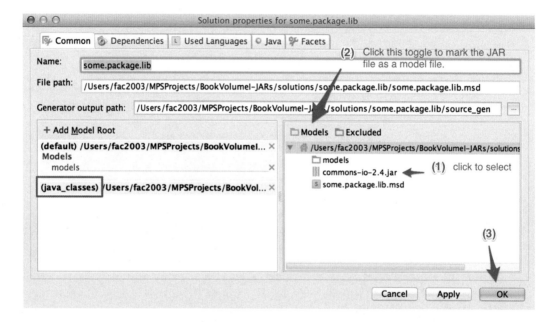

Figure 17.5: **Import JAR Files as Models, Step 2.** Continue to follow these steps to finish importing JAR files. Note that the Models and Excluded icons at the top of the right panel are toggles. Press them once to activate, press again to deactivate. Each JAR file you select can be marked as a model or excluded. Only JAR files marked as Models will be exposed as stubs in the solution.

6. Press OK to accept these changes.
7. Verify that you have correctly imported the JAR file(s). See Figure 17.6 for directions.

Figure 17.6: **Verify that the JAR file is Imported.** When you are in doubt if a JAR file is imported you should check that you can see the stubs under the solution or language where you imported these JARs. This snapshot shows the stubs for the commons-io.jar file we imported in this section.

After you have created a new model root and added JAR files to it, the models can be referenced from within MPS. Remember that to access any model/java stub(s), you first need to add the stubs to the dependency of the model you plan to use the stubs in. For instance, assume you have imported apache.commons.io.jar in the *some.package.lib* solution. If you need to use these imported models in language A, you need to open the Module Properties for this language, and add *some.package.lib* to the list of dependencies of the language. After you identify which aspect of the language needs the stubs, you need to add apache.commons.io@java_stubs to the dependencies of the aspect in language A.

17.3.2 Libraries

You can also import Java Classes as libraries. Some JAR files do not need to be imported as first class MPS models, but are used in the APIs that you have imported as models. This happens with JARs that you will reference from *baseLanguage* directly, but which need to be loaded when classes that you reference directly are loaded. For instance, assume you import class C as a first-class model. Instantiating class C needs to load class D because C creates instances of D in its constructor. In such a case, you do not need to create first-class models for D because you do not refer to D directly from your MPS models, but you still need to load the JAR file that contains class D so that the class loader can find class D.

You do this by adding the JAR file that contains class D as a Library. Follow these steps to do this:

1. From the project tab, create a new solution. You could call the solution *some.package.lib*. The name lib at the end will indicate that the solution contains JAR files. Leave this solution empty.
2. Select the new solution in the Project Tab and do: some.package.lib ⟩ right-click ⟩ Module Properties . When the dialog opens, select the Java tab.
3. Click on the + button at the bottom of the tab and select one or more JAR files in the dialog that opens. When you close the dialog the JAR files you selected will appear in the list of Java libraries for the module.

(R) Note that it is good practice to put all related models and libraries in one solution. You can import this solution in your languages and have a single place to update when new versions of the JAR files need to be imported.

17.4 Path Variables

When working with MPS, some of your sandbox models or code may need access to file or directories on the local machine. For instance, you may need to refer to the directory where the project was checked out from version control. This directory would typically not be constant from one machine to another, so you cannot store the absolute path to the directory and hope that checkouts by different people on different machines will work.

To solve this problem, you can use Path Variables. Path Variables can be defined by opening the MPS Preferences, finding the item named "Path Variables" and defining an association between a logical path name and the absolute path of the directory (or file) on the local machine. Follow the steps shown in Figure 17.7.

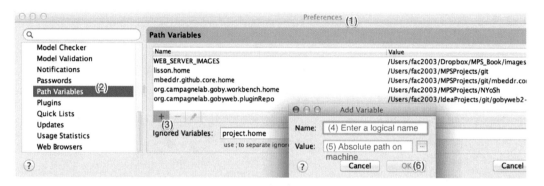

Figure 17.7: **Defining Path Variables.** Open the MPS Preferences and follow these steps to create a new Path Variable.

After you have defined a Path Variable, and imported `jetbrains.mps.util@java_stubs` in the aspect dependency, you can resolve the value of the variable in code with the following expression:

```
MacrosFactory.getInstance().getValue("a.path.variable")
```

This expression will return the value associated with the PathVariable, on the specific user machine. The value will change depending on what is defined in MPS Preferences. If the variable was not yet defined by the end user, an error message will be displayed that will link to Preferences.

Often more convenient, you can also expand paths stored as string properties, for instance when they follow the syntax: `${a.path.variable}/some/relative/path`:

```
MacrosFactory.getGlobal().expandPath(path)
```

The above expression will expand the path string and replace `${a.path.variable}` with the value obtained from the MPS Path Variable preferences.

Finally, you may also shrink a path. Shrinking a path replaces any prefix of the path that matches a defined PathVariable with a reference to the variable. For instance, if you shrink a path /data/some/path when the Path Variable DATA is defined to /data, shriking the string value "/data/some/path" will return "$DATA/some/path".

You can shrink path strings with the following expression:

```
string shrunk = MacrosFactory.getGlobal().shrinkPath(path);
```

In summary, Path Variables facilitate sharing of configuration across user machines and platforms.

17.5 Generate Executable Concepts

You can mark a concept that generates to a Java class with the IMainClass interface concept. When you do so, the generated class must implement a main method suitable to run the class. After you generate/build such a concept, right click on the concept and select Run <concept name>/Debug <concept name> to run or debug an execution of the generated code.

(R) Note that debug information must be generated together with the model for the Run/Debug actions to be shown when you right-click over a concept that implements IMainClass. Open the Generator tab under Preferences and make sure Generate Debug Information is enabled under TextGen Options (in MPS 3.2, look for this under Preferences ⟩ Build, Execution, Deployment ⟩ Generator).

17.6 Navigate to a Node

It some cases it can be useful to change the node displayed in the editor tab programmatically (the usual way to navigate to a node requires the end user to select the node in the Project Tab). The following code fragments show how navigation can be triggered programmatically:

```
IOperationContext context = editorContext.getOperationContext();
NavigationSupport.getInstance().openNode(context, node,
            true /* not documented, and does not seem
            to change anything),
            true  /* True selects content of node in
            editor and inspector*/);
```

To also select the node in Project Tab, use the following code fragment:

```
NavigationSupport.getInstance().selectInTree(
        editorContext.getOperationContext(),
        viewer,
        false /* The tree view is updated only when
        this flag is false. */);
```

Note that you will need to import the *jetbrains.mps.openapi.editor* language stubs before you can use NavigationSupport.

17.7 Generic View of Children and References of a Concept

In some case, it can be useful to process the children or references of a concept in a generic manner, that is without knowing how many children or references a concept has. This is useful for instance to create UML diagrams to present relationships between concepts in a graphical manner[2], but is useful anytime you need to create behavior that depends on the structure of a concept.

Concepts can be manipulated by holding a reference to `AbstractConcept Declaration`. Such references will auto-complete to a concept in a sandbox as long as the concept is part of a language defined in the sandbox dependencies (you need to add the structure aspect of the language under Dependencies). See also Section 7.5.4 for a discussion of the difference between the `concept<>` type and `node<AbstractConcept Declaration>`.

17.8 Undo/Redo Support and Access to Nodes

MPS implements a transparent mechanism to support undo-redo for nodes of a model. When you access nodes from behavior methods, you usually do not need to be concerned with this mechanism, which handles undo-redo actions transparently. However, in some cases, such as when you try to read, or write data from an AST node from Java code, you will find that you need to explicitly handle access to the nodes. You will notice that you have encountered such a situation when the code that you wrote triggers an exception such as:

1. Run in EDT (Event Dispatch Thread).
2. Cannot read from node (or ModelReadException).
3. Cannot write to node (or ModelWriteException).

To handle these situations, you should import the *jetbrains.mps.lang.access* language and use one of the following statements:

1. `read action` Use this when you only need to read the content of a node.
2. `write action` Use this when you need to modify the content of a node and need the change to be under control of the platform undo-redo mechanism.
3. `undo-transparent command` Use this when you need to modify the content of a node, but do not need the change to be recorded by the platform undo-redo mechanism. Changes performed in these actions will be done on the node, but will not be undoable or redoable by the end-user.
4. `execute command in EDT` Use this when you get an EDT failure. The command take an optional project argument, which is usually available when running code inside an MPS Plugin solution.
5. `execute in EDT` Use this when you get an EDT failure and need to run a code fragment on the event dispatch thread (EDT).

   Each of these statements protects a block of *baseLanguage* statements. You should perform access to the AST node inside this block.

---

[2]An simple example of generating UML diagrams from MPS concepts is available at `https://github.com/CampagneLaboratory/UML_Diagrams` and uses these techniques.

17.9 **Retrieving the Cursor Position**

It can sometimes be useful to retrieve the cursor position while the user is editing a string property. This can be achieved with code similar to the following:

```
EditorCell contextCell = editorContext.getContextCell();
int cursorPosition=0;
if (contextCell instanceof EditorCell_Label) {
  EditorCell_Label label = (EditorCell_Label) contextCell;
  int cursorPosition = label.getCaretPosition();
} else {
  cursorPosition = 0;
}
```

(R) Note that the MPS platform often refers to the cursor position as caret position.

(R) See `AddCellAnnotation` intention for an example of retrieving the cursor position and selection range.

17.10 **Migrating to a new version of MPS**

This section describes a strategy for migrating your languages to a new version of MPS. Assuming you have developed languages with MPS and a new major release of the platform is announced in the Early Access Program (EAP), what should you do?

I would suggest that you consider how experienced you are with the platform before you try to evaluate a new EAP release. The typical sequence of MPS releases look like this (using MPS 3.1 as the stable release for illustration):

- **Last Stable Release of 3.1** (some time ago)
- 3.2 EAP1
- 3.2 EAP2
- 3.2 EAP3
- 3.2 RC1
- 3.2 RC2
- **First Stable release 3.2**

Several months can separate the first EAP release from the final stable release. I would suggest that the more experienced users of MPS jump in sooner into the EAP cycle, and the less experienced wait for at least a late EAP or RC. I think that if you are more of a beginner, you probably have enough on your plate figuring out how a stable release of MPS works and don't need the extra complications that bugs in the platform could cause you.

For instance, while the first EAPs could work well when you create new projects and languages with them, they may still include subtle bugs that prevent them from working smoothly with languages developed in the previous release. Not only this, but documentation could be sparse for a while, so you may have nothing to walk you through the new features.

Finally, new features may still evolve from EAP to EAP (for instance, concepts may be renamed, other deprecated, etc).

When you have determined that you are ready to jump in an evaluate an EAP or RC, you should always make sure you have a backup of a language developed with the previous release of MPS before you open this language with the new release of MPS. The reason for this is that the new MPS may modify or migrate the model files in ways that will be incompatible with the earlier version of MPS that you were using. Bugs may cause the files to become corrupted. If this happened, you could loose the ability to open these languages. The easiest way to make sure you have a backup is to have language(s) and solution(s) into source control and create a branch in which you test the upgrade. It is convenient to name the branch according to the release you are testing the upgrade to. For instance, if you will try to upgrade to EAP2 of MPS 3.2, you could call the branch `MPS3.2_EAP2`. Even if you find no problems with the migration, I would not recommend merging this branch back into master before the version has been released in stable form.

The following section provide tips if you need to migrate languages from MPS 3.1 to MPS 3.3.

17.10.1   Migration from 3.1 to 3.2

- Review your projects for usage of nodes and concepts that were deprecated in MPS 3.1. Some previously deprecated concepts have been removed from MPS 3.2 and this will cause migration to fail. For instance, review any concept functions to make sure they are defined as presented in Section 17.2. Do these changes in the master branch of your project with MPS 3.2.
- If you ran the migration assistant in 3.2, it may fail to start with the reason that some property, child nodes or references exist on the nodes, but have no equivalent on the concept of the nodes. This is likely to happen if you have sandbox models you built while you were developing your languages and you renamed properties or children of your concepts without developing associated migrations. Save yourself some time and run the script `Tools` `Enhancements` `Delete Undeclared Links and Properties` on your development models, while you are still in 3.1. Check that everything is OK, then commit and create the migration branch off this commit (see `https://youtrack.jetbrains.com/issue/MPS-21497#` for more details).
- All modules (languages and solutions) needed by the project you will migrate must be visible to the migration assistant for migrations to complete successfully. It is preferable you post-pone migration and include all modules you need directly inside the project. If you run migration and find that some languages are missing a behavior aspect, you may have run into this problem. Check that the language was not included from a plugin where you ran the migration assistant. You will likely need to revert to the previous commit or fresh migration branch.
- If your languages use non-platform plugins, make sure you disable these plugins. The migration assistant does not seem to behave well when languages are provided by plugins (see `https://youtrack.jetbrains.com/issue/MPS-21070`). Instead, import languages and solutions provided by the plugins directly as modules. Make

sure these languages have already been upgraded to 3.2.

- If you run the 3.2 migration assistant and get errors that some concepts cannot be found, it could mean that you have moved the concept to another language and that the change was not tracked. You might be able to fix these issues in 3.2, but if you trying an early EAP release you would have to do this several times, once for each EAP. Instead, identify these nodes in the 3.1 branch, using MPS 3.1, and delete the nodes and recreate them with the latest concept. You can then commit the change to master and cherry-pick it in the migration branch. When you try the next EAP, these changes will have been done already.

- You will find that MPS 3.2 is stricter about self-imports or generator imports than 3.1 used to be. You will need to adjust dependencies of your languages to remove self-import (e.g., language A importing itself or one of its aspects).

- You may find that some nodes do not generate to the expected output. This is likely to be caused by a missing generator priority rule. MPS 3.1 was more permissive in this regard and grouped more generation steps together. See Section 15.7 for details about this.

17.10.2 Migration from 3.2 to 3.3

Migration of most projects to 3.3 should be mostly uneventful. Make sure you run the migration assistant on all projects.

- One change that may require adjustment is how annotations are propagated through generation. If you notice that TextGen complains that some annotation has no TextGen, you may need to drop the annotation before generation. See Section 15.8.9.

- If you notice that custom run configurations cannot be launched from the context menu, make sure all the plugins have been rebuilt to the version of MPS that you are using (see `https://youtrack.jetbrains.com/issue/MPS-23295`).

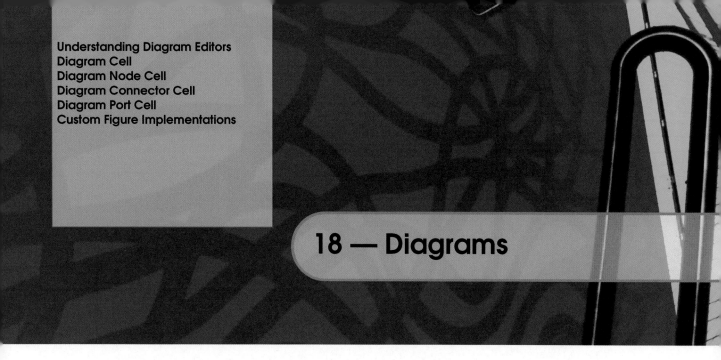

18 — Diagrams

Diagram editors were introduced in MPS 3.1. This chapter reviews the Diagram Editor capabilities introduced in the 3.1 EAP.

18.1 Understanding Diagram Editors

MPS implements diagrams by providing means to map from AST nodes described in some MPS language to a two dimensional (2D) editing user interface (UI). The 2D UI offers graph layout, rendering and editing capabilities. This UI will be familiar to you if you have previously used one of the many tools that let you represent graph data structures in a visual manner. Figure 18.1 presents a high-level view of the types of graphical elements found in MPS diagrams.

> **Definition 18.1.1** Graphs are a type of data structures that consist of nodes and edges. Edges connect nodes and can be either directed or undirected. A directed edge has different roles for the two nodes that it connects (for instance source and destination nodes). Undirected edges do not associate special roles to the nodes they connect and these nodes are indistinguishable.

Diagrams are a special kind of editor cell that you can insert in the editor of a concept. The cells of the diagram language are defined in the *jetbrains.mps.lang.editor.diagram* language (*diagram* language for short). You need to import this language in order to create these cells in the editor of your languages (see the next chapter to learn how to do this in practice). The diagram language offers editor cells to render parts of the AST into diagrams. A Diagram Cell provides the 2D surface onto which the nodes of the diagram will be rendered. A Diagram Node Cell maps individual AST nodes to a graphical element that represents the node on the diagram. Finally, Connector Cells define the rendering of the edges between nodes. The following sections describe these types of cells in detail.

18.1.1 Figure Implementation

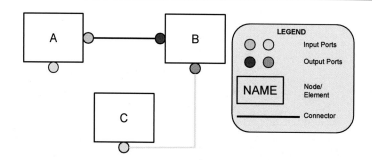

Figure 18.1: **Types of Graphical Elements in MPS Diagrams.** MPS Diagrams offer three types of graphical elements. Nodes represent entities that you need to display on the diagram 2D surface. Nodes may have one or more type of connectors. A connector is an anchor point where a connection to another node can be made. There are two types of connectors: output connectors from which a connection can be iniated, and input connectors to which a connection can end. An output connector can be connected to an input connector to establish a connection between a pair of nodes that hold these two connectors. In this figure, node A is connected to node B with a black edge, and node B is connected to node C with a yellow edge. Diagram semantic would associate a meaning to the edge colors and different types of connectors.

> **Definition 18.1.2** A figure implementation is responsible for rendering a specific type of diagram node. Figure implementations define how a type of diagram node will appear to the user on the diagram.

MPS provides a number of ready to use figure implementations in the solution *jetbrains .mps.lang.editor.figures.library*. It is also possible to define new figure implementations if none of the platform implementations are suitable. Defining a new figure implementation involves two steps:

1. Create a *baseLanguage* Class that implements the *jetbrains.jetpad .projectional.view .View* interface.
2. Create a new external figure root node in a solution. The ExternalViewFigure root node annotates the figure implementation so that it can be used in Diagram Node Cells.

These steps are described in Section 18.6. The following sections describe the different types of diagram editor cells.

18.2 Diagram Cell

You can add a diagram cell by typing "diagram" when a cell is required in an editor under construction. This ability makes it possible to construct hybrid diagrams where the diagram is embedded into a regular MPS editor (described in Chapter 5). Figure 18.2 presents a freshly created diagram cell. Figure 18.3 illustrates how you can combine a diagram cell with indent and constant cells.

Figure 18.2: **Freshly Created Diagram Cell.**
You will see this editor cell immediately after
you type "diagram" to insert a diagram cell
into a concept editor.

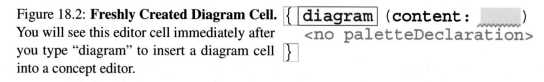

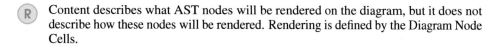

Figure 18.3: **Diagram Cell Mixed with Other Cells.** Notice how a diagram cell can be
mixed with regular Editor cells.

Diagram cells have several attributes. The attributes visible in the editor pane include
`content`, and the palette declaration. The diagram cell also has several important attributes
only exposed in the [2: Inspector]. Click on the diagram keyword in the cell and open the
Inspector Tab to view the attributes (these attributes include: `elements creation` and
`connector creation`).

18.2.1 Content

Content is a list attribute that is used to reference the AST node(s) that will be rendered
as diagram nodes. You can use auto-completion and accept the suggestion to query for
concepts, or you can press ⏎ over the pink cell to create another element in the content
list. Adding several concepts here is useful if you need to show different kind of diagram
nodes on the same diagram.

> (R) Content describes what AST nodes will be rendered on the diagram, but it does not
> describe how these nodes will be rendered. Rendering is defined by the Diagram Node
> Cells.

When you enter a query under content, you need to type an expression that will return
a sequence of AST nodes (of type `sequence<node<>>`). A typical expression to enter
here is `this.someChild` where `someChild` is a child attribute, with multiplicity 0..n or
1..n, of the concept for which the editor is being defined. For instance, if you define a
diagram in an editor for concept Computer, and the concept has children hardwareParts
and softwarePrograms, both with multiplicity 0..n, you can declare that both types of parts
should be shown on the diagram by entering content as a list: `this.softwarePrograms`,
`this.hardwareParts`.

> (R) If you find that you need to add a child to a diagram when the child has a multiplicity
> of 0..1 or 1..1, you could expose the child through a behavior method which returns a
> `sequence<node<>>` and call this method from the content attribute.

Note that if you need connectors to be displayed on the diagram, content should include at least one source for the connector AST nodes.

18.2.2 Elements Creation

The Element Creation attribute allows to control what happens when the end-user clicks on an empty area of the diagram. The default behavior is to do nothing. However, when you define a new element creation item, you can specify that diagram elements are created upon a click on the diagram surface. Remember that diagram elements render AST nodes on the 2D space of the diagram.

The Element Creation attribute is located under the 2: Inspector . The Elements Creation attribute contains an « ... ». Press ↵ over the « ... » to introduce an element creation description. Note that you can add multiple element descriptions by pressing ↵ several times. After you have pressed ↵ you should see a new element creation, as shown in 18.4. The following sections describe each of these attributes.

name

Enter a name for the type of diagram node that you would like to create. This will make it possible to refer to this type of diagram node from the palette.

```
elements creation:
name: <no name>
container: <query>
concept: <no specialized concept>
on create: (node, x, y)->void {
  <no statements>
}
```

Figure 18.4: **New Diagram Element Creation.** A freshly created element creation item is shown.

container

This attribute should point to the container of the elements in the node associated with the editor. The container must have type sequence<node>. This attribute duplicates the content attribute of the diagram, but describes where new diagram element of the type specified in concept will be stored when they are created by a user left-click on the diagram surface.

concept

This attribute is optional and should contain a reference to a concept. When provided, the attribute makes it possible to define a specific concept to hold data for the diagram element. Note that the concept selected must be a sub-concept of one of the concepts already referenced in the diagram content attribute. For instance, if the content attribute points to a child of type sequence<node<A», then an element creation concept attribute can only be defined with a concept B when the B is a sub-concept of A.

on create

This attribute is a concept function that let's you initialize a new diagram element. It has the following signature:

```
on create: (node, x, y)->void {
}
```

The method is called with a new diagram element instance in the node parameter. Nodes are created by clicking on the diagram surface. You may use the `on create` concept function to assign the *x* and *y* coordinates of the click to the new node instance and to perform other initialization. Note that when the concept attributes defines a sub-class of the content concept, this method is responsible for initializing the properties, children and references of the sub-concept. It would typically use constants or information from the super-class.

18.2.3 Connector Creation

The Connector Creation attribute allows to control what happens when the end-user clicks on a diagram port and drags across the surface of the diagram to another port. Note that connectors can be only be created by dragging the mouse from an output port to an input port. You cannot connect two input ports or two output ports, or connect an input port to an output port.

The Connector Creation attribute attribute is located under the 2: Inspector . The Connector Creation attribute contains an « ... ». Press ⏎ over the « ... » to introduce a connector creation description. Note that you can add multiple connector descriptions by pressing ⏎ several times. After you have pressed ⏎ you should see a new connector creation, as shown in 18.5.

The `name`, `container` and `concept` attributes are similar to the attributes of the same name which were described for element creation, but relate to connectors rather than diagram nodes/elements. See the description of these attributes in the previous section. The following sections describe the attributes which are specific to the *connector creation* item.

Figure 18.5: **New Diagram Connector Creation.** A freshly created Connector creation item is shown.

```
connector creation:
name: <no name>
container: <query>
concept: <no specialized concept>
can create: (from, fromId, to, toId)->boolean {
    <no statements>
}
on create: (node, from, fromId, to, toId)->void {
    <no statements>
}
```

can create

This attribute is a concept function that determines the semantic of diagram connector creation. The function must return a boolean value. Returning `true` in this method indicates that the connector can be created. Returning false indicates that the two ports that the user attempts to connect are not compatible in the diagram semantic.

The can create concept function has the following signature:

```
can create: (from, fromId, to, toId)->boolean {
}
```

The parameters are:

from This parameter provides access to the input node that holds the output port that would be connected.

fromId This parameter provides the identifier of the port from which the connector would originate. The parameter fromId has the type of the connector defined in the connector cell. (This type can be either an anonymous port or a port concept instance attached directly to a node, see Section 19.3 for an example).

to This parameter provides access to the input connector on the destination diagram node.

toId This parameter provides the identifier of the node that holds the input port where the connector would end.

on create

This attribute is a concept function that determines what happens when a new connector is created. The function will be called only when the can create concept function has returned true. The on create concept function has the following parameters:

```
on create: (node, from, fromId, to, toId)->void {
}
```

node This parameter holds the new connector node. You can use this parameter to set attributes of the connector instance for each new connector. If you have defined a specialized concept attribute, you should use this function to initialize the attributes of the sub-concept.

The other parameters have the same meaning as for the can create concept function. A typical implementation of the on create concept function would retrieve the nodes corresponding to the input and output connectors (provided in the from and to parameters). It would then create an edge between these nodes and store this edge in the AST that is rendered as the diagram.

18.2.4 Palette Declaration

The Palette Declaration attribute makes it possible to add a graphical palette on one side of the diagram. The palette offers tools that the end user can activate to add nodes or connections between nodes. MPS 3.1 EAP3 warns that the palette is a an experimental feature of the diagram language. You add elements to the palette and refer to element or connector creation items by their name.

18.3 Diagram Node Cell

A Diagram Node Cell describes how a diagram node/element will be rendered. You create these cells by typing "diagram node" when a new cell is needed in an editor. Figure 18.6 presents a freshly created Diagram Node Cell. The attributes of a Diagram Node Cell are described in the following sections.

`{` `(<< ... >>)` `inputPorts:` `<no inputPort>` `outputPorts:` `<no outputPort>` `}`

Figure 18.6: **New Diagram Node Cell.** A freshly created Diagram Node Cell is shown. You can create this type of cell by typing "diagram node" when a new editor cell is needed. The attribute on the left shown as a pink cell is called the figure implementation reference. The « ... » makes it possible to assign parameters to the figure implementation. See text for a description of these attributes.

figure implementation reference

Rendering diagram node/element on the surface of the diagram requires a figure implementation.

This attribute makes it possible to enter a reference to the figure implementation that will be used to render the node associated with the editor. MPS makes it possible to define custom figure implementations to define specific node renderings. However, the platform also provides a set of ready to use figure implementations. These implementations should be sufficient for simple rendering needs. You can use the figure implementations available in the MPS platform when you import *jetbrains.mps.lang.editor.figures.library* into the editor aspect where you are creating the Diagram Node Cell.

parameters

Figure implementations may expose parameters. See Section 18.6.2 to learn how to expose parameters when you create custom figure implementations. Assuming some parameters are exposed, you can bind these parameters to the model (AST node that the editor is rendering) by pressing ⏎ with the cursor over the « ... ». This will create a new parameter binding item that looks like this: `<no name>`: . You can use auto-completion to fill in the left and right parts of the item. The left part presents figure implementation parameters, while the right part presents properties of the AST node attached to the editor. Note that the properties presented on the right are constrained by the type of the property entered on the left.

You can also enter a `baseLanguage` expression in the right part of the item. This is useful if you need to calculate the value of the property with a behavior method on the node, need to use a constant, or need to calculate it in some other way. Type # to introduce an expression. You can use `this` inside the expression to obtain the edited node instance.

inputPorts

This attribute makes it possible to indicate how to obtain diagram ports used as input to the diagram node. You can either use auto-completion to locate children of the node that represent input ports, or enter an expression. Type # to introduce an expression. You can use `this` inside the expression to obtain the edited node instance.

outputPorts

This attribute makes it possible to indicate how to obtain diagram ports used as output to the diagram node. You can either use auto-completion to locate children of the node that represent output ports, or enter an expression. Type # to introduce an expression. You can use `this` inside the expression to obtain the edited node instance.

18.4 Diagram Connector Cell

The Diagram Connector Cell defines the source and destination nodes of Diagram Connectors. You create a new Diagram Connector Cell in an editor by typing "diagram connector". Figure 18.7 presents a freshly created Diagram Connector Cell. Connectors have a source and a destination attributes. Press ⏎ over either to insert a query. Type `this.` to locate a child of the edited node to use as source/destination of the connector, or type # to enter an expression.

Both the source and target attributes accept two items: *targetNode* (the item on the left) must provide a reference to a node that should be connected. The *pointId* (item on the right) is optional and may identify a specific port where the connector will attach (see below). Both the `targetNode` and `pointId` attributes let you enter an expression to retrieve the appropriate reference.

There are two ways to use connectors:

- When diagram ports are direct children of the diagram node, `targetNode` of the connectors directly references a port node (and `pointId` is not set).
- When diagram ports are not children of diagram nodes. Such ports are called anonymous ports. This case is more general. Anonymous ports can be of any Java Object type. In this case, the connector will refer to the node (using `targetNode`) and the optional `pointId` attribute must be an instance of the Java Object type that identifies the port. See Section 19.3.1 for examples of use.

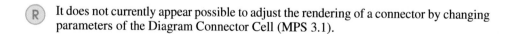

Figure 18.7: **New Diagram Connector Cell.** A freshly created Diagram Connector Cell is shown.

> (R) It does not currently appear possible to adjust the rendering of a connector by changing parameters of the Diagram Connector Cell (MPS 3.1).

18.5 Diagram Port Cell

The Diagram Port Cell defines the rendering of a diagram port. You create a new Diagram Port Cell in an editor by typing "diagram port". The diagram port editor is very simple: it is either **input port** or **output port**. You can switch the type of the port from output to input by placing the cursor at the beginning of the keyword and invoking auto-completion.

Figure 18.5 presents a freshly created Diagram Connector Cell.

 It does not currently appear possible to adjust the rendering of a port by changing parameters of the Diagram Port Cell (MPS 3.1 EAP1).

18.6 Custom Figure Implementations

This section describes how to implement a custom figure implementation to customize the rendering of diagram nodes.

18.6.1 Creating a Figure Implementation

To create a new figure implementation, you create a *baseLanguage* Class that implements the *jetbrains.jetpad .projectional.view.View* interface. When you have done this, you should mark the class with the **@Figure** annotation. This is achieved with the intention called "Add Figure Attribute". Figure 18.8 presents a figure with the suitable structure, but no custom rendering defined.

```
@Figure
public class NewFigureImplementation extends View {
}
```

Figure 18.8: **Minimal Figure Implementation.** Note that the class extends View, (defined in *jetbrains.jetpad .projectional.view.View*) and is marked with the **@Figure** annotation.

Property Fields

A Figure implementation class may have fields that map to the AST node that the diagram node needs to render, or that control some visual characteristic of the diagram node. You can define primitive property fields following the instructions in the caption of Figure 18.9. The figure illustrates how to create a width property of type integer initialized with value 100.

```
@FigureParameter
public Property<Integer> width = new ValueProperty<Integer>(100);
```

Figure 18.9: **Figure Property Field.** You define new figure property fields by adding a field to the class, declaring the type of the field to be Property<PrimitiveType> and initializing the field with a new Property<PrimitiveType> object. The value given to the constructor is the initial value of the property. The default value must have the type of PrimitiveType.

Property Value Mappers

If you define new Property Fields in your implementation of *View*, you should define and register a Property Value Mapper. Mappers are responsible for synchronizing changes in the AST node (the model) with the view. Figure 18.10 presents a minimal MyView implementation that defines and registers a Property Value Mapper. Take a look at existing Figure implementations to learn how to define synchronization behavior (for instance, navigate ⌘N to NamedBoxFigure or to BoxFigure.

```
@Figure
public class MyView extends View {
  @FigureParameter
  public Property<Integer> width = new ValueProperty<Integer>(100);
  public MyView() {
    this(new MyViewFigureMapperFactory());
  }
  public MyView(MyView.MyViewFigureMapperFactory mapperFactory) {
    <no statements>
  }
  private static class MyViewFigureMapperFactory implements MapperFactory<MyView, MyView> {
    public Mapper<? extends MyView, ? extends MyView> createMapper(MyView figure) {
      return new MyViewFigureMapper<MyView>(figure);
    }
  }
  protected static class MyViewFigureMapper<T extends MyView> extends Mapper<T, T> {
    protected MyViewFigureMapper(T figure) {
      super(figure, figure);
    }
    @Override
    protected void registerSynchronizers(Mapper.SynchronizersConfiguration configuration) {
      super.registerSynchronizers(configuration);
      // fetch property values from configuration and regenerate rendering elements to update
      // the diagram node display
    }
  }
}
```

Figure 18.10: **Figure Implementation With Mapper.** This figure presents a figure implementation called MyView, which uses a FigureMapper to update property field values and refresh its rendering.

Composing JetPad Views

JetPad Views are designed to be composable. This means that you can reuse other views to create parts of the rendering of a new View implementation. Assume that you are implementing ViewA. To reuse another view implementation (let's assume you will reuse PolyLineView), you create a field with the type PolyLineView, initialize this field with a new instance of PolyLineView, and add this instance to ViewA's children. The field children is defined by the *View* interface in the jetpad.projectional.view package (see https://github.com/JetBrains/jetpad-projectional).

18.6.2 Creating an ExternalViewFigure

In the solution where you will develop the new figure implementation, do: solution-name ⟩ New ⟩ j.m.l.editor.figures ⟩ ExternalViewFigure . This will create a new ExternalView Figure (see Figure 18.11 for a freshly created ExternalViewFigure). After you create the ExternalViewFigure, you can expose the Figure implementation parameters to make them visible to the Diagram Node Cell. You do this by pressing ↵ inside the « ... ». Immediately after you pressed ↵, you should see <no fieldDeclaration>; . Place the cursor before <no and use auto-completion to reference a Figure implementation property

field which you have already defined in your View implementation. Only fields that you expose in this way will be visible when you edit the Diagram Node Cell in an editor.

Figure 18.11: **Freshly Created External ViewFigure.** Place the cursor at the beginning of `<no classifier>` and use auto-completion to locate the reference to a Figure Implementation classifier. Press ⏎ over the « ... » to expose new property fields for this implementation.

```
view class <no classifier> {
    << ... >>
}
```

19 — Diagrams In Practice

Since you need to already have a concept defined to develop a diagram editor, we will assume that you have a language with the following concepts:

1. **Node** A node will connect to one or more other nodes, via edges.
2. **Edge** An edge will connect two nodes.
3. **Project** This concept will hold collections of Nodes and Edges that will be rendered in the diagram.

In this chapter, we will build a diagram editor to display the Project node as a 2D surface, the node instances will be shown as diagram nodes and the edge will be shown as MPS diagram connectors. Let's start by creating these concepts, as shown in Figure 19.1 and Figure 19.2.

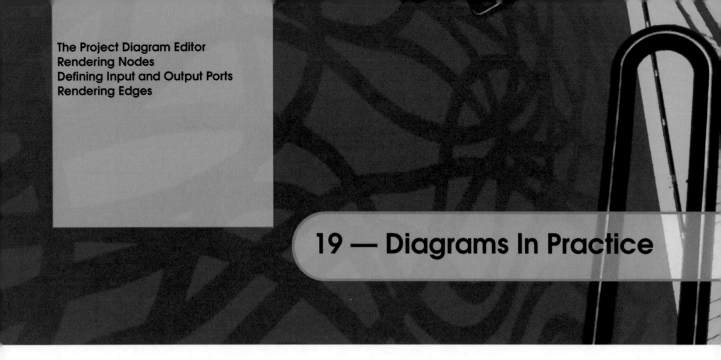

```
concept Edge extends      BaseConcept
          implements <none>

  instance can be root: false
  alias: <no alias>
  short description: <no short description>

  properties:
  << ... >>

  children:
  << ... >>

  references:
  source      : Node[1]
  destination : Node[1]
```

```
concept Node extends      BaseConcept
                 implements INamedConcept

  instance can be root: false
  alias: node
  short description: <no short description>

  properties:
  << ... >>

  children:
  << ... >>

  references:
  << ... >>
```

Figure 19.1: **Structure of Node and Edges.** This snapshot presents the structure of the Node and Edge concepts. Create these concepts before continuing with the tutorial. Note that the Node concept implements INamedConcept.

```
concept Project extends        BaseConcept
                   implements <none>

  instance can be root: true
  alias: <no alias>
  short description: <no short description>

  properties:
  << ... >>

  children:
  nodes : Node[0..n]
  edges : Edge[0..n]

  references:
  << ... >>
```

Figure 19.2: **Structure of Project Concept.**
The project concept holds nodes and edges as
children.

19.1 The Project Diagram Editor

We start by creating the Project Diagram Editor. Navigate to the Project Concept (⌘ + N)
followed by "Project"), click on the Editor Tab and create a new empty editor. This editor
will be automatically bound to the Project concept.

Place the cursor over the editor aspect of the language and press ctrl + L . This will
prompt you for the name of a language to import in the editor aspect model. Enter "diagram"
to locate the language *jetbrains.mps.lang.editor.diagram*. You will need to press ctrl + L a
second time to locate the language among the platform languages (or click the checkbox at
the top of the dialog). Accept the suggestions for other imports.

Place the cursor at the beginning of `<choose cell model>` in the editor window
(editor for the Project concept). Type "diagram" to lookup the Diagram Cell and accept the
choice that reads "diagram" to associate a Project node to a diagram rendering area.

When you have done this, the Project editor will appear as shown in Figure 19.3.
Select the pink area immediately after content and invoke auto-completion. Accept the
"DiagramElementBLQuery" suggestion (this is the only choice). Accepting the suggestion
will replace the pink block with a `<query>` item. Put the cursor at the beginning of `<query>`
and type `this.nodes`. Follow the steps shown in Figure 19.4 to Figure 19.5. You should
obtain the final editor shown in Figure 19.5.

```
<default> editor for concept Project
    node cell layout:
        { diagram (content:         )
            <no paletteDeclaration>
        }

    inspected cell layout:
        <choose cell model>
```

Figure 19.3: **New Project Diagram Editor.** The Project
Editor will appear like this
immediately after you have
typed "diagram".

```
{ diagram (content: this.nodes)
    <no paletteDeclaration>
}
```

Figure 19.4: **Diagram Cell With Node Content.** The Project editor will appear like this after you have linked the content item to the Project Nodes. Press ⏎ to add a new content item, accept the "DiagramElementBLQuery" auto-completion and add a link to the edges children.

```
{ diagram (content: this.nodes, this.edges)
    <no paletteDeclaration>
}
```

Figure 19.5: **Final Diagram Cell.** The Final Diagram Cell is shown linked to the project nodes and edges children.

19.2 Rendering Nodes

In this section, we will define an editor for the Node concept. Before we can do this, we need to define a sub-concept of the Node concept, which we will call NodeRendering, that will hold attributes needed to render the node on the diagram. For instance, rendering a node on the diagram requires x and y coordinates. While it is possible to add such attributes to the Node concept described earlier, a cleaner design consists in extending the Node concept and providing the rendering attributes in the sub-concept.

Create a new concept called NodeRendering that extends Node and provides two properties, x and y of type integer. After you have done this, create an editor for this concept and enter "diagram node" at the beginning of <choose cell model>.

19.2.1 Import the Figures Language

To proceed, you need to import figure implementations into the editor aspect. Start by selecting the language in the Project Tab. Open the language properties and add jetbrains .jetpad to the language Dependencies. Continue by adding jetbrains.mps.lang .editor.figures.library (hint: use "figures.library" to locate it easily). Continue and add the figures.library language to the editor aspect of the language (see Figure 19.6).

Figure 19.6: **Model Properties for Editor Aspect.** Enter this dependency in the editor aspect of the language.

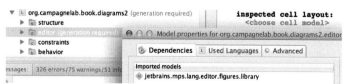

19.2.2 Define the NodeRendering Editor

You can now locate a figure implementation called NamedBoxFigure. Place the cursor at the beginning of the pink area in the NodeRendering editor and invoke auto-completion.

Select the `NamedBoxFigure` choice.

When you have performed this step, you should see the content of Figure 19.7. Bind each parameter in turn by pressing ⏎ over the « ... » or between the parentheses. A new Parameter will appear as <no name>: _____ . Place the cursor at the beginning of <no name>: and use auto-completion to see which parameters the figure defines. The pink box on the right of the colon character is where the value will be entered.

Start by binding the `POSITION_X` parameter. You need to bind this parameter to the x integer property that we have defined in the `NodeRendering` concept. Place the cursor over the value item and invoke auto-completion. You will see each property visible in the `NodeRendering` concept. Choose x and accept the selection. When the parameter is bound, you should see `POSITION_X:x`.

Set the `POSITION_Y` parameter in the same way (bind it to the y property). Bind the `nameText` attribute to the `NodeRendering` name property (name is inherited from the `Node` concept).

Some figure attributes need to be set to constant values. Add them as usual, but instead of navigating to the property of the concept, type # to enter an expression. For instance, to indicate that the figure should allow editing the `name` parameter, enter #true in the value of the `editable` parameter (to enter #true you need to press ⏎ between # and true).

```
<default> editor for concept NodeRendering
  node cell layout:
    { NamedBoxFigure (<< ... >>) inputPorts: <no inputPort> outputPorts: <no outputPort> }

  inspected cell layout:
    <choose cell model>
```

Figure 19.7: **NodeRendering Editor with Figure Implementation.** The `NodeRendering` editor will appear as shown after you have bound the "diagram node" cell to the `NamedBoxFigure` implementation. When shown in the editor, the background of the cell will be light-brown and a warning message will indicate that some figure parameters are undefined. Place the cursor at the beginning of the « ... » and press ⏎ to bind these parameters.

Continue to bind parameters to yield the result shown in Figure 19.8

```
<default> editor for concept NodeRendering
  node cell layout:
    { NamedBoxFigure (POSITION_X:x, POSITION_Y:y, nameText:name, editable:#true, figureHeight:#50, figureWidth:#100,
        lineWidth:#3) inputPorts: <no inputPort> outputPorts: <no outputPort> }

  inspected cell layout:
    <choose cell model>
```

Figure 19.8: **NodeRendering Editor with Bound Parameters.** Binding all available parameters resolves the error which was present in Figure 19.7.

19.2.3 Define Create Element

Open the Project editor, click on the diagram cell and open the ⊞ 2: Inspector . Scroll down until you see the `element creation:` section. Press ⏎ to add one item in this section. Define the item to match the content shown in Figure 19.9.

Figure 19.9: **Element Creation Definition.** The content shown declares that an instance of NodeRendering is to be created when a user clicks on the diagram. The instance will be stored in the concept nodes role. Coordinate of the user click are used to initialize the x and y properties of the new node. We also set a default name for the new node to make it easier to click on the name and change it.

```
elements creation:
name: CreateNodeRendering
container: this.nodes
concept: NodeRendering
on create: (node, x, y)->void {
    node.x = x;
    node.y = y;
    node.name = "NEW";
}
```

19.2.4 Rebuild the Language

Rebuild the language at this point. If no errors are reported you should be able to create a Project AST root in a sandbox, see an empty diagram surface, and see new NodeRendering elements created when you click on the diagram surface (left-click). Figure 19.10 shows how diagrams render after the first build.

Figure 19.10: **Diagram After the First Build.** This snapshot shows a diagram after we have clicked twice on the diagram surface. We renamed the first NodeRendering instance to Box1.

19.3 Defining Input and Output Ports

Edges can only be created from an input port to an output port. To support edges on a diagram, we need to extend the NodeRendering concept to provide ports. There two ways to define ports: as anonymous ports or as concept ports.

19.3.1 Anonymous Ports

Any Java Object can serve as an anonymous port. In this example, we use a Java String to represent a port. You define ports by defining a behavior method that returns the list of ports available in a node. Define the following method in the behavior aspect of the RenderingNode concept:

```
public list<Object> retrieveInputPorts() {
    return new arraylist<Object>{"Input"};
```

```
}

public list<Object> retrieveOutputPorts() {
  return new arraylist<Object>{"Output"};
}
```

These behavior methods define one anonymous input port, implemented with the Java String "Input" and one anonymous output port, implemented with the Java String "Output". When you use anonymous ports, you can set `pointId` on the connector to the value of one of the elements of the collection in order to identify a specific port.

19.3.2   As Children of NodeRendering

You can define ports explicitly as children of the `NodeRendering` concept. For instance, if we add two children to the `NodeRendering` concept, of role input and output, and type `InputPort` and `OutputPort` respectively (both cardinality 1), we can return these concepts instead of Java Strings.

```
public list<Object> retrieveInputPorts() {
  return new arraylist<Object>{this.input};
}

public list<Object> retrieveOutputPorts() {
  return new arraylist<Object>{this.output};
}
```

The ports are no longer anonymous and can be retrieved for specific nodes. Figure 19.11 shows the concepts after this change.

```
concept NodeRendering extends     Node
                   implements <none>
                                                concept InputPort extends     BaseConcept
                                                                  implements <none>
   instance can be root: false
   alias: <no alias>
   short description: <no short description>      instance can be root: false
                                                  alias: <no alias>
   properties:                                    short description: <no short description>
   x : integer
   y : integer                                    properties:
                                                  << ... >>
   children:
   input  : InputPort[1]                          children:
   output : OutputPort[1]                         << ... >>

   references:                                    references:
   << ... >>                                      << ... >>
```

Figure 19.11: **Updated NodeRendering and InputPort concepts.** We added InputPort children to NodeRendering. Note that InputPort (and OutputPort, not shown) are empty concepts with no attributes.

19.4 Rendering Edges

19.4.1 The EdgeRendering Concept

To render edges, we also create a new concept that will hold the rendering attributes. We call this concept EdgeRendering and make it extend Edge. See Figure 19.12 for this new concept. Note that we specialize the source and destination roles because we know that they will hold NodeRendering instances.

Figure 19.12: **The EdgeRendering Concept.** Specialization of the source and destination types makes it possible to access NodeRendering through the references without casting to the specific type.

```
concept EdgeRendering extends      Edge
                               implements <none>

instance can be root: false
alias: <no alias>
short description: <no short description>

properties:
<< ... >>

children:
<< ... >>

references:
source        : NodeRendering[1] specializes: source
destination : NodeRendering[1] specializes: destination
```

When you have done this, create an editor for this concept and enter "diagram connector" to create the diagram cell.

19.4.2 Configuring the Connector Cell

We need to bind the source and target of the connector to nodes/elements of the diagram. To do this, place the cursor in one of the pink cells and invoke auto-completion ctrl + SPACE. Accept the ConnectionEndBLQuery. Type this.source to connect the source to the source Node of the edge, and this.destination to connect the target to the destination of the edge.

At this point, we have bound the connector to the source and destination NodeRendering instances that the connector links. As configured, the connector will appear to originate from the center of source node and terminate in the center of the destination node. It is often more aesthetically pleasing to have connectors start connect ports. To do this, we need to bind the pointId parts of the connector editor cell. The pointId element requires a port. If you have defined ports as children of NodeRendering as shown in Figure 19.11, you can simply navigate to each port from the node. See Figure 19.13 for a complete editor for the EdgeRendering concept. If you have defined anonymous port, you can use an expression to return the object that represents each port.

19.4.3 Second Build

Rebuild the language. You will now be able to see ports on each node that you create (see Figure 19.14). Input ports are shown as small rectangles of a light grey color. Output ports are shown as darker grey color rectangles. You will not yet be able to connect ports. The reason is that we have to configure what happens when a user interacts with the diagram to connect ports.

```
<default> editor for concept EdgeRendering
  node cell layout:
    { connector (source this.source # this.source.output target: this.destination # this.destination.input) }

  inspected cell layout:
    <choose cell model>
```

Figure 19.13: **EdgeRendering Editor.** Note that the `source.output` port is connected to the connector source, and the `destination.input` port is connected to the target input.

Figure 19.14:   **Diagram With Connectors.** This diagram is obtained after the second build and shows one input (light-grey) and one output port (darker grey) on each node.

19.4.4   Connector Creation Behavior

To make it possible create connectors on the diagram, you need to define a connector creation behavior. To do this, navigate to the Project editor, select the diagram cell, and in the 2: Inspector, locate the section `connector creation:`. Press ⏎ over the « ... » of this section to introduce a connector creation behavior element.

Enter the content shown in Figure 19.15.

```
connector creation:
name: CreateConnector
container: this.edges
concept: EdgeRendering
can create: (from, fromId, to, toId)->boolean {
  true;
}
on create: (node, from, fromId, to, toId)->void {
  node.source = from : NodeRendering;
  node.destination = to : NodeRendering;

}
```

Figure 19.15:   **Connector Creation Behavior.** The concept function on `create` casts `from` to the `NodeRendering` type and assigns it to the `EdgeRendering` instance (`node`).

19.4.5   Final Diagram

Rebuild the language one more time. Now that we have defined a connector creation behavior, if you click on an output port (darker grey), hold the button and drag the mouse over to an input port (lighter grey), you should see a connector established between the two ports that you have selected. The result is shown in Figure 19.16. Try to create more nodes and additional connections between them. Move the nodes around and notice how the edges are reorganized dynamically.

  We do not define an editor for input and output ports because port editors have no parameters that we can override and the default editor is sufficient to display the port.

Figure 19.16: **Final Dia-**
gram Rendering.   Notice
that the connector joins output and input ports.

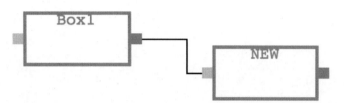

Exercise 19.1 Modify the diagram editor so that each time that you bind a port on a
node, another port of the same type is added to the node. You should obtain a result
similar to the following:

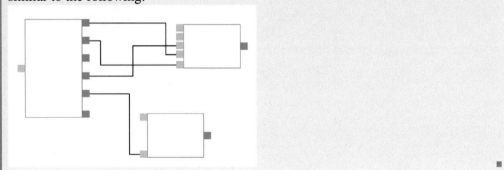

20 — MPS Key Map

Windows or Linux	MacOS	Action
⌥ + 0-9	⌥ + 0-9	Open corresponding tool window
ctrl + S	⌘ + S	Save all
ctrl + ⌥ + F11	N or A	Toggle full screen mode
ctrl + ⇧ + F12	N or A	Toggle maximizing editor
ctrl + BackQuote	ctrl + BackQuote	Quick switch current scheme
ctrl + ⌥ + S	⌘ + Comma	Open Settings dialog
ctrl + ⌥ + C	⌘ + ⌥ + C	Model Checker

Table 20.1: General

Windows or Linux	MacOS	Action
⌥ + F7	⌥ + F7	Find usages
ctrl + ⌥ + ⇧ + F7	⌘ + ⌥ + ⇧ + F7	Highlight cell dependencies
ctrl + ⇧ + F6	⌘ + ⇧ + F6	Highlight instances
ctrl + ⇧ + F7	⌘ + ⇧ + F7	Highlight usages
ctrl + F	⌘ + F	Find text
F3	F3	Find next
⇧ + F3	⇧ + F3	Find previous

Table 20.2: Usage and Text Search

Windows or Linux	MacOS	Action
`ctrl` + `M`	`⌘` + `M`	Import model
`ctrl` + `L`	`⌘` + `L`	Import language
`ctrl` + `R`	`⌘` + `R`	Import model by root name

Table 20.3: Import

Windows or Linux	MacOS	Action
`ctrl` + ` `	`ctrl` + ` `	Code completion
`ctrl` + `⌥` + `click`	`⌘` + `⌥` + `click`	Show descriptions of error or warning at caret
`⌥` + `↵`	`⌥` + `↵`	Show intention actions
`ctrl` + `⌥` + `T`	`⌘` + `⌥` + `T`	Surround with...
`ctrl` + `X` or `ctrl` + `⇧` + `⌦`	`⌘` + `X`	Cut current line or selected block to buffer
`ctrl` + `C` `ctrl` + `Insert`	`⌘` + `C`	Copy current line or selected block to buffer
`ctrl` + `V` `⇧` + `Insert`	`⌘` + `V`	Paste from buffer
`ctrl` + `D`	`⌘` + `D`	Up current line or selected block
`⇧` + `F5`	`⇧` + `F5`	Clone root
`ctrl` + `↑` or `↓`	`⌘` + `↑` or `↓`	Expand or Shrink block selection region
`ctrl` + `⇧` + `↑` or `↓`	`⌘` + `⇧` + `↑` or `↓`	Move statements Up or Down
`⇧` + `Arrows`	`⇧` + `Arrows`	Extend the selected region to siblings
`ctrl` + `W`	`⌘` + `W`	Select successively increasing code blocks
`ctrl` + `⇧` + `W`	`⌘` + `⇧` + `W`	Decrease current selection to previous state

Table 20.4: Editing (Part 1/2)

Windows or Linux	MacOS	Action
`ctrl` + `Y`	`⌘` + `Y`	Delete line
`ctrl` + `Z`	`⌘` + `Z`	Undo
`ctrl` + `⇧` + `Z`	`⌘` + `⇧` + `Z`	Redo
`⌥` + `F12`	`⌥` + `F12`	Show note in AST explorer
`F5`	`F5`	Refresh
`ctrl` + `MINUS`	`⌘` + `MINUS`	Collapse
`ctrl` + `⇧` + `MINUS`	`⌘` + `⇧` + `MINUS`	Collapse all
`ctrl` + `PLUS`	`⌘` + `PLUS`	Expand
`ctrl` + `⇧` + `PLUS`	`⌘` + `⇧` + `PLUS`	Expand all
`ctrl` + `⇧` + `0-9`	`⌘` + `⇧` + `0-9`	Set bookmark
`ctrl` + `0-9`	`ctrl` + `0-9`	Go to bookmark
`Tab`	`Tab`	Move to the next cell
`⇧` + `Tab`	`⇧` + `Tab`	Move to the previous cell
`Insert`	`ctrl` + `N`	Create Root Node (in the Project View)

Table 20.5: Editing (Part 2/2)

Windows or Linux	MacOS	Action
ctrl + B or ctrl + click	⌘ + B	Go to root node
	or ⌘ + click	Go to declaration
ctrl + N	⌘ + N	
ctrl + ⇧ + N	⌘ + ⇧ + N	Go to file
ctrl + G	⌘ + G	Go to node by id
ctrl + ⇧ + A	⌘ + ⇧ + A	Go to action by name
ctrl + ⌥ + ⇧ + M	⌘ + ⌥ + ⇧ + M	Go to model
ctrl + ⌥ + ⇧ + S	⌘ + ⌥ + ⇧ + S	Go to solution
ctrl + ⇧ + S	⌘ + ⇧ + S	Go to concept declaration
ctrl + ⇧ + E	⌘ + ⇧ + E	Go to concept editor declaration
⌥ + Left or Right	ctrl + Left or Right	Go to next or previous editor tab
Esc	Esc	Go to editor (from tool window)
⇧ + Esc	⇧ + Esc	Hide active or last active window
⇧ + F12	⇧ + F12	Restore default window layout
ctrl + ⇧ + F12	⌘ + ⇧ + F12	Hide all tool windows
F12	F12	Jump to the last tool window

Table 20.6: Navigation (Part 1/2)

Windows or Linux	MacOS	Action
ctrl + E	⌘ + E	Recent nodes popup
ctrl + ⌥ + Left or Right	⌘ + ⌥ + Left or Right	Navigate back or forward
⌥ + F1	⌥ + F1	Select current node in any view
ctrl + H	⌘ + H	Concept or Class hierarchy
F4 or ↵	F4 or ↵	Edit source or View source
ctrl + F4	⌘ + F4	Close active editor tab
⌥ + 2	⌥ + 2	Go to inspector
ctrl + F10	⌘ + F10	Show structure
ctrl + ⌥ +)	⌘ + ⌥ +)	Go to next project window
ctrl + ⌥ + (	⌘ + ⌥ + (	Go to previous project window
ctrl + ⇧ + Right	ctrl + ⇧ + Right	Go to next aspect tab
ctrl + ⇧ + Left	ctrl + ⇧ + Left	Go to previous aspect tab
ctrl + ⌥ + ⇧ + R	⌘ + ⌥ + ⇧ + R	Go to type-system rules
ctrl + ⇧ + T	⌘ + ⇧ + T	Show type
ctrl + H	ctrl + H	Show in hierarchy view
ctrl + I	⌘ + I	Inspect node

Table 20.7: Navigation (Part 2/2)

Windows or Linux	MacOS	Action
ctrl + F9	⌘ + F9	Generate current module
ctrl + ⇧ + F9	⌘ + ⇧ + F9	Generate current model
⇧ + F10	⇧ + F10	Run
⇧ + F9	⇧ + F9	Debug
ctrl + ⇧ + F10	⌘ + ⇧ + F10	Run context configuration
⌥ + ⇧ + F10	⌥ + ⇧ + F10	Select and run a configuration
ctrl + ⇧ + F9	⌘ + ⇧ + F9	Debug context configuration
⌥ + ⇧ + F9	⌥ + ⇧ + F9	Select and debug a configuration
ctrl + ⌥ + ⇧ + F9	⌘ + ⌥ + ⇧ + F9	Preview generated text
ctrl + ⇧ + X	⌘ + ⇧ + X	Show type-system trace

Table 20.8: Generation

Windows or Linux	MacOS	Action
ctrl + O	⌘ + O	Override methods
ctrl + I	⌘ + I	Implement methods
ctrl + /	⌘ + /	Comment or uncomment with block comment
ctrl + F12	⌘ + F12	Show nodes
ctrl + P	⌘ + P	Show parameters
ctrl + Q	ctrl + Q	Show node information
ctrl + Insert	ctrl + N	Create new ...
ctrl + ⌥ + B	⌘ + ⌥ + B	Go to overriding methods or Go to inherited classifiers
ctrl + U	⌘ + U	Go to overridden method

Table 20.9: BaseLanguage and Editing

Windows or Linux	MacOS	Action
ctrl + K	⌘ + K	Commit project to VCS
ctrl + T	⌘ + T	Update project from VCS
ctrl + V	ctrl + V	VCS operations popup
ctrl + ⌥ + A	⌘ + ⌥ + A	Add to VCS
ctrl + ⌥ + E	⌘ + ⌥ + E	Browse history
ctrl + D	⌘ + D	Show differences

Table 20.10: Version Control System and Local History

Windows or Linux	MacOS	Action
F6	F6	Move
⇧ + F6	⇧ + F6	Rename
⌥ + ⌫	⌥ + ⌫	Safe Delete
ctrl + ⌥ + N	⌘ + ⌥ + N	Inline
ctrl + ⌥ + M	⌘ + ⌥ + M	Extract Method
ctrl + ⌥ + V	⌘ + ⌥ + V	Introduce Variable
ctrl + ⌥ + C	⌘ + ⌥ + C	Introduce constant
ctrl + ⌥ + F	⌘ + ⌥ + F	Introduce field
ctrl + ⌥ + P	⌘ + ⌥ + P	Extract parameter
ctrl + ⌥ + M	⌘ + ⌥ + M	Extract method
ctrl + ⌥ + N	⌘ + ⌥ + N	Inline

Table 20.11: Refactoring

Windows or Linux	MacOS	Action
F8	F8	Step over
F7	F7	Step into
⇧ + F8	⇧ + F8	Step out
F9	F9	Resume
⌥ + F8	⌥ + F8	Evaluate expression
ctrl + F8	⌘ + F8	Toggle breakpoints
ctrl + ⇧ + F8	⌘ + ⇧ + F8	View breakpoints

Table 20.12: Debugger

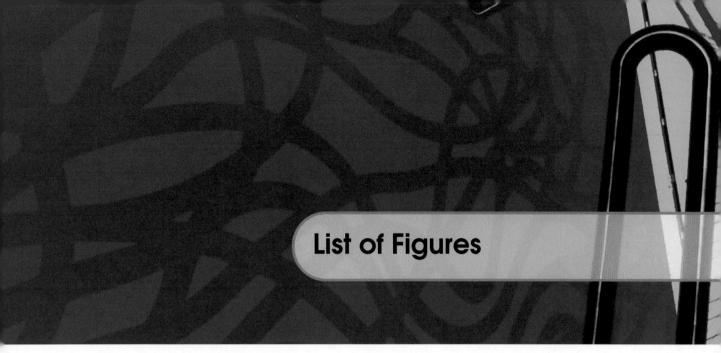

List of Figures

Bibliography

[BC15]   Victoria M Benson and Fabien Campagne. "Language workbench user interfaces for data analysis". In: *PeerJ* 3 (2015), e800. URL: `https://peerj.com/articles/800/` (cited on page 17).

[Cam15]   Fabien Campagne. *The MPS Language Workbench*. Volume II. Fabien Campagne, 2015. URL: `https://play.google.com/store/books/details?id=NPwyBwAAQBAJ` (cited on pages 24, 31).

[CDS15]   Fabien Campagne, William ER Digan, and Manuele Simi. "MetaR: simple, high-level languages for data analysis with the R ecosystem". In: *bioRxiv* (2015), page 030254. URL: `http://biorxiv.org/content/early/2015/11/04/030254` (cited on page 17).

[Cit]   CitationStyles. *Citation Style Language (CSL), an open XML-based language to describe the formatting of citations and bibliographies*. Online; accessed 22 February 2014. URL: `http://citationstyles.org/` (cited on page 183).

[Con]   The Apache Consortium. *http://velocity.apache.org/*. Online; accessed 29 December 2013. URL: `http://www.stringtemplate.org/` (cited on page 32).

[Dmi04]   Sergey Dmitriev. *Language oriented programming: The next programming paradigm*. 2004. URL: `http://www.jetbrains.com/mps/docs/Language_Oriented_Programming.pdf` (cited on pages 15, 16).

[Ele+01]   Bjorn Elenfors et al. *Refactoring*. Online; accessed 28 December 2013. 2001. URL: `http://en.wikipedia.org/wiki/Code_refactoring#List_of_refactoring_techniques` (cited on page 24).

[For+04]   Paul Ford et al. *Domain Specific Language*. Online; accessed 28 December 2013. 2004. URL: `http://en.wikipedia.org/wiki/Domain-specific_language` (cited on page 16).

[Gac+04]   Gachet et al. *Software Framework*. Online; accessed 28 December 2013. 2004. URL: `http://en.wikipedia.org/wiki/Software_framework` (cited on page 17).

[Gos+05]   James Gosling et al. *Java(TM) Language Specification, The (3rd Edition) (Java (Addison-Wesley))*. Edited by James Gosling. Addison-Wesley Professional, 2005. ISBN: 0321246780 (cited on pages 30, 81).

[GP15]   Evgeny Gryaznov and Vaclav Pech. Online; accessed March 17 2016. 2015. URL: `https://confluence.jetbrains.com/display/MPSD33/Pattern` (cited on page 131).

[KSC16]   Jason P Kurs, Manuele Simi, and Fabien Campagne. "NextflowWorkbench: Reproducible and Reusable Workflows for Beginners and Experts". In: *bioRxiv* (2016). DOI: `10.1101/041236`. eprint: `http://biorxiv.org/content/early/2016/02/24/041236.full.pdf`. URL: `http://biorxiv.org/content/early/2016/02/24/041236` (cited on page 17).

[Lam+06]   Monica Lam et al. *Compilers: Principles, Techniques, and Tools*. 2006 (cited on page 19).

[LW94]   Barbara H Liskov and Jeannette M Wing. "A behavioral notion of subtyping." In: *ACM Transactions on Programming Languages and Systems (TOPLAS)* 16.6 (1994), pages 1811–1841 (cited on page 135).

[Par]   Terrence Parr. *StringTemplate*. Online; accessed 29 December 2013. URL: `http://www.stringtemplate.org/` (cited on page 32).

[SC14]   Manuele Simi and Fabien Campagne. "Composable languages for bioinformatics: the NYoSh experiment". In: *PeerJ* (2014) (cited on page 45).

[Sim95]   Charles Simonyi. "The death of computer languages, the birth of intentional programming". In: *NATO Science Committee Conference*. 1995. URL: `http://research.microsoft.com/apps/pubs/default.aspx?id=69540` (cited on pages 15, 16).

[SCC06]   Charles Simonyi, Magnus Christerson, and Shane Clifford. "Intentional software". In: *ACM SIGPLAN Notices*. Volume 41. ACM, 2006, pages 451–464 (cited on page 16).

[Sta]   Standards Office of the Library of Congress. *Metadata Object Description Schema (MODS) is a schema for a bibliographic element set*. Online; accessed 8 March 2014. URL: `http://www.loc.gov/standards/mods/` (cited on page 183).

[Str00]   Bjarne Stroustrup. *The C++ Programming Language*. Edited by Bjarne Stroustrup. 3rd. Boston, MA, USA: Addison-Wesley Longman Publishing Co., Inc., 2000. ISBN: 0201700735 (cited on page 80).

[Voe13]   Markus Voelter. "Language and IDE Modularization and Composition with MPS". In: *Generative and Transformational Techniques in Software Engineering IV*. Springer, 2013, pages 383–430 (cited on page 16).

[VS10]   Markus Voelter and Konstantin Solomatov. "Language modularization and composition with projectional language workbenches illustrated with MPS". In: *Software Language Engineering, SLE* (2010) (cited on page 16).

[Voe+13]   Markus Voelter et al. *DSL Engineering, Designing, Implementing and Using Domain-Specific Languages*. 1st Edition. CreateSpace Independent Publishing Platform (January 23, 2013), 2013. ISBN: 978-1481218580 (cited on page 17).

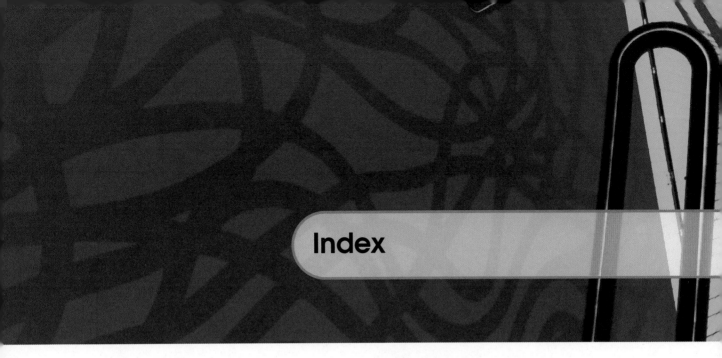

Index